# ERIC STANTON

## & THE HISTORY OF THE BIZARRE UNDERGROUND

# ERIC STANTON

## & the History of the Bizarre Underground

RICHARD PÉREZ SEVES

Schiffer Publishing Ltd

4880 Lower Valley Road · Atglen, PA 19310

Copyright © 2018 by Richard Pérez, Richard Pérez Seves: research, story, exclusive film rights

Library of Congress Control Number: 2017955754

ISBN: 978-0-7643-5542-4

Printed in China

Published by Schiffer Publishing, Ltd.
4880 Lower Valley Road
Atglen, PA 19310
Phone: (610) 593-1777; Fax: (610) 593-2002
E-mail: Info@schifferbooks.com
Web: www.schifferbooks.com

Cover design by Matthew Goodman
Type set in Vitesse/Optima/Times

For our complete selection of fine books on this and related subjects, please visit our website at www.schifferbooks.com. You may also write for a free catalog.

Schiffer Publishing's titles are available at special discounts for bulk purchases for sales promotions or premiums. Special editions, including personalized covers, corporate imprints, and excerpts, can be created in large quantities for special needs. For more information, contact the publisher.

We are always looking for people to write books on new and related subjects. If you have an idea for a book, please contact us at proposals@schifferbooks.com.

"Without deviation from the norm,
progress is not possible."

– FRANK ZAPPA

# CONTENTS

# FOREWORD
## My Introduction to the Bizarre Underground

I can't exactly say when I first came across the work of Eric Stanton. As a long-time collector of risqué vintage magazines and artifacts largely focused on the sexploitation era—that is, pre-1970, pre-hardcore or XXX— it may have been in an old digest or "girlie" magazine published by Stanton employer Leonard Burtman. I did notice a passing resemblance to the work of another artist, John Willie, creator of the illustrated fetish serial known as *Sweet Gwendoline;* an artist with whom Stanton is often confused.

Word on the Internet was that John Willie was a genius, a visionary; he had somehow isolated and inadvertently christened an entire fringe culture with the name of his self-published magazine, *Bizarre*, several copies of which I finally spotted on eBay and paid a high price for. Soon enough I realized this unique culture deserved some serious investigation: although rooted in sexuality, vintage fetish art was not obscene. In fact, it was quite tasteful, elegant, and beautiful—only alien to the mainstream and tainted by its sublimated connection to sex. Publishers of such material I later found out were maligned as "sleaze" merchants, spat upon as common criminals, called "pornographers," brought to trial, although nothing they published was explicit. Supporting characters in the formation of this underground culture other than John Willie were Irving Klaw; Bettie Page; the father of commercial fetish publishing, Leonard Burtman; Times Square bookstore owners and operators Edward Mishkin and Stanley Malkin; and artists Gene Bilbrew and Steve Ditko. And there were others even lesser known but just as significant, like Charles Guyette.

I finally realized the one connecting thread weaving together all these stray narratives was Eric Stanton, because here was an influential and pioneering artist who had been there from the beginning. Following the arc of Stanton's life would provide an understanding of what was then labeled as "bizarre." I needed to create an in-depth and detailed biography to bring to light a secret cultural history. Soon enough, my interest in Stanton's life and work took on an obsessive quality all its own.

*Eric Stanton & the History of the Bizarre Underground* was created with the full participation of the late artist's surviving family and through interviews with them over a four-year period, particularly his daughter Amber, son Tom, and widow Britt. It is both a history of New York City trailblazers and a study/biography of a misfit artist in search of an identity. As per my own interest, the book focuses on the pre-hardcore era, the true "underground" age, a time when producing fetish art—from a social, moral, and legal standpoint— was an act of bravery, if not rebellion.

# INTRODUCTION
## Tracking a Ghost

Transgressive artist, cult figure, fetish illustrator, deviant—
none of these descriptions seem to capture the essence of a
man who, to this day, remains enigmatic at best.

What seems clear is that the individual who started his life as Ernest Stanzoni Jr., who by the late 1960s reimagined himself as "Eric Stanton," was an unconventional man, a nonconformist. If ever there was a sexual fantasist ahead of his time, it was Stanton. There is no question he was a pioneer, an audacious interpreter of psychosexual fantasy, a subversive insurrectionist of identity and gender, and to this day remains one of the most pirated underground comic artists in the world.

Biographical facts about his life are often contradictory and murky; sometimes he would contribute to this misinformation personally, often in an attempt to maintain a shroud of secrecy he felt necessary to protect his family from scrutiny and condemnation. (And he was wise to do this.) Strange as it may seem, for many years there was even some question of his physical existence when it was suggested that "Stanton" was just a front for another, more mainstream artist.

When it comes to the birth of commercial fetish art, there are few traces of recorded history. Stanton lived and operated in an underworld where people rarely kept records and everyone functioned under a multitude of aliases. This was the dicey time largely preceding true porn—hardcore or XXX—when any association with "adult entertainment" could get you locked up. In this period, operations connected with producing this sort of "smut" were aggressively tracked by government agencies, postal inspectors who acted as censors with strong ties to the local police, and even the Catholic Church (hugely influential then).

And these same underground publishers/producers/distributors *were* targeted and raided: Irving Klaw's Jersey-based warehouses, Leonard Burtman's Manhattan editorial office, Stanley Malkin's Queens paperback warehouse; and virtually anything connected to Times Square operator/book shop owner Edward Mishkin was under surveillance and sooner or later put under wraps—at least temporarily. Even the working studio shared by Steve Ditko and Eric Stanton was subjected to a police raid, with all the priceless artwork confiscated and much of it destroyed.

It would be difficult, even impossible, to fully convey Stanton's life without showing him in the context of his times and the culture in which he operated, which might require straying into the lives of those connected to him. But make no mistake, this is Eric Stanton's chronicle, and with it, I hope to dispel the many myths surrounding the man, once and for all correct the many errors in biographical fact, and shed light on the life of an artist who for too long has been relegated to the shadows.

With Stanton, things were not always what they seemed. But as with any life account, we need to rewind the clock, settle down, and recall the dream from the beginning . . .

# The Early Years: Let's Examine the Records

Eric Stanton was born on November 30, 1926, to parents Anna T. Stanzoni and Ernest Stanzoni. He was named Ernest Stanzoni Jr.—a designation fraught with irony, as we will understand later. Born at home at 1893 Pacific Street, Brooklyn, New York, he was delivered by his grandmother, Sophie, a neighborhood midwife and bootlegger of some repute. His mother was nineteen years old, and according to the birth certificate, had given birth to a previous child that died in infancy.

Anna and the future Eric Stanton

By 1930, the family was in Ozone Park, Queens, New York, and Ernest Jr. had been joined by a sister, Sophia. As noted in that year's census report, Ernest Sr. was Italian American, while the birthplace of Anna's side of the family is listed as:

Poland Poland Poland Russian

"Russian," is written under the heading: "Language spoken in home before coming to the United States." This simply suggests that Stanton's maternal lineage originated from a Polish region near Russia, possibly Congress, Poland, territory that later became part of the USSR.

Stanton's grandmother, Sophie, was twenty-six when she immigrated to the US in 1911; his mother, Anna, was four (possibly five) years old at the time. Anna's father—Stanton's grandfather—was a man named Nicholas Pelsewski, another male presence who drifted out of the household as insubstantially as a puff of smoke.

As for the matriarch, Sophie, she had known hardship as a girl. After her mother died, her father expected her to be a mother to the younger children according to Stanton's niece, Cathy Hysell. Apparently, a family incident involving a table fork resulted in her being blinded in one eye.

Life in America did not seem any easier, and she had to find ways to make ends meet. According to Stanton's sister, Eleanor, Sophie became uniquely skilled with a sewing machine and could reproduce, without a pattern, any dress, blouse, or shirt on sight. She was a neighborhood midwife. Her bootlegging activities became the stuff of family legend. "Vodka was made in the bathtub from rare alcohol. Some she'd flavor with fresh lemon and some straight," Cathy explained. Amber recalled her father telling her that at times he had to use a neighbor's tub to bathe because their own was routinely filled with a batch of her famous brew.

For a time she appeared to have run a speakeasy, with the New York City mayor rumored to be among her customers.

Details are sketchy, but some time by 1931, there was an upheaval in the Stanzoni home, and abruptly the marriage between Anna and Ernest Sr. ended. Exit Mr. Stanzoni. By 1932, Anna's final child, Eleanor, was born, but the father of Eleanor was a Russian émigré by the name of Nikodem Kochengin.

Born in Tashkent, Russia, he first visited America as a crew member aboard the ship *Siljan*, hailing from Singapore, China, his occupation noted on surviving vessel documents as "cook." The following year (1927) he immigrated to the United States.

Known variously as Nicholas, Nicolai, Nickolay, and Nick, he was the only father Stanton could call his own. And even so he was scarcely seen.

According to 1940's census report, Nick and Anna were comfortably ensconced in Brooklyn. Their address—which would remain unchanged for at least a decade—was 213 Lincoln Avenue.

Also listed at the residence was Grandma Sophie, Eleanor, and Ernest Jr.

Mysteriously absent from the document was Stanton's sister, Sophia.

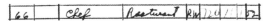

The census further provides stepfather Nick's occupation, as well as evidence of his workaholic tendencies: "66" was the number of hours he worked in a week and "52" represented the number of weeks he worked in a year.

Cathy related how her grandmother and Nick met: "Anna and her sister, May, were out dancing and Nick was working out back in the kitchen. Anna went out to smoke a cigarette passing through the kitchen." It was a display of her boldness, and Anna wasted no time. It was her first serious involvement with a man who spoke her native tongue. Soon Russian became the only language spoken in the home, which proved a problem for young Stanton when he was legally obliged to attend school. As he recalled in later years, whenever his teachers spoke he had no idea what they were saying.

Compounding language problems was his proneness to getting sick. Later he recollected that while attending PS 171 he succumbed to pneumonia no less than three times. Likely connected to his many childhood illnesses—and only worsened by neglect—were his ruined teeth, which would result in Stanton wearing full dentures before the age of thirty.

Anna, Nick, and Sophie, 1951

PUBLIC SCHOOL. NO. 171, RIDGEWOOD & LINCOLN AVES., BROOKLYN, N. Y.

Now that her bootlegging years were behind her, Grandma Sophie took control of domestic duties and watched over Ernest Jr. while he played big brother to Eleanor. "I used to worry about him and he used to worry about me," she recalled about her brother. Occasionally, Stanton's beloved Aunt May (right) pulled babysitting duty. As Cathy related, "Anna was not home a lot. She could be gone for days at a time."

As for stepfather Nick, Eleanor remembered, "He worked seven days a week. And, I think, every couple of weeks he'd have a day off. But that was his life." According to Eleanor, he worked at The Balalaika, Two Guitars, The Russian Tea Room—at one point even purchasing a restaurant. "But he hated it, sold the restaurant, and went back to work at those other places," Eleanor recalled. "There weren't too many Russian restaurants, but whatever there were, he would work for them, sooner or later. And he was always the head chef."

As for Anna: Where was she? As Cathy explained: "Off with more than likely whomever she was dating or seeing at the time. She loved her men!"

## Salvation in Cartoons: 1938

Nephritis and Scarlett Fever were among the childhood illnesses feared in the pre-antibiotic era, and evidently young Stanton would contract both. But in 1938, it was Eleanor's turn to be sick.

Quarantined for weeks on end because of his sister and left with nothing to do, Stanton sought a way to deal with the crushing boredom. If he never considered cartooning before, he thought of it then: "I grabbed some comic books and did some tracings and things like that. That's how I started to learn."

Strange as it may seem today, comic books were a brand new medium, having only been invented five years before in 1933.

The character Superman made his initial appearance in 1938, the year Stanton did his first sketches. Batman followed a year later. Stanton's interest in art coincided with the birth of the superhero.

But men, as superheroes, did not interest him—would never interest him.

"He didn't really have powerful men around him. He didn't really have a steady, solid father figure," explained Amber. "So he probably got this wishy-washy impression of men."

Perhaps this might explain why almost immediately he gravitated toward dynamic females, seeking inspiration not only in comics, but lurid pulps, exotic matinee serials, and even risqué men's magazines as they existed then. And not always with the approval of his stepfather, who was otherwise creatively inclined.

Stanton's mother, while not an artist, was a liberated woman who cast aside doubt: "Let him draw what he wants." And he needed her encouragement, too, because cartooning and illustration did not come easily to him. Soon his fixation with drawing brazen, leggy femmes would earn him a nickname at school: "Dirty Ernie."

As for Nick, his contribution to Stanton's creative development, over time, was to instill a ferocious work ethic, and on his rare day off, his stepfather also dabbled in art, although his taste was more traditional.

"My father used to oil paint," Eleanor recalled. "We all were artistic, except for my mother." In the absence of creative talent, Anna was nothing if not supportive. "'Do whatever makes you happy,' she'd say," as Amber recalled her father telling her. And years later, he recognized the impact of her constant approval: "That's how I kept on drawing."

Almost at once Stanton recognized that art provided a unique satisfaction he did not experience in real life: not only access to a special fantasy world, but a sense of personal power: "I had control . . . I could have the people I drew do anything I wanted," he reflected in later years. "I was king of my world." Control and powerlessness—as mirrored in the secret subculture of the sexual fantasist—would become a major theme in his art.

Scraping through grade school, Stanton transferred to Franklin K. Lane High in June 1941. An examination of his high school records reveals his name at this point was "Ernest A. Stanzoni." The initial "A." standing for "Armond," a middle name not on his birth certificate, nor any previous documents; the "Jr." meanwhile had been dropped, as there was no longer a visible Ernest Sr. in his life. And even though she was already married to Nick, "Stanzoni" appeared as Anna's last name on school paperwork, as if to justify the last name of her misfit son. Meanwhile, Eleanor's last name was "Kochengin."

## Comics and the War against Japan and Germany

World War II signaled America's last undeniable good fight, and a flood of comic book heroes swept up into the propaganda machine. Some, like Captain America, seemed uniquely created to sell war bonds. But if there was one comic book character that intrigued Stanton and informed his art for years, it was conceived by an errant psychologist with progressive and unconventional ideas about the role of women in society.

Created by William Moulton Marston, and first appearing in December 1941—the same month of Japan's attack on Pearl Harbor and America's entry into the war—Wonder Woman proved an unexpected and immediate success with the public, introducing an eccentric fantasy world of protective Amazons, a golden lasso expressly designed for compelling obedience,

and most importantly, the revolutionary notion that a superhero could be female. Wait: a woman who could be physically superior yet utterly feminine? This contradiction not only deeply pleased Stanton, it turned him on!

Despite once describing himself as "an awkward, gawky kid; I guess you could even say ugly," Stanton was in many ways a normal American teenager during high school. According to Amber, his favorite movie was *The Wizard of Oz,* "Because of all the fantasy elements and the play of extreme characters: the wicked witch, the good girl." He enjoyed Frank Sinatra records, and encouraged by his mother, took up singing. Prompted by his mother's enjoyment of horse racing, he groomed a nascent passion for gambling. His love of big American cars compelled him to obtain a driver's permit as soon as possible in 1942. That same year what many consider the best of the Republic Pictures serials was released in fifteen parts, *The Perils of Nyoka*. A sequel to another of his favorites, *Jungle Girl*, it became another youthful obsession—and one he would reference repeatedly in future artwork.

Like many sensational matinee serials, *Nyoka* featured exotic locales, overheated melodrama, and suspenseful situations more often than not devolving into capture and bondage. The lead character, Nyoka, was spirited, yet consistently endangered and reduced to a damsel in distress; this duality of fiery willfulness and undeniable physical vulnerability captivated Stanton through repeated viewings. Vultura ("Ruler of the Arabs"), Nyoka's glamorous and imperially beautiful nemesis (below) also clearly marked his imagination.

As for other Stanton favorites of the period, they included, according to family friend Paul Quant, peculiar, lesser known screen actors Gale Sondergaard and Victor McLaglen. Quant related:

> It once surprised me to hear Eric say that, so I argued, "What? *Gale Sondergaard?*—she's got no *beauty*!" And he said, "Yeah, but she's got *character*!" And I understood it once he explained it to me. She did have this very strict, very odd dramatic presence. As for Victor McLaglen, Eric said, "Look at his face. He's got *fifty* faces in one. So much expression there." And Eric loved that: someone who could give a lot of expression.

Curiously, actress Gale Sondergaard had once even tested for the role of the wicked witch in *The Wizard of Oz*. Stanton would reference Sondergaard's unconventional looks in future comics.

In summer 1943, while still in high school, Stanton took his first legit job—at Machpelah Cemetery in Ridgewood, Queens. According to son, Tom, part of his duties as groundskeeper was taking care of magician Harry Houdini's grave site. It was no small irony that Houdini had made a name for himself escaping from various forms of bondage and that he died the same year Stanton was born. If nothing else, working in a cemetery reminded Stanton of the cycle of life, and that in the end no one escaped their fate.

Among his numerous duties Stanton dug graves. He was paid $14.00 a week. Not that it was all work, according to Tom: "They would play games, like pretend they were coming out of graves. Put dirt on their faces and scare people who were coming into the graveyard." When not clowning around, Stanton also took note of some of the tragic sadness and misery of the visitors and learned his first real lessons in empathy.

World War II was still raging and people were dying on an unimaginable scale. And at age sixteen, it must have occurred to Stanton that his number was coming up. Sooner or later he would get the call to serve.

THIS APPLICATION TO BE MADE OUT IN APPLICANT'S OWN HANDWRITING

# APPLICATION FOR ENLISTMENT OR INDUCTION
## INTO THE NAVAL SERVICE

9 _____ Congressional District, County of _____ King _____ State of _____ N Y _____
(Information to be Supplied by Recruiter)

Last school grade completed: _12 yrs._

Reason for enlistment: _WAR_

Language qualification: _NONE_

What is your trade? _NONE_

U. S. New York (Recruiting Station)

27 JUL 1944 _____, 19 _____
(Date)

Term of service _____ years

**USN - I**

Name in full (print) _ERNEST ARMOND STANZONI_
(First) (Middle) (Last)

Date of birth _SEPT. 30 1926_ Place of birth _B'KLYN N.Y._
(Month) (Day) (Year) (City) (State)

**USN -SV    USNR -SV**

What is your race? _White_ Religion? _CATHOLIC_ Are you now a U. S. citizen? _YES_

If you were born in foreign territory, how did you acquire citizenship? _____

When did you acquire citizenship? _At Birth_

Have you resided continuously in U. S. since initial entry? _YES_

Have you anyone solely or partially dependent upon you for support? _NO_

Are you married? _NO_ Have you ever been married? _NO_

Status: (Married) (Divorced) (Legally separated) (Widowered)

Local Board # _____ Address _N. Reg._

Your address when registered? _N. Reg._ S. S. Classification _____

**1st enlistment    re-enlistment**

Home address: _213 LINCOLN AVE._ _BROOKLYN_ _N.Y._
(House Number) (Name of Street) (City or Town) (State)

Where was your father born? _AMERICA_ Where was your mother born? _RUSSIA_

Is your father living? _YES_ Is your mother living? _YES_
(Yes or No) (Yes or No)

Are your parents divorced? _YES_ Separated? _YES_ Have you a stepfather? _YES_ Stepmother? _NO_
(Yes or No) (Yes or No) (Yes or No) (Yes or No)

**USN    USNR    7141022**

Name of next of kin or legal guardian: _MRS. ANNA KOCHENGIN_

Relationship: _MOTHER_ Full home address of next of kin or legal guardian:

_213 LINCOLN AVE._ _BROOKLYN_ _KINGS_ _N.Y._
(House No.) (Name of Street) (City or Town) (County) (State)

ATTENTION IS INVITED TO THE INVESTIGATION OF EACH APPLICANT BY THE FEDERAL BUREAU OF INVESTIGATION.

Have you ever been arrested or in the custody of police? _NO_ If so, for what? _____

Have you ever been convicted of any crime? _NO_

Have you ever been in a reform school, jail or penitentiary? _NO_

Have you previously been processed for enlistment or induction into the Armed Forces? _NO_

Have you ever served in the U. S. Navy _NO_ Marine Corps _NO_ Army _NO_ Coast Guard _NO_

Naval Reserve _NO_ Naval Militia _NO_ National Guard _NO_ Marine Corps Reserve? _NO_

Character of discharge _____ Date of last discharge _____

**Service Number**

(Applicant sign full name here) X _Ernest Armond Stanzoni_

Consent _7/19_                     Fingerprints _____

Birth Verification _VH_             Proof of divorce _Filed_

Custody _such_                      Citizenship _____

Guardianship _____                  X-ray _____

Proof of death _Filed_              Examination _____

Mother's name _____

June 1944 finally marked Stanton's high school graduation. That same month (June 22), the Servicemen's Readjustment Act—also known as the GI Bill of Rights—became law, and less than one month after finishing school, on July 27, 1944, Stanton confronted the inevitable when he marched into a recruiting station, cut short the suspense, and filled out his application (see previous).

If Stanton had no choice about being drafted into the Second World War, he could at least choose which branch of the military to serve. But as he was underage (seventeen years, ten months old) he still needed his mother's consent, which she finally provided, no doubt with sadness, two days later.

Why the naval branch of service, it might be asked? Consider that the man whose name he carried, Ernest Stanzoni, had also enlisted in the Navy at the same age. So like father, like son?

Not exactly. As her boy was going off to war and there was a very real possibility she might not ever see him alive again, Anna felt obliged to make a confession: Ernest Stanzoni was in fact not his father.

One can only imagine Stanton's confusion. As Tom related, "All his life he was told Ernest Stanzoni was his dad." But now his mother revealed that his biological father was someone completely different.

And who was he? Just some fellow, a prospective horse trainer she was seeing at the time, along with Stanzoni. His name was Edward D'Andrea.

According to the 1930 census, Edward D'Andrea was also living in Ozone Park, Queens, where Anna and Ernest relocated after Ernest Jr. was born in Brooklyn. Was it a coincidence that Ozone Park was where Anna chose to relocate after leaving Brooklyn? Was Anna chasing him? Or was Edward chasing Anna?

In any event, knowledge of her infidelity somehow became evident to Ernest Stanzoni and likely resulted in the end of their marriage some time following the date of the 1930 Federal Census.

This knowledge would also help clarify the disappearance of Sophia—Stanton's sister—after that date.

An important piece of the family puzzle was contributed by Eleanor, who admitted she had not met the missing family member—Sophia—until she was twelve. As Cathy recalled her mother's story:

> One day my grandmother told my mom to get dressed, that she wanted her to meet someone. She took her to a diner, and a girl was there with some man. They introduced the two, and my mom was told "Eleanor, this is your sister, Sophie." When my mom got a little older, she asked my grandmother about her sister and why she didn't live with them. My grandmother explained how Sophie's father came and took her away and warned if she tried to get her back he would send her away where she would never see her again, so my grandmother let him keep her.

Sophia—born one year after Ernest Jr.—was evidently his biological offspring, while Jr. clearly was not, which explained why Ernest Sr. never went back for him.

So where did this leave Stanton? With no father or name?

## Origin of Armond

After his marriage to Anna ended in divorce after 1930, Ernest Stanzoni remarried in 1934, and in 1936, had a son whom he named "Armond"—a name Ernest Jr. adopted as his own not long after.

Was Stanton indulging in some fantasy in which he imagined he was the "true" son? Did he undergo some crisis of identity? Or was he merely being wishful?

Ernest Stanzoni Sr. eventually relocated to Long Island, taking his new family with him, including Armond. In contacting Armond Stanzoni for this book, he seemed unaware of a man named Ernest Stanzoni Jr., although he did admit to a "half sister" by the name Sophia.

# Growing Pains: Stanton vs. Manhood

World War II would bring various changes in the perception of women, and initially propaganda was behind much of it.

"Rosie the Riveter," a symbol and term that first appeared in a 1942 popular song by the same name, proclaimed that any American woman was physically capable of stepping into a male dominated trade and proving herself just as effective and tireless as any man. The intent behind this media campaign was to spike morale, but few anticipated that shock waves would be projected into the future—that by altering the perception of a cultural stereotype of women as physically useless, frail, and dependent creatures things might never be the same.

Alternately, the World War II era saw the preeminent rise of the pin-up, whose primary focus, again, was to raise spirits and project hope, this time by recasting sexually provocative and risqué imagery as a tool for good and thus

Varga Girl, July 1944 © 1944, 1991 Hearst Corporation

giving soldiers—mostly anxious, homesick, and inexperienced boys—something to fight for.

Meanwhile, in lower Manhattan, a man proclaiming himself to be the "Pin-up King"—Irving Klaw—was testing the limits of the craze and gathering a measure of attention.

"Cheesecake is a good morale factor," one commanding officer was quoted as saying in an AP article dated from 1943. "I want to distribute these photographs in the recreation room . . ."

## Seaman's Rite of Passage

If Stanton had an identity crisis, or any reason to question his existence previously, it hardly seemed to matter while he was in the Navy.

Measuring in at sixty-five inches and weighing 125 lbs. (eight pounds more than he weighed six months previously, according to Navy papers), apprentice seaman Stanzoni, Ernest A., service #714 10 22, reported for active duty on 15 September 1944, and was transferred that same day to the US Naval Training Center in Bainbridge, Maryland—rotten teeth, poor vision, and all.

After surviving his first assault at the hands of a Navy dentist (as per records twelve cavities filled in a single day), Stanton adapted surprisingly well to the regimented life of the service, gaining friends and some measure of self-respect after enduring the mandatory eleven weeks of recruit training.

While stationed in Maryland, where he remained until spring 1945, the need to make art asserted itself, and Stanton contributed drawings to the naval newspaper *The Bainbridge Mainsheet*, the first time he saw his work in print. "It was a comic strip about plane recognition," he later recalled.

His actual tour of duty was soon to begin, and fortunately for Stanton, would be largely uneventful and swift, with his full naval history clearly traced alongside that of his war vessel, the brand new USS *Turner*, which, according to the *Dictionary of American Naval Fighting Ships*, was first laid down in November 1944, in Bath, Maine.

On 12 June 1945—the same day the ship was officially commissioned—Stanton (as Stanzoni, Ernest A.) was reported on board. Record of his attendance from this point on can be found in the ship's surviving "muster roll"—the ship's crew list—recorded "Jul 1945," "Oct 1945," "Jan 1946," and "Apr 1946," with his final appearance being May 1946.

As per the *Dictionary of American Naval Fighting Ships*:

> Immediately following her commissioning, Turner began undergoing conversion to a destroyer picket ship at Boston while her crew attended intensive specialized schools in preparation for picket duty. In mid-July, she arrived at Guantanamo Bay and, while she was undergoing shakedown in Cuban waters, Japan capitulated, ending World War II.

Was it lucky timing that it should be over this quick? In Stanton's case, yes. But by then the war had charted a long chain of events. Following the Hiroshima atomic bombing of August 6, the subsequent bombing of Nagasaki, and the Soviet invasion of Manchuria, it was curtains for the Japanese. The date was 14 August 1945, and as Stanton was radioman aboard the USS *Turner*, he was the very first to hear of the Japanese surrender.

According to his widow Britt, the first person he told was the ship's cook, who in passing the radio room had dangled a snack. Then Stanton shambled to tell his commanding officer, who appreciated hearing the important news firsthand, finally eyeing him suspiciously: "Say, you didn't *tell anyone else*, did you?!. . ."

The history of the USS *Turner* continued with Stanton experiencing it in tow:

> Late in August, the ship returned to Boston for post-shakedown availability. In the second week of September, she resumed training exercises in the Caribbean and in Atlantic coastal waters. On 8 October, she departed Norfolk and steamed—via Pensacola, the Panama Canal, and San Diego—to Hawaii, arriving at Pearl Harbor on 28 November. There, she prepared for duty in the Tokyo area and, on 10 December, departed the Hawaiian Islands and proceeded to Japan.

The *Turner*, with Stanton on board, remained a picket ship for this voyage. And what exactly is a picket ship? This Navy illustration (below), courtesy of young Stanton, might help explain.

But not all was fun and games, as it turned out. Regarding the Japanese, there was still an atmosphere of intense hostility and distrust, and it was en route to Japan that Stanton was injured as a result, although in the end it was his own inattentiveness that was mostly to blame.

According to family friend, Jim Chambers, the incident unfolded one night just after Stanton had finished two back-to-back, eight-hour watches, was exhausted, and had just fallen asleep:

> Suddenly there was the cry of "Battle Stations! All hands!" That meant there was some place he had to be for an attack. He was so sound asleep at first that he didn't hear the alarm—should've already been where he was supposed to be.

Barely able to open his eyes, Stanton was racing to his battle station, cutting past a massive antiaircraft gun, when—*Boom!*—it fired, and on recoil, an ejected shell struck him in the chest. "A five-inch shell casing," as Stanton recollected in 1978, "and that laid me up for a long time." The end result, as Tom heard it: "He passed out through the whole action." Jim reiterated and finished the story:

> A large gun fired off and a shell casing came out and knocked him down and he'd hit his head, and when he woke up he was fine except that he couldn't see colors, he could only see in black and white. That lasted for a while. Finally when he regained the ability to see colors, mostly it was primary colors— like bright red, bright blue, bright green, bright yellow, and as a result a lot of his artwork had all primary colors and a lot

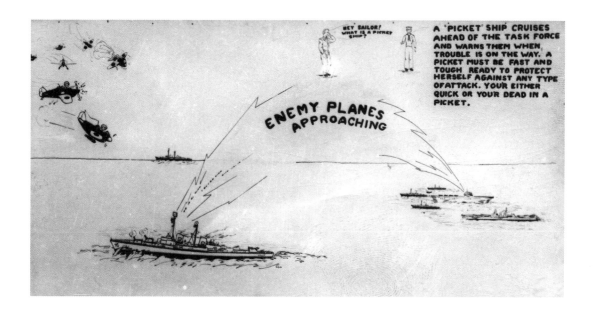

of people liked that about his artwork, but it was a result of his head injury. And I can remember the time when he bought Amber a set of colored pencils, and he was astonished. He remarked to me, "I can't believe it, I can see the different shades of color!" It came back to him, just like that. I'm gonna say Amber was maybe early teens at that time . . . It had to be like almost forty years later. It took that long for his brain to reconnect.

## Birth of a Dream Merchant

Aboard the seafaring USS *Turner* there was not much to do, so Stanton tried to fill his leisure time with drawing, and soon others took notice and began making requests.

"It was the pin-up era, and you have nothing on the ship," remarked Amber, "and if there's an artist who can draw women, thank God, 'cause that's what they wanna see, that's what they miss. So it started out fairly innocently like that and then it evolved . . ." What began on scraps of paper progressed to handkerchiefs, and as word got around that Stanton could provide these little harbingers of hope demand grew until, as he later said proudly: "I was making a dollar a handkerchief on board."

The true career of Stanton—as dream merchant of erotic longing—may have begun at that time, with those first modest commissions from his shipmates.

## Stanton the Solo Artist

During his high school days, Stanton's enjoyment of big band music and crooners like Sinatra held strong, and by graduation, his involvement in singing even led him in a city-wide competition against Queens-born peer Antonio "Tony" Benedetto (later known as Tony Bennett). What finally turned Stanton off to stage singing occurred while in the Navy, when he realized he just did not need to have the audience on his side, he needed to have the musicians as well. During one particular performance it seemed the band members had

decided to sabotage his style, playing the music at the wrong tempo—fast when he needed it slow and vice versa. "The band didn't back him up properly," related Tom. And it was deliberate. Once again, it would be an issue of control or powerlessness. "I guess that's when he decided not to be in the music business," according to Amber. "Up till then, he enjoyed drawing and singing. But then he realized he was really the kind of person who needed to work alone."

## Japanese Leave

As for the crew of the USS *Turner*, they had been on board ship for a long time, and they were relieved to finally pull in to shore. "They were in port in Japan," according to Jim Chambers:

> . . . and they told them, "Whatever you do, don't eat anything" . . . they let them go ashore, but were specific: "Don't eat anything while you're there!" Well, the food on board wasn't too good, so they said, "Hell, we're gonna eat some nice Japanese food." They went out, had Japanese food, came back to the ship, and got deathly ill. And why? Because—surrender or no surrender—the Japanese hated the Americans and tried to poison them! Eric said he was terribly ill, but he recovered, survived. A lot of guys got sick, but they didn't die.

Time passed, and boredom prompted the sailors to venture out again, somewhat older and wiser. On leave in Japan, Stanton managed to see as much of the country as time and protocol allowed. Quite naturally, he also sought out diversions apart from what had only been drawing and gambling. According to Tom, his father did have a sexual dalliance with a young woman, most likely a geisha.

But Japan was not where Stanton lost his innocence. That trauma had already transpired years before, courtesy of his only uncle, brother of Anna. As per family folklore, Uncle Willie was an aspiring boxer who had changed his name from William Telesewski to "William Tell." Later he resided in the Baltimore area and died on a railway. He was also sex obsessed.

It was when Stanton had just turned twelve that Uncle Willie decided to make a man out of him, according to Tom: "He took my dad to a whorehouse to celebrate." And it was there that a professional quickly took charge of the minor, who was understandably disoriented. The end result, as Tom concluded: "My dad said he wasn't sure if he peed or came."

According to Jim Chambers:

> After that, maybe the first time he had sex was with a big woman who attacked him, knocked him down, and forced him to have sex with her. Whether that imprinted on him, or whether he already had a predetermined desire for that, or it was just in his nature or his temperament or something, who knows. But that might've been where his fascination with domination began.

"Who really knows," Stanton once remarked himself, regarding this very question and how sexual preferences are formed. "I think it goes back beyond even what is considered the probable imprint period of adolescence. Maybe it can even be genetic—something recurring along the genetic bloodline. I used to think my fantasy began at eleven, then I said no, it was five. Then I thought I might have enjoyed that at two or three. I believe that."

# Seaman Stanzoni First Class, Over and Out

As for the rest of the USS *Turner*'s (and Stanton's) tour, according to public record:

> She operated out of Japanese ports with Task Group 55.4, Task Force 54, and other elements of the 5th Fleet until 24 March 1946 when she departed Yokosuka and proceeded via Midway to Pearl Harbor.

San Francisco followed in April. In May, records show Stanton parting the USS *Turner* for good—transferring to San Diego.

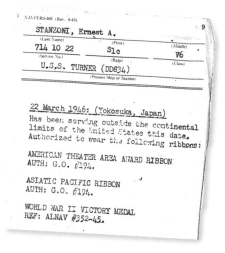

According to his final physical examination and release papers completed at the USN Personnel Separation Center in Lido Beach, Long Island, Seaman First Class, Stanzoni, Ernest A., service #714 10 22, with a dodgy eye condition and now measuring sixty-seven inches and weighing in at 134 lbs. (that is two inches taller and nine pounds heavier), was honorably discharged and reintroduced to civilian life. To what purpose? On his Notice of Separation form dated 22 June 1946, Stanton shared his ambition:

Under the GI Bill this would be possible, but it would wait.

# Nowhere Man: Knife-Throwing and Boody Rogers

"After the war, Eric thought he might apply for disability," according to Jim Chambers:

> He tried to explain to them that he got hit with a shell casing, got a concussion, and that he couldn't see color. And as an artist that really was a disability. They essentially said, "You're a faker, there's nothing wrong with you, you're fine," so he got nothing.

Life wasn't all bad for Stanton. One of the generous provisions of the GI Bill was known as the 52-20 Clause: "20" meant $20.00, and "52" meant the number of weeks a vet was eligible to collect while he looked for work. In other words, this amounted to unemployment compensation for veterans returning from the war.

Stanton, now twenty years old, collected his VA allotment while he looked for grown-up employment—or at least faked it. In the meantime, he lived at home, back on 213 Lincoln Avenue, with his mother Anna, Nick, and Grandma Sophie. Eleanor (right) was now in high school.

Stanton continued to draw, caught up on movies, Sinatra records, Jungle Girl and Amazon comics. He joined a softball team and bummed around the neighborhood. His restlessness took him to other parts of the city. Along the way, he struck up a friendship with future actor Walter Matthau, who shared a passion for shooting dice.

"They used to shoot craps together behind the soda jerk place where Matthau worked," related Tom. "They were always gambling together."

Stanton took a stab at applying to college in September 1947, but by then his year of unemployment ran out, and so did his excuses at home. Soon he was working with his stepdad, Nick, at the Casino Russe, a night club run by the Russian Tea Room, on 157 West 56th Street. From busboy, Stanton progressed to waiter. But it was just a matter of time before he felt a creeping unrest that led him to try his hand again at performance. This was a night club, after all, and if he could not make it as a stage crooner, he could at least try his luck as part of the flamboyant Russian-themed cabaret. What did he have to lose?

Twice nightly "he did the Russian dance with boots, performing for customers," according to Britt. From there he progressed to "dagger dancer," throwing knives: "He used to do it with his mouth. A knife in his mouth. Throw it at a board," recalled Eleanor. "God forbid he made a mistake, he would've killed somebody." Years later Stanton recalled his performance days and why he had to quit: "Women were jumping at me with this knife-throwing thing but I started to get a sore lip." Not to disappoint his stepfather, he remained at the Casino Russe for at least a year, but he was marking his days.

# Boody

As it turned out Stanton would not have to wait forever. One of his softball teammates, who had seen his drawings, revealed that his uncle was a comic illustrator, and that he was looking for an assistant. The job was modest, involving lettering and adding backgrounds to unfinished cartoon panels, but Stanton saw an opportunity to set his creative ambitions back on course. He took the job, which paid strictly by the hour. He would hop the Long Island Railroad from Brooklyn. Boody Rogers was the uncle's name. The year was 1948. By now Stanton had turned twenty-one.

At this time, Gordon "Boody" Rogers was lead assistant for Zack Mosley, a former art college roommate and creator of a syndicated strip called *Smilin' Jack*. While working for Mosley, Rogers had invented a few characters of his own, both superhero parodies: *Sparky Watts*, a plain-clothes send-up of Superman, and *Babe*, a *Li'l Abner*-inspired burlesque centering on a hillbilly gal endowed with Wonder Woman strength.

*Sparky Watts* was published by Columbia Comics, while *Babe* was published by Crestwood (which also published *Young Romance*). These were stapled fifty-two-page comic magazines, not syndicated strips, although between 1940/'42, *Sparky Watts* was syndicated in forty newspapers, including *The Brooklyn Eagle*, where Stanton might have seen it.

Boody Rogers' idea of cartooning befitted one of the original contributors to *The Funnies*—an unstapled comic anthology produced weekly on newsprint, starting in 1929—much like those appearing in Sunday tabloids years later. To Rogers, cartooning was about "making people laugh," so his work expressed that, being deliberately "zany" and ostensibly aimed at kids. Rogers also managed to push the envelope, as far as story concepts, and in this Stanton fanned the flames, contributing what Rogers must have realized at the time was a unique perspective.

At least three of Rogers's most bizarre stories can be traced to Stanton:

**1.** "Mrs. Gooseflesh": in issue #4 (Dec./Jan. '48/'49) of *Babe*—being a narrative about an entertainingly psychotic, neck-breaking lady wrestler that even featured Stanton, appropriately self-cast, as a cartoon character: a female wrestling promoter (next page).

**2.** "Hideout!": in issue #8 (Oct./Nov. 1949) of *Babe* (then renamed *Babe, Darling of the Hills*)—being an escapist romp involving the borderline subject of male cross-dressing.

**3.** "The Mysterious Case of Mystery Mountain!": also issue #8 (Oct./Nov. 1949)—involving a spoof of "pony play," an elaborate (one might say "bizarre"), gear-heavy form of animal role play.

Stanton's year with Boody Rogers unquestionably provided a valuable learning experience. He was introduced to the mechanics of professional comic illustration, and apart from the job he was hired to do, was even allowed to contribute original pencil and ink work, test his skills with watercolors (a medium he would come to favor), and even invent recurring characters, like "Teddy Tripod," a three-legged, pint-sized Neanderthal hatched from an egg first appearing in issue #7 of *Babe*.

While working for Rogers another significant event transpired. The area of Long Island known as Wantagh, where Rogers resided at this time, was promoted as "The Gateway to Jones Beach," and it was at Jones Beach, at a 1949 party not far from his employer's home, where Stanton met his first serious paramour, Grace Marie Walter.

Inspecting Rogers's comics for evidence of Stanton's hand, undoubtedly the most charming trace appears in *Babe, Darling of The Hills* #8, when in the next to last panel (below) of "The Mysterious Case of Mystery Mountain!"—the pony-play story—he passed a message to his sweetheart.

# Stanton Meets Isadore Klau (a.k.a. Irving Klaw)

Some of the most popular "girlie" magazines of the 1940s were published by Robert Harrison, a man probably best remembered for creating the scandal rag *Confidential*, but who years earlier had managed to successfully combine pin-up artistry with elements of burlesque and fetishism in a series of magazines that today have become highly collectible artifacts of Americana: *Beauty Parade, Eyeful, Wink, Titter, Flirt,* and *Whisper*.

It was likely in spring 1949, in "*Whisper* or one of those," as Stanton recalled, that he spotted an advertisement that stopped him cold. It was from Irving Klaw, the self-proclaimed "Pin-up King." This was nothing new in itself, as Klaw had been advertising in these magazines for years.

What made this ad uniquely of interest was that it went beyond "glamour" pin-ups, beyond cheesecake and "unretouched" girlie photos, to advertise a cartoon serial—in fact a fetish cartoon serial—something Stanton had apparently not seen before. He placed an order. "It cost me something like .50 cents a page," he remembered. "Each page or episode was an 8 × 10 in. photograph of a strip." When it arrived he was unimpressed: "What the other guy had drawn wasn't bad, but he didn't know how to do the 'sexy' thing with the two girls." Writing to Irving Klaw, Stanton declared that as an artist he could do better, even explaining why: "because I was into fighting girls and the last

guy wasn't." A second version of that story, told in 1978, had Stanton stating: "What happened was . . . I wrote and told him I thought I was a better artist than the one whose work was in the ad and I would like to do something for him."

Either way, the end result was an invitation from Klaw to present some artwork of Stanton's own based on the same theme, which was "battling women." And Stanton admitted, "It took me a week to draw it. I think I did eight pictures . . . I turned it into Klaw and he took one page and paid me $8.00, and it took me a week!"

But Stanton was far from discouraged. And so, hitting the pavement: "I went into bookstores and found some magazines like *Wit, It, Dash*— magazines that had some fighting girls. I got some wrestling magazines. Instead of men, I drew women

in these poses." So it went, with the artist applying himself. "Within a month or two Irving was paying me $10.00 a page. After . . . he went up to $15.00 per page."

"Pretty soon it didn't take me a week to do these little cartoon pages. I could do twenty in two or three days."

Stanton's first Klaw-issued comic contribution was *Battling Women*, no. 4 (above). Mention of it first appeared in a June 1949 Klaw advertising bulletin. In all, there would be twenty episodes or pages.

*Battling Women* was followed by *Fighting Femmes* (right).

## The Birth of "Stanton"

It was upon his involvement with Klaw (perhaps even suggested by him?) that Stanton, still known as "Ernie Stanzoni," considered adopting a fresh identity, a pseudonym or "artist's name." Making art—even comic art—was an act of reinterpretation, after all, so why not figuratively reinvent himself in the process? According to Eleanor, "He thought 'Stanzoni' was not a good name for an artist, so he changed it to 'Stanton.' He called himself 'Ernest Stanton.'" "Ernie Stanton" was how his name appeared on an illustration (above) drawn for his sister, obviously while employed by Boody Rogers.

**S TANTON**

How did he settle on "Stanton"? Circa 1949, there is evidence to suggest that he toyed with a magician-like variation of "Stanzoni" (above) and simply dropped the final letter. And in years to come Stanton would tweak the name again, adding another "o" to create "Stantoon"—his own *brand* of cartoon. (A later caricature of himself was a wrestling dummy/playtoy named "Stantooney." ["Stantooni."]) In connection with Klaw, it was

not until the newly titled, year-end advertising catalog *Cartoon and Pin-Up Parade* (Nov./Dec. 1949) that the name "Stanton" first appeared. And just the last name, like "Houdini." Klaw was not just a perceptive businessman, but a showman who understood the value of PR and keeping things simple.

## Who Was Irving Klaw?

Irving Klaw had established a self-named business—initially at 209 East 14th Street in Manhattan—largely to sell movie star photos, "glamour" girl pin-ups, and Hollywood ephemera. Circa 1948, on the suggestion of a customer, he entered the fetish art trade, building his distinctive catalog with anything he could get his hands on: customer/practitioner's contributions produced outside or inside his store (where he set up monthly shoots), back catalog and European-acquired material originally sold by Charles Guyette (a local "burlesque and theatrical" specialty shop owner and Klaw's predecessor), and in 1949, licensed material—illustrations and fetish photography—by John Willie (a.k.a. John Alexander Scott Coutts).

## Irving Klaw Timeline: In Brief

1910, 9 November: born Isadore Klaw (original family name "Klau") in Brooklyn.

1933–1937: employed as a furrier while running his first mail order business, Nutrix Novelty Co. (c. 1935– 1936), under the alias, "Irving Leder." Both were unsuccessful business ventures.

1938: married Natalie Youdelman, and with younger half-sister Pauline (Paula), opened a used magazine and book shop, which promptly switched to the sale of Hollywood movie stills.

1940s: aggressively developed his mail order business, out-spending pin-up competitors in advertising.

1945: opened new location at 212 East 14th Street to be named "Irving Klaw Pin-Up Photos."

1947/48: absorbed understanding of fetish sub-categories from Robert Harrison's publications, particularly *Titter*, *Wink*, and *Flirt*; others shaping Klaw's visual aesthetics included predecessors Charles Guyette and John Willie, both of whom contributed to Harrison's magazines.

1948: entered the fetish art business when it was suggested by a prominent businessman and associate of Guyette and Willie, later referred to as "Little John" or "J.J.B." Weekend photo shoots facilitated by Klaw in which devotees/fetishists were allowed creative control in exchange for Klaw keeping photo negatives resulted in the rapid accumulation of a back catalog.

1949: a decisive year, evidenced in two key advertising catalogs: *Movie Star News* 29th Edition (May/June) and *Cartoon and Pin-Up Parade* 30th Edition (November/December), in which Klaw's fetish art trade clearly dominated his interest.

1949: Issued the first of his fetish fantasy cartoon chapter serials. Early commissioned artists included C. W., Arista, "G." (George), and finally Stanton.

# Stanton Does Bondage Fantasy

Stanton's earliest serials for Klaw were thematically similar and the kind of comics that he naturally preferred: *Battling Women*, *Fighting Femmes*, *Dawn's Fighting Adventures*, and *Dawn Battles the Amazons*. But along the way, Klaw suggested that Stanton try his hand at producing a different kind of illustrative art. "He gave me a bunch of photographs and showed me how the bound women should look and how the rope should be tied," recalled Stanton. The year was still 1949, and Irving Klaw had just acquired the rights to *Sweet Gwendoline*, which also appeared in Harrison's magazine, *Wink*. "Of course we had John Willie's work to look at and I did."

"The first thing I drew on the bondage theme was a girl tied up in just bra and panties."

For his part, Stanton saw that what Klaw asked for was not so far removed from the matinee serials of his childhood. In fact, in recalling *The Perils of Nyoka*, the chapters were even called "episodes." For Klaw, it was just a matter of cutting to the chase. Since customers could buy each page separately, each page needed a cliff-hanger.

Starting in 1950, Klaw issued Stanton's first solo bondage serial, *Jill, Undercover Girl*, followed by *Poor Pamela*, with the first five pages contributed by another artist "G." (George). While Stanton penciled and inked these "damsel in distress" serials, the scripts were suggested by others, including Irving Klaw, who listened carefully to customer requests.

## The End of Boody Rogers

Times were tough in the humor comics genre. By mid-1949, Columbia Comics, publisher of *Sparky Watts*, had folded, ending the run with issue #9. Rogers took one last stab at creating a new comic, *Dudley*—his take on *Archie*. First published by Crestwood in November/December 1949, Dudley lasted only three issues. Almost simultaneously, *Babe, Darling of The Hills* ceased in 1950, with the March/April issue. Clearly his prospects were drying up.

It might be apparent that by late 1949, Stanton had made his choice: taking on Irving Klaw as his primary role model and guide. It was Klaw, for better or worse, who had opened up a brave new world for Stanton—one that piqued the imagination of the inherent sexual fantasist he no doubt already was. And in retrospect, it is easy to see where his story contributions to Boody Rogers originated, from the burlesque female impersonator photos to the reproductions of pony-play art by French illustrator "Carlo"—sold under-the-counter or via mail order by Irving Klaw.

As for Boody Rogers? Faced with starvation, he retired from cartooning, moved to Arizona, and opened up an art supply shop, where for the first time in his life he earned a sound income. He lived until age ninety-one.

# A Warning to Klaw:
# The Influence of Charles Guyette

If Stanton was molded to some extent by Irving Klaw, then it might be said that Klaw was shaped by Charles Guyette, who, despite being a trailblazer in the history of American sexploitation culture, remains a shadow figure.

What is known about Charles J. Guyette is in the early to mid-'30s, he sold "theatrical" costumes and supplies, and like Klaw, also ran his own successful, wide-ranging mail order business specializing in psychosexual fetish prints and photo sets. In fact, his operation was the first of its kind in America, dealing in what was then generally regarded as "deviant" European-inspired material.

Ads in the influential fetish-friendly magazine *London Life* announced: "We have costume studies of all kinds. Lingerie, corsets, high heels, etc. Female boxers and wrestlers in action. Also other types. 5/- per dozen. 30 photos for 10/-. Send cash or International Postal Order. C. Guyette, 116 East 11 Street, New York City."

Guyette's conspicuous success was short-lived. As reported by tabloids, on August 19, 1935, he was indicted for "offering to supply photographs of boxers, strong women, and other 'interesting subjects.'"—a charge—one of several—to which Guyette pleaded guilty, and for which he ultimately served time in a federal penitentiary.

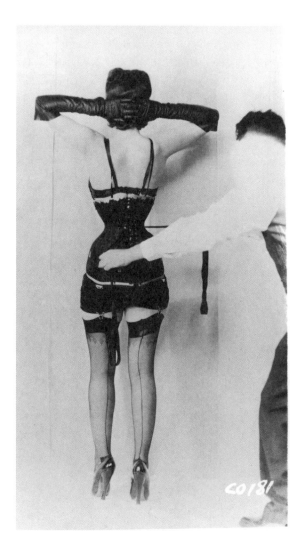

Charles Guyette—whose place of business was only three blocks away from where Irving Klaw would establish his own—served as a cautionary tale for anyone choosing to enter the fetish art trade.

## Klaw Takes Precautions

No doubt Guyette was very much on Klaw's mind when he entered the fetish game circa 1948. Klaw knew that if he was to avoid Guyette's fate, he needed to adhere to strict self-imposed limitations regarding what he sold, particularly through his mail order business.

First was a no nudity policy. Second, no sex (not even implied) in any material he sold. Third, to ensure compliance with obscenity standards, the material would not feature men and women together. In a rule well-suited to Stanton, men were excluded or diminished in what became purely a female-centered universe. Ladies playfully wrestling, ladies strutting about in skyscraper heels and kidskin boots, ladies calmly rolling on a pair of seamed silk stockings, ladies fitting on corsets, ladies tying each other up—all that was welcome. If men appeared at all, it was likely as female impersonators.

As for promoting his new line of fetish cartoon serials? Even here Irving Klaw showed restraint

Sweet Gwendoline.

Faithful Frederick (our hero)

Sir d'Arcy d'Arcy (the foul fiend)

Dad (poor but honest)

the Mysterious Countess.

" Ah! who will save her ! "

Charles Guyette makes most of the G-strings; sells them for $30. As he provides a variety of styles, he has a virtual monopoly on this item

at first. To play it safe, the word "bondage" was not used at all. Perhaps studying the approach of John Coutts (a.k.a. John Willie, creator of *Sweet Gwendoline*), Klaw relied on more ambiguous terms like "melodrama" and "damsel in distress" in his earliest advertising. There was a tradition of such femmes-in-peril storylines that extended back to medieval times. There was no nudity, no sex—not even men!—in his comic serials. So who should complain?

As far as the content of Irving Klaw's early bondage serials, it might be worth noting that nearly all of it was derivative, in one way or another, of the work of John Willie. *Zaza's Perilous Adventures*, *Paula's Perils Out West*, *Gale Girl Reporter*, *Poor Pamela*, *Miss Adventure*, *Jane's Jungle Adventures*—all wouldn't exist without Willie's *Sweet Gwendoline*. Stanton, too, was obliged to walk in his footsteps, at least to make Klaw happy. As it turned out, it was an adopted persona—one of several in Stanton's life—that he would not mind at all.

**CARTOON SERIALS OF ADVENTURE AND DAMSEL'S IN DISTRESS!**
Illustrated below are some of my various cartoon serials of ADVENTURE, OLD FASHIONED MELODRAMA, and CAPTIVE GIRLS, drawn by various artists in episode form. Each episode is complete on 8 x 10 glossy photograph paper format and may be purchased separately at price of 50¢ each episode.

# Working-Class Fantasist: Stanton vs. John Willie

While for most of his lifetime John Coutts was obliged to regard his high-minded artistic aspirations as a hobby, from the start Stanton was determined to earn a living from making art; this, in many ways, is what differentiates the two. To that end, Stanton would cast all pretentions aside, and always consider himself a commissioned artist— a fantasist for hire—and hustle as any ordinary Joe might.

While still living at home at 213 Lincoln Avenue, Eleanor's memory of Stanton was of someone who never stopped working: "My brother—for as long as I can remember—spent all his time drawing. And he worked alone in the cellar. He had an art table down there. And lights." She recalled:

> I'd come to the top of the stairs and I'd yell out 'Ernie, you need me today? Do you want me to do anything?' He'd say, 'Yeah, come on down here. I got some stuff for you to do.' So I'd go downstairs and he would tell me what to do. I was just a kid."

Sometimes Stanton had his obliging sister erase stray pencil marks. "Then he'd ask, 'How'ya like it?' And I'd say, *Oh, y'know* . . . I would give him my opinion . . ."

By late 1950, Stanton had finished at least seven serials, with the nineteen episodes he contributed to *Poor Pamela* (in the style of "G.") being among his best early "damsel in distress" pen and ink efforts. To pick up extra pocket change and not lose touch with reality, he also worked alongside Irving and his sister, Paula, at Irving Klaw Pin-Up Photos. According to Tom, "My dad said he did anything he could for the family. He worked the register there, at the store." Other artists saw Irving Klaw's Hollywood movie stills, pin-ups, and "art studies" as a valuable resource and visited the shop with increasing frequency. With the new art college called Cartoonists & Illustrators School opening up just nine blocks away, "Irving's" became just the place to be.

# Art School: Stanton Meets Ditko, Bilbrew, and Robinson

The year 1951 marked many significant changes in Stanton's life. First was a legal name change, allowing him to shed the ghost of "Stanzoni" once and for all. He had already chosen to reinvent himself as "Stanton" at least as far back as 1949, but in 1951, he played with a subtle variation. Under the name "Stanten" (with an "e") he enrolled full time at Cartoonists & Illustrators School, likely with Klaw's encouragement, beginning in April.

If the choice "Stanten" seemed somewhat shifty, it was intentional: he wanted a name that was close enough to his "real" self—the artist taking form— yet different enough that it could provide a cover. Being elusive, as Stanton understood then, was critical to an underground artist, especially one operating under the radar of the law. Now Stanton could work at Irving's, continue to draw chapter serials, and for the first time receive some formal art training. The GI Bill provided the opportunity.

## Stanton, Bilbrew, and Ditko

In 1950, Cartoonists & Illustrators School moved to a four-story building on the corner of 23rd Street and Second Avenue, and it was here, one year later, that Stanton received his first serious trade instruction.

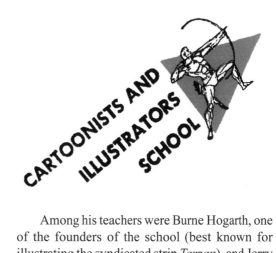

Among his teachers were Burne Hogarth, one of the founders of the school (best known for illustrating the syndicated strip *Tarzan*), and Jerry Robinson (best known for his work on the *Batman* syndicated strip). No less significant, it was at C&I where Stanton met two artists who would figure prominently in his life: Stephen "Steve" John Ditko and Eugene "Gene" Webster Bilbrew. Steve Ditko, with support from Stanton (as we shall see), later created Spider-Man for Marvel Comics; Gene Bilbrew, a black artist, became a comrade, fellow innovator, and even a friendly competitor for any illustrative fetish-themed art. Together, Stanton and Bilbrew would create the most significant sexual fantasist art of the 1950s and 1960s. Long before adult comics—then renamed "comix"— became accepted in the 1970s, they represented the vanguard.

Because of his propensity for excess Bilbrew would have a tragic life. A former member of the vocal group the Basin Street Boys (see p. 38), he had just recently turned to art. As fate would have it, it was Stanton who prompted Bilbrew's true calling.

Their first meeting, as related to publisher J. B. Rund, took place in mid-1951, when Stanton spotted his fellow student working on a drawing unrelated to the class they shared (likely Robinson's). It was an illustration with exotic elements of fetishism (including bondage), and it got them talking and made them aware that they were kindred spirits—equally curious about exploring subversive cartoon art.

## 'Diggin'' The Cash Box...

HOLLYWOOD, CALIF.—Diggin' *The Cash Box* is Leon Rene (center), President of Exclusive Records, and the Basin Street Boys. Prexy Rene is justly proud of his artists' fine showing in *The Cash Box's* recent record poll. The Basin Street Boys were consistent favorites with their Exclusive recording of "I Sold My Heart To The Junk Man" and Johnny Moore and his Three Blazers placed first in their field in *The Cash Box's* annual awards for '46. Left to right: Ormand Wilson, Reuben Saunders, Leon Rene, Gene Bilbrew, Arthur Rainwater.

Upon meeting Stanton, Bilbrew was working for Will Eisner (according to cartoonist Jules Feiffer, "as a troubleshooting background artist, called to help on deadlines"); he had also recently taken over a comic created by Feiffer called *Clifford*. But he was being poorly paid. With an interview arranged by Stanton, Bilbrew presented sample sketches to Irving Klaw; the reaction was positive, and reinventing himself as "Eneg" (Gene spelled backward), he joined Stanton in producing Klaw chapter serials.

Three years older, more experienced, and evidently possessing greater natural ability as a draftsman, in truth, Bilbrew had the jump on Stanton, who had to sweat each increment of artistic progress through sheer persistence. As Stanton later admitted of his friend: "Listen, he was a better artist at the time than I was. Much better." In retrospect, Stanton could accurately say, "But I think I improved more than he did."

(Artwork by "Carlo")

## The Inspiration of Robinson

If there was one thing that Stanton and Ditko shared from the beginning, it was their enthusiasm for their instructor, Jerry Robinson, whom Stanton acknowledged as a great influence: "Fabulous teacher," he would say years later. "You can draw all your life, but if you don't get the basics rubbed into you, you don't have any room for improvement." This seemed to echo the sentiments of Ditko, who stated: "Until I came under the influence of Jerry Robinson I was self-taught, and you'd be amazed at the hours, months, and years one can spend practicing bad drawing habits." Stanton would say: "You have to learn good planning, how to develop a page, and Jerry Robinson is it."

As for how Stanton and Ditko met? Stanton could not seem to recall a specific incident. Two earnest misfits, they simply gravitated toward each other (more in chapter nineteen). Both were from the same social class and unpretentious, and both had grown up in the shadow of the Great Depression. There is no doubt that Stanton saw similar qualities in Ditko that he saw in his stepfather and even in Irving Klaw, both of whom were no-nonsense workaholics. In many ways Stanton would grow closer to Ditko, whom he seemed to regard as a positive role model, than Bilbrew.

Did Ditko ever recall meeting Bilbrew? In contacting him for this book, he answered directly: "Yes, Gene was one of the students in Jerry Robinson's class." In 1976, when asked by publisher J. B. Rund how he and Stanton came together as friends, Ditko replied simply enough, "I liked the way he drew women."

## Stanton and Comics Reexamined

Although Stanton showed little interest in male super-hero comics throughout most of his life, while at C&I he would reassess the work of several mainstream cartoonists and note some favorites. "Ogden Whitney. Ogden because I thought his girls were full and round and voluptuous . . . very attractive. He had a good hand for girls . . . I liked Dan Barry. I didn't care for a lot of artists who overdid muscles and things like that. Like Hogarth, even though I was taught under him."

While he had the opportunity, Stanton also appraised the art of Alex Raymond (best known for illustrating the syndicated strip *Flash Gordon*) and Hal Foster (best known for illustrating the syndicated strip *Prince Valiant*), both coincidentally old favorites of Ditko. From 1951 on, Stanton's work for Klaw reflected this new-found awareness—with direct references.

When it came to fetish art, the ingenious French illustrator Carlo was still undoubtedly a strong influence (just as he remained for John Willie), and while at Irving's, Stanton studied every sample he could find, in addition to other "bizarre" illustration of European origin. The "Cartoon Artist Series"—eventually numbered CA-1 to CA-60—issued by Klaw starting in 1949, would reproduce, as stated in advertisements, "artists which appeared in foreign publications many years ago, which have been out of print for some time." These included obscure names like Esbey, Selby, and Wighead. Stanton also once related to J. B. Rund a memorable occasion while working for Klaw in which both he and Gene Bilbrew, in the name of research, were dispatched to the residence of "Little John," the important fetish art collector and enthusiast who had initially suggested the business to Klaw in 1948. Apparently that visit proved an eye-opener.

## Jungle Girl Heyday

As far as referencing kinky sub-currents in popular comic magazines: "Wonder Woman probably had the most satisfying bondage scenes," according to Stanton. But elements of fetishism also appeared in other strips as well, in particular jungle girl comics, which from the late 1930s to the early 1950s (Stanton's artistic formative years) were in their glory.

While Ditko adored Will Eisner's *The Spirit*, Stanton frequently cited his other best-known co-creation, *Sheena*, originally drawn by Mort Meskin and later by "good girl art" specialist Matt Baker. The commercial success of Sheena soon created a cottage industry of copycat jungle vixens whose names have long since passed from history, but whose brief collective appearance left an indelible mark on Stanton's consciousness. And what was the appeal beyond the suggestive, leggy girl art? Obviously the pleasure of seeing a subversion of the Tarzan formula. These jungle princesses—Rulah, Camilla, Cave Girl, Tiger Girl, et al.—were self-reliant, bold, in touch with their primal selves, and often gratuitously violent. In fact, one might see that comic books in the pre-code era were much like latter day exploitation movies in how they tapped subconscious fantasy. And it was subconscious fantasy that largely appealed to Stanton from the beginning, especially if it went contrary to normal cultural expectations.

It might be worth noting that Sheena's American comic debut—three months after Superman in 1938—coincided with Stanton's sudden interest in comics.

## Diana's Ordeal

While attending Cartoonists & Illustrator's school, Stanton continued to illustrate serials for Klaw. His first success came midway 1951, with *Diana's Ordeal*, a serial involving a guileless damsel and her "guided tour" of imaginative bondage exhibits on display in a menacing wax museum named Inquisition Castle. The popularity of the comic was such that Klaw swiftly commissioned a sequel that became *Perils of Diana*, produced that very summer.

Today, *Diana's Ordeal* is probably most noteworthy in how it marked Stanton's technical improvement as an artist between February and June 1951—obviously as a result of his schooling. Compare a panel from the first page installment to the final page of the serial (opposite), and one can see how much more interesting and sophisticated it is on every level, from the more realistic muscle tone of the ladies, to the facial expressions, to the composition, etc.

Amusingly, while in a cartooning class at C&I, Stanton was stealing a moment to alter a page of *Diana's Ordeal* when he got caught by the instructor, who berated him for working on such trash, as opposed to more respectable comic art. Although the bondage exhibits in *Diana's Ordeal* only featured wax dummies and not the real thing (i.e., damsels), it seemed realistic enough to warrant being sent to the "principal's office." Burne Hogarth (no stranger to sensational pulp art) then sat Stanton down and gave him a perfunctory lecture about how he ought to be more careful about his choice of material and how he ought to consider his "career."

# Wedding Bells

On a more personal note, the fall of that year marked the marriage of two Kochengin siblings. In the case of Eleanor, it was on her birthday in September that she married a young man she originally met at a neighborhood swimming pool. Less than a month later, on 20 October 1951, it was Stanton's turn. The embossed names appearing on the chunky wedding album proclaimed, "Grace and Ernie." A local community news item that followed declared: ". . . Grace Marie Walter of Ozone Park and Ernest Stanten of Cypress Hills are Honeymooning in Florida following their marriage in St. Sylvester's R. C. Church . . ."

Following the couple's return, they moved into a new apartment in South Ozone Park. Stanton's mother and stepfather also left Brooklyn, granting Eleanor and her new husband the familiar 213 Lincoln Avenue residence. For the rest of the 1950s and early 1960s, Stanton more or less resided in working-class Queens, a detail that Steve Ditko played on years later when the two would finally become studio mates.

# 8

# Enter the Muse: Bettie Page

Following Stanton's honeymoon, as fate would have it, another notable event transpired: the appearance at Irving's of the one fetish model who served as Stanton's life-long inspiration.

Although it is uncertain exactly when Stanton became aware of Betty Page (as her name was spelled then), references first began to appear in his artwork in 1952, as evidenced in the serial *Phyllis in Peril* (see p. 44). From that point on, her image and name would recur, often in dreamlike mutations, almost obsessively until the end of his career.

"I never was in love with anybody else like I was in love with Betty Page," Stanton confessed years later. But this was in the idealized sense: an infatuation "from a distance." He admitted, "I think I must have placed her too high on a pedestal in my mind at the time. I was married too. So . . ." His constant presence at Irving's afforded him recurrent exposure and a firsthand view of her growing catalog of work, and finally an opportunity to meet. "I just put her in bondage a few times," Stanton related. "Only once did I ever do something to her and that was because

IRVING KLAW
Featuring the Largest Variety of Popular Model Photos
212 East 14th Street — GRamercy 7-8526
NEW YORK 3, N. Y.

*Betty & me a dream till today Eric Stanton*

I was expected to. We had her tied up and her breast was falling out of her bra, so I kind of snuggled it back . . ."

The possibility of forming a deeper bond was made all the more improbable because of Klaw's business policy of keeping the artists who worked for him apart, as Stanton acknowledged: "Klaw didn't like the artists fraternizing with the other artists or the models, even though I would help out on some of the shoots. When the shoot was over she'd get dressed and leave. When she finished she went immediately to another job. She worked all the time." As Stanton recalled years later, she also kept most people at arm's length: "Nobody really knew her. Not even Irving . . . You'd sit and talk with her, but it was business. All business."

The chief orders a third degree form of questioning for Vultura!

Bettie Mae Page arrived in New York City, for the second time in September 1950, determined to make it in show business. Tired of the monotony of secretarial jobs, she followed in the path of Cocoa Brown and June King (both future Irving Klaw hires) and became a camera club model. From there, she progressed to Robert Harrison's publications (*Beauty Parade*, *Eyeful*, *Wink*, *Titter*, *Flirt*, and *Whisper*), where starting in August 1951, she eventually made more than seventy-five appearances. As with Harrison's publications, it was through a camera club photographer that she was introduced to Irving Klaw.

The photo shoots that Stanton recalled generally took place once a month on the third floor of the building occupied by Klaw at 212 East 14th Street. According to photographer Jack Bradley, husband of Klaw model Joan Rydell, Klaw would change up spots (possibly as a security measure): "He had two or three different locations, but only one at a time." Irving Klaw was rarely involved in the shoots personally, and like Charles Guyette before him (despite claims to the contrary) *never* the photographer. In those early years, the creative end was entrusted to fetish devotees who were knowledgeable, if not expert, in the study and placement of ropes and knots; and others, like

Stanton, who were called in to pose "his bondage and fighting girls." Stanton firmly acknowledged: "I did pose a lot of pictures for Irving."

Such responsibilities, entrusted to him in the name of artistic research and apprenticeship, would serve him well with future employers (and even his own future mail order business), as well as socially. According to fetish photographer Eric Kroll, "Sometimes the models would try and date Stanton in hopes that it would lead to more assignments."

Although Stanton never connected with Bettie romantically, it was with great pride that he admitted, "I had her make an 8mm film for me at Irving's. It was a fighting girl movie."

# Four Serials and Steve Ditko

Being Irving Klaw's favorite son had its disadvantages, as Stanton was to find out. The first bit of unpleasantness occurred when Klaw approached him to police the work of the somewhat erratic artist he had personally recommended that same year: Gene Bilbrew. This would very likely create the first tension between the two.

The material in question was Eneg's serial, *Princess Elaine's Terrible Fate*. Upon close examination, Klaw noticed what seemed like indecent references in the artwork, the likes of which—as he had made plain—were forbidden. As Stanton recalled years later: "Klaw asked me to cover some of what he thought were phallic symbols . . . Gene didn't like that . . ." No doubt Bilbrew liked it even less when Stanton was called upon again to censor the sequel, *Dangerous Plight of Princess Elaine*.

Even more upsetting, and something Stanton would dwell on until the end of his life, occurred in 1952, when Klaw purchased—outright—the original artwork of what many consider a John Willie masterpiece, *The Missing Princess* (to be renamed *New Adventures of Sweet Gwendoline*), and assigned Stanton the unwelcome task of "amending" it for publication, which at first Stanton refused to do.

To a man like Irving Klaw, this was just business; there was nudity in the artwork and the nudity posed a legal risk, so had to be covered up. To Stanton this was practically criminal: "I felt miserable, but what was I going to do? He would

have had someone else do it." According to publisher J. B. Rund: "Stanton proposed that acetate sheet overlays should be used, so as not to mutilate the originals, but this recommendation was rejected."

The end result: this achingly beautiful work—one of only two chapter serials that John Willie would complete in his lifetime—was in effect "sanitized," or some would say permanently defaced—and by another fetish artist, no less. On at least thirty-two episode/pages, Stanton was obliged to provide underwear or otherwise conceal pretty derrieres and breasts. (On episode/page 37, going even farther, he altered a punishment apparatus, removing a menacing sharp-toothed saw and adding a gentler, almost comical spring-loaded paddle.) All that remains of the untouched nude originals today are black-and-white photocopies.

On a cheerier note, despite the demands of school and married life, Stanton's personal productivity continued. His sister Eleanor recalled paying visits and even lending assistance: "I would go there no less than once every two weeks, sometimes more . . . I would visit him, and he had a pile of work." As she recollected: "Pen and ink, pen and ink—everything in black-and-white."

# "NEW ADVENTURES of SWEET GWENDOLINE"

(Gwendoline by John Willie, underwear by Stanton)

As for the edgier Klaw material, Stanton became guarded: "My brother didn't want anybody to know what he was doing because at that time, those comic strips were dangerous . . . maybe too *racy*? Yeah. So he didn't advertise the fact that that's what he did."

Completed by late 1952 were *Sheba, The Slave Girl*, the aforementioned *Phyllis In Peril*, *Bizarre Museum*, and *Priscilla, Queen of Escapes*.

Of these, *Bizarre Museum* and *Priscilla, Queen of Escapes* demonstrated Stanton's rapidly developing skills as a draftsman, and much less acknowledged, as an inker. Both serials show considerable precision and polish.

*Bizarre Museum* (below), with the lead character "Countess Bizarre" inspired by Stanton's favorite movie actress, Gale Sondergaard (see chapter 1), was another serial in the "tour of horrors" bondage subgenre, which included the previous year's

*Diana's Ordeal* and *Perils of Diana*, but this time done in a single-panel format, illustrating with a kind of stylized Halloween-like ghoulishness a catalog of loosely connected "bizarre" bondage predicaments purportedly inspired (if we are to believe the text) by a "real-life" Bizarre Museum based in nineteenth-century London, England.

By contrast, *Priscilla, Queen of Escapes* was a more conventional attempt to combine a damsel in distress narrative with a noir-style melodrama. The circus setting in which it all takes place enabled Stanton to inject a good deal of Saturday matinee-inspired excitement by pitting the heroine, in quasi-jungle girl fashion, against a parade of menacing circus animals (including a tiger, a bear, a gorilla, and an elephant) in league with a shadowy gang of female thugs headed by Leona (see p. 48), the animal trainer-cum-dominatrix.

*Queen of Escapes* also afforded Stanton an opportunity to pay homage to Harry Houdini (whose grave, it might be recalled, he maintained as a teenager) in referencing his famous milk can escape (below), a straightjacket escape—and his overall ingenuity and skill at managing ropes, chains, and locks: the stuff of theatrical bondage.

It is worth mentioning that although Stanton was well acquainted with Coney Island, he had never once attended the circus, but was able to recreate illustrative details for the comic from B-movie recollections and the circus movie stills sold at Irving's. Houdini photos were also available through Irving Klaw. In fact, one of Klaw's earliest businesses had been the Nutrix (as in "new tricks") Novelty Company, through which he sold magic tricks via mail order, but that venture had failed.

## Duchess of The Bastille and Jasmin's Predicament

The year 1953 saw not only the end of Stanton's art school days, but the last of his Klaw serials done in a more-or-less conventional "comic strip" style.

*Duchess of The Bastille*, first distributed between February and June 1953, marked a high point for Stanton. Said to be inspired by the 1935 film version of *A Tale of Two Cities* and staged in an all-female universe recalling the epoch of the French revolution, *Duchess of The Bastille* is a visually dynamic adventure tale full of powerful narrative arcs, essentially matching two iron-willed women: the righteous and unsentimental Baroness Lorraine against the cruel and despotic Mercedes, Duchess of the Bastille.

Proving that there is a fine line between super-heroines and fetishists, the Baroness Lorraine operates from a subterranean haunt, and in true renegade style, adopts a mask (next page) when called upon to perform her patriotic duty, which usually involves some bondage related activity—either tying or untying someone. (Elsewhere that alter ego is referred to as the "Purple Avenger.")

Later in the story, while trying to set free an innocent captive, Lorraine is captured and sentenced to prison (opposite, top), and after being forced to suffer severe indignities, finally turns the tables by sparking a climactic third-act revolt in the fashion of *Spartacus*.

Marking an end to Stanton's C&I influenced cartoon strip work is *Jasmin's Predicament*, a Klaw serial whose story of revenge involves the headmistress of a harem, Jezebel, who is jealous of a court dancer named Jasmin, and therefore sees to it that the woman is wrongly imprisoned and put through a litany of tortuous ordeals. As Jezebel states at one

## "DUCHESS OF THE BASTILLE"

EPISODE 19

point: "You displaced me in the Sultan's favor by your youth and dancing ability, but when I get through with you, you won't even be fit for a galley slave." Several times in the narrative Jasmin escapes from Jezebel's byzantine dungeon, only to be recaptured, like in some hellish nightmare (or horror movie), and put through even worse torment.

Although a lesser work than *Duchess of The Bastille* as far as page layout, with virtually every panel trying to top the next with some bondage terror befalling either Jasmin or some other innocent prisoner (to the effect of numbing overload)—*Jasmin's Predicament* is nevertheless significant for one reason: it is the first clear collaboration between Stanton and another recent graduate of C&I. As first stated in *Irving Klaw Bulletin* #73, advertising the work: "Popular artist Stanton has collaborated with new artist Omar to draw up a new Bondage cartoon serial . . ." And who might "Omar" be?

J. B. Rund, who reprinted most of the Klaw serials during the 1970s and '80s, answered this question directly: "It was Eric who told me that 'Omar' was Steve Ditko."

In comparing *Jasmin's Predicament* to *Duchess of The Bastille*, what is obvious is that Ditko not only contributed to the inking on this serial, but also original artwork. To appreciate the difference in style between Ditko's work and that of Stanton's, compare the portrayal of the turbaned "Jezebel" (above). Stanton's interpretation (center) was inspired by the darkly glamorous character Vultura ("Queen of the Arabs") from his favorite childhood serial, *The Perils of Nyoka*.

Whether it was to visit his pal or just thumb through bins of Hollywood movie stills in the name of research, Ditko frequented Irving's. Cartoonist great Al Williamson, who also attended Cartoonists & Illustrator's school, recalled visiting the shop in those days, and at least on a few occasions bumping into the artist there.

## Steve Ditko— an Irving Klaw Artist?

It may have been possible that Irving Klaw even expected Ditko to join his rebel crew of bizarre artists, as Bilbrew had done a few years earlier. Unlike Bilbrew and Stanton, Ditko's interest was in mainstream comics, and in fact, that same fall (1953) his first published narrative—a six-page contribution titled "Paper Romance"—appeared in Gillmor Magazine's *Daring Love* #1.

Nine years later, in reprinting the serial in a different format, Klaw wrote: "We have just re-issued popular artists [*sic*] Stanton's best-selling chapter serial 'Jasmin's Predicament' which was written by Omar the bondage author . . ." And what to make of this? Maybe this was Klaw's way of explaining "Omar's" short-lived involvement—the previously touted "new" Klaw artist who never produced more fetish art? Or did he?

The truth is Steve Ditko did, both for Irving Klaw and a host of others, as we shall see.

# Reimaginings: Stanton's First Milestone

By design, installments of Klaw chapter serials were issued concurrently or nearly so: that is, twelve or twenty episodes of one serial were offered for sale at the same time that two or ten episodes of another were made available.

Always a showman, Klaw felt it created more drama to unspool chapter serials gradually rather than all at once. The point was to keep devotees hooked—and coming back for more. Such was the case in 1953, when between the months of August and November—overlapping with the release of *Jasmin's Predicament*—Klaw unveiled (under a rather lackluster/generic title) a Stanton breakthrough: *Bound In Leather*. After pushing the limits of the cartoon strip format with *Duchess of The Bastille*, Stanton sought to try something new, and so proposed a variation to Klaw inspired by the illustrated novella. His new layout would have running text neatly allotted to one space, art another. Word and thought balloons, and other intrusive elements, could therefore be eliminated, and he would be free to re-imagine these fantasies and create distinctive interpretive art without the clutter. Irving Klaw, being a practical businessman, resisted this suggestion at first, indicating that the sequential comic strip design had been popular enough—and why tamper with success? Yet Klaw was never one to rule out an innovation that might potentially profit him.

And so, in June 1953, it happened that Klaw came into possession of a manuscript that changed everything. It was so well-written—or at least unique and bizarre—that he realized it might best be served the way Stanton had suggested.

The author of this manuscript (although Stanton would not know it for years—as the artists were kept apart) was another early contributor to Klaw's catalog, a bondage and "human doll" fantasist known as "B&G." In real life his name was Joe Cross, whose day job was in advertising, although he had once also written for the *Buck Rogers* radio program.

Evidence suggests (above) that in the beginning, B&G made an earnest attempt to illustrate the story himself, but then, abandoning it upon realizing his own artistic shortcomings, or possibly just through the urging of Klaw, Stanton was brought in.

*Bound In Leather* pulls damsel-in-distress fantasy straight down the rabbit hole of the surreal, a zone—as a young artist wanting to be tested—Stanton was curious and eager to explore. As he later acknowledged in an interview: "I attacked that story with relish."

In taking the trip ourselves: the fantasy begins at a theater (a place of unreality), where the protagonist, Mr. Walk ("Klaw" spelled backward), meets a mysterious, elegantly dressed woman. Beyond being beautiful, what is apparent is that she is also an adherent of fantasist culture. At the close of the play's first act more details of this woman's devotion to the "bizarre" are revealed (as expressed in episode/chapter 4's adjoining text):

# BOUND IN LEATHER

As the house lights came up, I turned to my companion and remarked, "I thought that was terrific, didn't you?"

"It was pretty funny, alright, but I would have liked it better if that had been a real gag," she answered.

"What do you say we go over to the bar and have a drink, instead of sitting in this hot theatre?" I asked.

She made me very happy by agreeing.

The waiter captain at the bar knows me, but he knew my companion even better.

"Good evening, Mrs. Roberts," he said, bowing. Then he led her to a booth; I followed along behind, feeling considerably dashed by the knowledge that she was married. But then I cheered up. Maybe she had been divorced.

As we sat down, I said, "So you're Mrs. Roberts?"

"That's right. Mrs. Richard Roberts, happily married and the mother of a daughter."

"Is that right?" I asked.

She started talking about her husband.

"My husband insists on high heels for my carriage, corsets for my figure, bondage to make me helpless, and a gag to assure that silence which is a guarantee of assent."

"How about your daughter? Is she being brought up the same way?"

"Being brought up? She won't have it any other way. At times she insists on such severe treatment that we're afraid she will do herself permanent injury. But she justs laughs, or would, if she could make a sound, and wants her gag and bonds pulled tighter."

"She sounds like a thoroughly delightful girl," I said, wistfully.

"Oh, she is, she just lives for bondage and figure training."

She paused and I waited. This was the moment.

"Would you like to meet her?" asked my pretty companion.

Restraining a strong, but I think natural, desire to yell "Yes!" at the top of my voice, I answered, "If she's anything like you, I'd be delighted."

"Well, I suggest we finish our drinks and then go home."

"Sounds like an excellent idea."

For her pat she told me her name was Victoria, Vicki for short. Her daughter was Nicole, or Nicki. Her husband, Dick, who ran a brokerage house, was away for a couple of days on business; that was why she had come to the theatre alone.

We were soon in a cab heading for an address uptown.

When we arrived at the address Vicki had given me, I was impressed to see it was a private house, rather than an apartment.

"I don't know what your daughter may look like, but you look utterly charming. I've never seen such a figure—that tiny waist and full bust."

"Oh, this figure?" she answered me in an oddly detached tone. "This is just the figure I wear in public—can't stop traffic, you know. But wait till we get inside."

"Would you unlock the door, please? My glove are so tight that it's very difficult for me. Use the big flat key."

I soon had the door swinging open and she stepped inside. I followed. I heard a pleasant, slightly French accented voice begin speaking as I followed her in.

"Madame is back so soon, surely, the play cannot be over? But of course not; madame didn't stay beyond the second act, that is when the interest ceases."

"Fifi, this is a new friend of mine. You may be seeing a good deal of him. His name is Mr. Walk."

Fifi looked at me, giving me a warm, inviting smile. Meanwhile, I was looking at her, well, maybe staring was a better word.

Believe me, this Fifi was worth a long stare any day. Actually about medium height, she appeared to be tall, by reason of the slim six-inch heels on her pretty ankle-strap sandals, of black patent leather, shackled at wrists and ankles with dainty cuffs and chains.

"Show Mr. Ted into the living room, Fifi. Then come upstairs and help me. I'm going to slip into something more comfotable."

Fifi watched her mount the stairs to where they turned at a landing, then she turned to me and breathed, "Madame is so lovely. But then, Mamselle Nicki is lovely, too . . ."

Then she waited.

"You're lovely, too, Fifi," I assured her.

"Thank you, monsieur, I was beginning to think you would not say it."

She opened the door with a grand gesture, ushered me through.

"This is the living room, monsieur," she informed me.

She was interrupted by Nicki's voice, calling from above.

"Fifi! Stop flirting, come up here and tend to your job!"

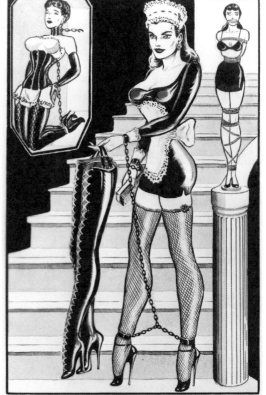

CHAPTER 4

# NEW BONDAGE CARTOON SERIAL!
## "JASMIN'S PREDICAMENT" drawn by Stanton & Omar

Popular artist Stanton has collaborated with new artist Omar to draw up a new Bondage cartoon serial called "Jasmin's Predicament". In this new cartoon the story centers around the perils, troubles and predicaments that Jasmin, the Sultan's favorite harem dancer goes through at the hands of the Sultan's jealous head mistress of the harem.

There are only 12 episodes available at present at price of 50¢ each 8x10 episode, but more will be drawn up next month.

Scenes from "Jasmin's Predicament" drawn by Stanton and Omar.

# New Combination Bondage Story and Drawing Serial!

## "BOUND IN LEATHER"

Now at last in response to many requests, we have had popular artist Stanton draw up a new series of illustrations done in the new wash technique to illustrate an unusual bondage story which was specially written to please the many Irving Klaw customers. This new Bondage serial is called "Bound In Leather" and tells what happens when a young man makes a casual pick-up of a high heeled booted woman in a theatre and the bizarre and thrilling events and circumstances which followed when they both found out they were bondage enthusiasts. When Ted visits Vikki's home which has been dedicated to various bondage gadgets and apparatus and is introduced to Vikki's daughter Nicki and their French maid Fifi, his adventure reaches a new high. Artist Stanton has put several illustrations on one side of each Chapter to illustrate the story material typewritten alongside; only the first 10 chapters of Bound in Leather are available at present at 50¢ each 8x10 chapter. This serial is a must for all collectors of bondage material.

Illustrations from "Bound in Leather" drawn by Stanton

(Advertisements appearing in Irving Klaw Bulletin #74)

As for her engagement ring? Walk makes clear:

> "You can't wear it on your finger, for your arms will be behind you almost all the time, so I think a diamond nose-ring is a neat substitute, don't you?"
>
> She nodded and offered her mask again. This time I obliged and Nicki and I were engaged.

(As for that nose-ring, consider the year: 1953.)

As illustrated by Stanton, not only is the mistress of the house a fetishist, so is the maid. In fact, in an *Addams Family*-like unveiling, the entire eccentric clan is touched by the same obsession—bondage and "figure training"—no family member more so than the daughter, Nicki (first presented in episode 9, above), the top portion of her body encased in a trunk:

> Guided by Fifi, this vision strutted into the room, taking steps not much over six inches long. The reason for the short steps was evident. The extremely thin heels on the boots were over eight inches high.

In the end, *Bound In Leather* is a bizarre romantic comedy in which Walk is so smitten with the masked fetish-obsessed daughter (who never actually reveals her face) that he asks for her hand in marriage. As usual with a Klaw commissioned fantasy, there is no sex depicted or implied anywhere.

Peculiarities abound in *Bound In Leather*, and not just in the highly descriptive writing. The very look of the artwork was a departure from anything Stanton had produced before and seemed to channel modernist and surrealist art. In fact, everything about it looked strangely foreign, except for the whimsical *Looney Tune*-like comic touches added throughout: lamps, lighters, ashtrays alive with a kind of anthropomorphism (note p. 52, the Bettie Page staircase ornament).

Departing farther from comic strip convention and his training at C&I, Stanton also heavily favored the technique of wash (as he would from this point on), when nib pen and ink was considered the standard in cartooning. And in various drafts of the artwork—perhaps inspired by the psychological realism of John Willie's *The Missing Princess* (whose artwork he was obliged to study closely before censoring)—Stanton also experimented with subtleties of human expression, as if trying to distinguish between levels of fear and desire, panic and pleasure (next page).

In the hierarchy of serials sponsored by Irving Klaw, *Bound In Leather* holds a unique place: it would become his all-time bestseller, a true American underground classic (when the term "underground" implied subversion and risk). It was Stanton's most celebrated accomplishment of the period. As he would say in later years: "I wasn't really as proud of any of my other work. I don't think much of it approached what I did with *Bound In Leather*."

It should be noted that *Bound In Leather* also featured the first appearance of masculine characters when they were strictly forbidden in Klaw serials. As the original script was told from a man's point of view (maybe for the first time in any Klaw serial) this was inevitable, and it must have been a technical challenge that Klaw and Stanton discussed in detail.

In the end, the male inclusion in the narrative was handled subtly, with Stanton finding ways to obscure the man's face, or diminish his presence whenever possible. Ultimately, the suggestion as presented in the illustrations, is that the male is there only in a gentleman-like capacity as a courteous agent of wish fulfillment in this surrealistic fantasy, offering his services and only present to serve and fulfill the ladies' largely unspoken desire of being strictly bound and contained.

In assessing this work in the scope of his career, one could say that *Bound In Leather* marked the first time Stanton fully demonstrated his unique ability to absorb and translate the fixations of another fantasist. According to Britt, her husband was personally never interested in bondage (strange as that may seem), except as a basis for art. And in years to come, the artist's ability to intuit and render other people's more sexually remote imaginings was a skill he would only improve at.

# 11
# Further Explorations into Bizarre Art

With the success of *Bound In Leather,* it was inevitable that a sequel would follow. *B.I.L., Book Two,* highlighted the fantasist wedding between main characters, Vicki and Walk. In a play on the Cupid and Psyche myth ("Love cannot live where there is no trust"), the bride-to-be promises to reveal her face to the groom only after the wedding. Meanwhile, the bizarre fairy tale ceremony would be officiated by a High Priestess of the Society:

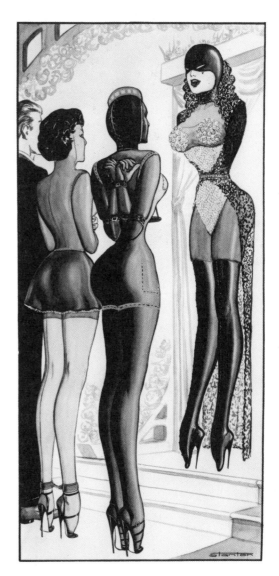

"Social Register Society?" I inquired doubtfully.

"Oh, no. Another kind of society altogether . . ."

"Subjects and gentlemen, we are gathered here this evening to witness the formal acceptance of this Human Puppet before me by the young man beside her."

Speaking to me, she asked solemnly:

"Do you, Edward Walk, take this puppet to be your property, to lace and to corset, to gag and to bind, in satin and in silk, in leather and in steel, from this day forth?"

"I do," I answered, my heart pounding with excitement . . .

After the ceremony, the father-in-law offers this advice to the young husband: "The best of luck, my boy and remember, in marriage there's nothing that can't be settled by a smaller corset, a higher heel, a tighter restraint, or a more severe gag. So long."

Off to their honeymoon, where the bride's promise is fulfilled: her mask is stripped away, her face revealed, and a first bare-lipped kiss is shared in a symbolic deflowering, after which they are free to play more secret games—involving bondage fantasy, of course. The maid, Fifi, also reappears and plays a part. At one point, in dreamlike fashion, she mysteriously morphs into an incarnation of Bettie Page and lends her assistance in fettering the new bride (while taking furtive pleasure in a little bondage play herself).

*B.I.L., Book Two*—although not on the level of its predecessor as far as detail and polish—still afforded Stanton license for some imaginative, even childlike, flights within the context of the genre. Technically (and sometimes with mixed results), it also allowed Stanton a chance to further experiment with textures, washes, and evidently various ink colors (rather than the standard comic book black). For the first time ever, this serial also permitted the artist an opportunity to render—unobstructed—a man's face (actually several). It is likely that Klaw allowed it since this narrative featured a wedding, and in the formality of the circumstances, the male presence could hardly be perceived as obscene.

*B.I.L., Book Two* was issued starting in January 1954, concurrent with two other serials: *Mrs. Tyrant's Finishing School* and *Pleasure Bound*.

While both are technically excellent for the genre—and even share themes of the nightmare "training school" variety—it was *Pleasure Bound* that would achieve a popularity to rival *Bound In Leather*.

In *Pleasure Bound*—also with text supplied by B&G—Stanton returned to the all-female universe, the elegance and sensitivity of his artwork underscoring a uniquely feminine perspective. The story begins:

> Little did I realize until too late what I would let myself in for when I answered an ad appearing in an issue of *Pleasure Bound*, a magazine devoted to correspondence and articles for enthusiasts of high heels, tight lacing, figure training, kid gloves, bondage, and other equally strange, but to me, fascinating and interesting subjects . . .
>
> Being a young girl of twenty-four with too much money and soured on the male sex, I longed for excitement of a different kind . . .

Beyond signifying that this may be an exploration of lesbian interest, it is also evident that the character's curiosity extends to the exacting demands, constraints, and discipline so apparent in bizarre culture.

> Though I admired smartly dressed girls in their high heeled shoes and trim slim-waisted figures, I had let myself go sloppy both mentally and physically, that now, I had no will-power to do what was necessary to correct my many faults, among which was my newly developed craze for alcohol.
>
> "If some young girl would only take me in hand and by force if necessary, help me to correct my faults!" I had thought to myself and then I stumbled on the ad which read:
>
> "'If you are a young girl over seventeen years and under twenty-five and desire assistance in improving your physical and mental deficiencies, write to Box 21 New York and you will be given further details . . .'"

The young protagonist answers the ad, waits several nights, and then, as in fulfillment of her prayer, her doorbell rings. Standing before her is a bizarre emissary of restraint (dressed in strict fetish fashion, of course). Beneath her white fur cape she is tightly bound in rope. In her girdle belt, the protagonist soon notices, is a letter. It reads:

> Dear Joan,
> The messenger who brought you this letter will give you some idea of the method of training to which you will be subjected at my establishment . . .

The letter continues, offering the protagonist a choice:

> If the ideas suggested frighten you, do not enroll, but if they awaken some secret desires in you, sign the enclosed enrollment agreement, make out your check and seal them in the enclosed envelope . . . It would be best to advise what friends or relatives you have, that you intend to take a trip for about a year. Your new Mistress, Armande

Joan, eager to satisfy her curiosity, enrolls. That same week, two stylishly dressed women appear at her home to take her away. Waiting in the purring limousine, this time as "chaufferette," is the messenger. Joan is blindfolded and gagged, and before long, she is delivered to Head Mistress Juliana, where Joan is obliged to shed her old identity by surrendering her clothes in favor of a more appropriate bizarre uniform: a prototype Catwoman suit of supple, skin-tight "black kid leather." And at this point Joan is still delighted.

Little by little, the true nature of this training school is revealed: it is not simply about fashion, it is about austere discipline and constraint. Introduced "to the stringent routine at this school and the restraints it entails," Joan begins to grasp that this may be more than she bargained for, especially when told of a system of demerits "so drastically severe" that it clearly crosses the line.

As illuminated by page after page of provocative Stanton art, all this proves far more than she can take, particularly when gagged and bound to a wheelbarrow at one point and subjected to a "gauntlet of hands and paddles" for perceived disobedience (i.e., yelping in fear at being fettered and suspended).

In the end, Joan becomes aware that perhaps she made a mistake in renouncing her freedom, and by episode 27, her curiosity about this lifestyle more than satisfied, plots revenge on her captors. Allowed to attend Head Mistress Juliana as her servant, Joan drugs her one morning, and in a significant twist assumes her place. As in a dream, Joan is so convincing that no one at the school is able to tell the difference. The head mistress in turn is subjected to the same treatment she inflicted on her pupils, and by the end Joan learns an important lesson: "Careful who—and precisely what—you surrender to." In this way, *Pleasure Bound* is a rare bondage fantasy: one that underscores personal responsibility while being a cautionary tale that exemplifies the dangers inherent in naively yielding control to just anyone.

In her journey toward self-awareness, Joan has also learned that she can capably be her own mistress. The evolution of her character was complete when she adopted the identity of head mistress and comfortably displaced her. Maybe Joan has learned that, for now, she would much rather identify as dominant than submissive?

*Pleasure Bound*, especially early on, marks some of Stanton's most gracefully beautiful artwork in the context of a Klaw serial, and again demonstrates his chameleon-like ability to adapt his style according to the demands—and unique perspective—of the fantasist.

That same year (1954) Stanton also produced, under the beginning of what appeared to be some duress at home, another serial, *A Hazardous Journey* (released July/October). And extending into 1955, two more serials would follow: *Leather Boot Club* (November '54/February '55) and finally, *Pleasure Bound, Book Two* (November '54/May '55).

Fall 1954, marked a significant event, although its full importance would not be grasped for some time. This was the appearance of a sixty-four-page publication, much like the periodical the character Joan was reading at the beginning of *Pleasure Bound* ("a magazine devoted to correspondence and articles for enthusiasts of high heels, tight lacing, figure training, kid gloves . . ."). In fact, this magazine was inspired by John Willie's *Bizarre*, while consisting of pilfered material from Willie, but even more so Stanton. "Leon

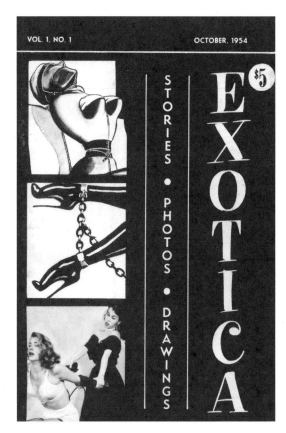

Brenner" was listed inside as the digest's editor, but in truth his name was Leonard Burtman, a man who would not only play a major role in Stanton's life, but in the history of clandestine publishing. (It seems Irving Klaw also took notice of this publication: not just to assess its pirated content, but its general design, and always the practical businessman made a few notes that he filed away for future use.)

It was earlier that year, at the tail end of summer, that news of a different kind had rocked the artist Stanton's household: the announced pregnancy of Grace with their first child. Had Stanton's career standing been more secure and his financial situation not so precarious, this might have been good news. As things stood, clearly it was not.

# Storm Clouds: Stanton and Klaw under Siege

If things had been a little strained between the couple before the pregnancy, things were about to get much worse. The problem, as summarized by Stanton's first-born son, Rick Vincel: "My mother couldn't deal with the way Eric lived. How he made his living."

Grace + note, circa 1949

As Stanton was all too aware, his wife did not approve of him. But such was not always the case.

Not only was there mutual affection and love in the beginning, but evidence to suggest that she was sympathetic, if not encouraging, of his creative ambitions. But by 1954, clearly things had begun to sour, almost as if all at once her patience had run out.

Grace was not an artist, had no need or desire to re-imagine the world, and in the end just wanted what everyone else had: something predictable, something "normal." Above everything she wanted a family, which meant children, as Rick heard her say: "'cause that was the only reason to be married."

All this was a terrible blow to Stanton's spirit, first because he felt guilt and shame at not being able to provide for his wife in the traditional sense, and second because it became more and more obvious that his outlook was at odds with hers: being closer to that of his restless mother, whose temperament was largely bohemian. Whereas Grace wanted security, being alive to Stanton meant never quite knowing what was ahead. It meant

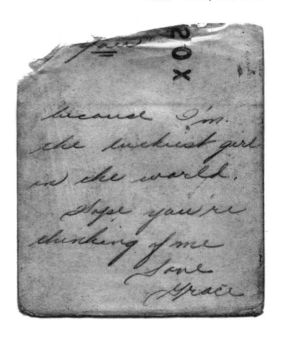

gambling and creating art. It meant offering himself up to chance. And what else could he do but follow his natural curiosity?

## Subcommittee Hearings

When Stanton was not drafting and inking serials for Klaw, he was busy at the shop (the lady holding the cup is Grace, circa 1954). Yet try as he might to make good, it obviously was not enough; and Grace, for all her good qualities, simply didn't understand her husband, couldn't even *begin* to comprehend the significance of this bizarre fantasy world he seemed so comfortably immersed in.

In truth, being a staunch Catholic and an adherent of dichotomous thinking (right/wrong, good/bad), she took a conformist's view of his taste and interests, and at times could be brutally unkind. (Years later, according to Rick, she would refer to his art simply as "filth.") To be fair, we should not forget that this was still the 1950s, when the gyrations of Elvis Presley were denounced as obscene, married couples could not share the same bed on TV, and sex was not considered an appropriate subject for open discussion in America ever, except maybe in some smoky burlesque joint or seedy bar.

By 1955, things were about to take a downward turn both for Stanton and his employer, Irving Klaw. On May 19, much to his surprise, Klaw was subpoenaed to appear before a Senate subcommittee hearing purportedly centered on the causes of juvenile delinquency. Bettie Page was also subpoenaed to testify. "I sat with her in Irving's office at the time," Stanton recalled years later. "She wanted to know what to say. She was so tearful . . . It was the only time I ever saw Bettie upset."

The previous year, this very same Senate subcommittee had focused on the evils of comic books, resulting in the evisceration of the industry. Chairing the subcommittee, again, was Tennessee Senator Estes Kefauver, who several years earlier had gained such wide attention as chairman of The United States Senate Special Committee to Investigate Crime in Interstate Commerce (1950-51), that he was able to launch a bid for the Democratic presidential nomination in 1952. Although he had failed in his first attempt, he was back to try again, using this latest investigation as a platform for national exposure.

As he addressed the public in his opening statements regarding this latest pernicious menace and internal threat to national security—"pornography"—he paraphrased the fear-mongering sentiments of J. Edgar Hoover:

> I think it is time that this whole sordid business in insidious filth be brought into the open . . . The impulses which spur people to sex crimes unquestionably are intensified by reading and seeing filthy material. Certainly something must be done about this filth. [Page 41 of the published subcommittee report.]

Irving Klaw was summoned to appear on the first day of the hearing (May 24), and in accordance with the subpoena, asked to present "certain books," which no less amounted to a truckload:

State and Federal income tax returns for the years 1950 to 1954, inclusive: records of your business, including bank books, bank statements, checkbooks and check stubs, profit and loss statements, statements of assets and liabilities, and all documents reflecting your interest in property, real, personal or mixed.

On the recommendation of counsel, Klaw's tactic was to refuse, invoking the fifth and fourth amendments to the constitution in his own defense. This of course infuriated Estes Kefauver, who in auditioning for the part of president before the media was trying to appear above challenge. Finally he commanded Klaw: "You will remain under continuing subpoena to appear here at 9 o'clock Thursday morning with the books and records described in this subpoena. Is that clear?" By no accident Klaw's follow-up appearance was staged immediately after the emotional testimony of Clarence Grimm, father of an unfortunate seventeen-year-old who was murdered the year before by an unidentified assailant. As the body of the dead teenager—described as an innocent "Eagle Scout"—was found in suspension and "trussed up in a very unnatural position," it was the suggestion of the subcommittee (simply by association) that Irving Klaw, underground disseminator of fetish and bondage art, was responsible.

Reaching for evidence, a copy of the Klaw catalog *Cartoon and Model Parade* was entered into the record, and it was Kefauver who called attention to the work of one artist in particular (p. 68) whose renderings were apparently emblematic of the sort of stuff that might drive a maniac to murder:

**Chairman Kefauver:** It gives a little example of what it is you are going to see; and then it says that after being bound and blindfolded, "Joan is led away in an automobile driven by a bound and gagged chauffeurette, taken to a training school." The price is 50 cents, each chapter, size 8 by 10, so that you order by number, and then you get a large picture and a series of the similar kind of picture here. That is what this catalog is.

**Mr. Grimm:** That's right.

**Chairman Kefauver:** I think it is interesting to look at this. This seems to be the 97th edition. The catalog itself costs 50 cents.

**Mr. Grimm:** Yes. Obviously, I believe you will agree with me—I am no expert on this sort of thing, but I have been around a little bit in my life, in the type of work that I do—it doesn't take an expert to recognize that as not a wholesome, cultural type of literature. It definitely was not displayed or sent through the mails for that reason at all, to add to the cultural uplift of the country at all. It is evil; it is no good.

**Chairman Kefauver:** Well, it speaks for itself.

**Mr. Grimm:** That's right.

Irving Klaw, alleged operator of $1,000,000 a year pornography business, pleaded Fifth Amendment at hearings.

When his turn finally came up, a perspiring Irving Klaw solemnly stated his full name and address, and afterward (again, on recommendation of counsel) pled the fifth to all questions posed to him, even as Estes Kefauver tried every tactic of intimidation at his disposal, including allowing flash photographs when Klaw had the right to deny them (Kefauver: "The photographers have a right to take your picture") and harping over and over (no less than twenty times) that Klaw would be cited "under penalty of contempt of the Senate" for not answering any or all questions directed at him.

Although Kefauver proved nothing, the damage from the bad publicity on Irving Klaw cannot be underestimated. It was a trial in the public eye, in which Klaw was shown to be a "bad man" by association.

In fact, "Get Klaw!" seemed to be the general theme of the subcommittee hearing from that point on, with his name invoked again and again (particularly by William C. O'Brien, an assistant solicitor from the Post Office [pages 287, 288, 306, 308, 309, 310, and 311 of the published report]) in recommending aggressive action:

I have a copy of the charges we have pending against him, and if we supported the charges—I am the complainant—if we support these charges, an order can be issued that will stop all mail addressed to Irving Klaw. That means, of course, his mail-order business in this type of pornography, what I call pornography, in which he has been indulging, these pictures, photographs, slides, and so forth, will be in the past.

And what of Klaw's "alleged" annual earnings (estimated without the benefit of examining actual bank statements or business records and bandied about as 1.5 million or 1 million annually)? "Obviously you can't believe what the government tells you," cautioned longtime Klaw historian and publisher, J. B. Rund. "Irving Klaw lived in an apartment in the Brighton Beach section of Brooklyn. If he's making a million dollars a year, I think he could've moved up in the world."

## Stanton Gets a "Real" Job

Unsure of the future of his business, Irving Klaw became cautious of sponsoring more artwork that year. This left Stanton with little opportunity, considering his specialty. In 1955, only two more Stanton serials—*Madame Discipline* (February/May) and *Girls' Figure Training Academy* (June)—were issued in full by Klaw. With bills and pressures mounting, Stanton saw no other solution but to look outside of Irving's.

Pan American World Airways was a company on the move; that year they would invest in their future with the Boeing 707, ordering twenty such planes, and the Douglas DC-8, ordering twenty-five.

In other words, Pan Am was in rapid growth and hiring. So largely to please his wife and no doubt prove he was a responsible husband and father, Stanton put his calling on hold. He went from fugitive artist to being a routine parts clerk at $62.00 a week. Also to please his wife, he moved the family to a larger home (the new address indicated on the baby pic).

Grace was happy. And could it be said that Stanton was happy, too? After all, he had a steady paycheck now. He had love from his wife. He had a bright-eyed child.

What was so good about being in the arts, anyway?

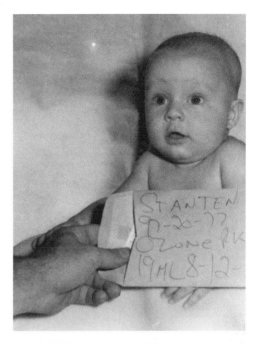

# Klaw's Mail Block and Edward Mishkin

Of course it could not last. The love from Grace was conditional, and the desire of wanting to be an artist burned too strongly in Stanton. But for the time being, Stanton did what was required. He faked it, he lied; he learned to compartmentalize his life and keep secrets, at least for the sake of his wife and son. According to Rick (in Stanton's arms), "My mother told me so many stories about Eric that I didn't know what to believe. My mother told me that Eric never wanted children. Eric told me all he ever wanted was children."

Regardless, Stanton reverted to his mild-mannered alter ego—Ernie Stanten—and performed his duty, shuffling daily from Ozone Park to Jamaica, Queens. His engagement with Klaw during 1956—no doubt to the relief of Grace—was sporadic and minimal. Several installments of two Stanton serials were offered through Klaw's monthly bulletin—*Marie's Unique Adventure* (April) and *Fifi Chastises Her Maids* (May)—but both projects were left unfinished and would remain so for years. Another offering appeared in September, *Diary Of A Lady Wrestler* (p. 222), which consisted of twelve single-panel episodes first advertised in a bulletin for Lovelies Inc., a new company Irving Klaw had formed in reaction to the fallout from the Kefauver inquiry.

On 16 July 1956, according to the *New York Times*, the postal department carried through on its threat to block all mail addressed to Irving Klaw, but earlier that year Klaw had braced himself, incorporating several new businesses (listing Paula, his sister, and Jack Kramer, his brother-in-law, on the paperwork). In February 1956, Klaw established "Ikay Products, Inc." in Jersey City, New Jersey, to handle any fetish art related material; that same month in New York he also established "Lovelies, Inc.," and finally "Movie Star News," which was the name of his catalog preceding *Cartoon and Model Parade*. Now that the name "Irving Klaw" had been dragged through the mud and permanently sullied, it was obvious he needed to rename his store. Irving Klaw Pin-Up Photos—used interchangeably with simply "Irving Klaw"—would at last be rechristened Movie Star News.

## Irving Klaw: Sexploitation Pioneer

So much attention has been focused on Klaw's involvement with the fetish subgenre that few realize his importance in the development of American sexploitation culture as a whole. From the start, a large portion of Klaw's business was cheesecake pin-ups and burlesque related material, and besides Bettie Page, his best known models included burlesque/cabaret greats Tempest Storm, Lili St. Cyr, and Blaze Starr.

Part of Klaw's legacy was his output of films, which ultimately amounted to five theatrically distributed features and roughly 350 shorts (films generally ranging from 100 to 300 feet, most often shot on 16 mm, with some later reproduced as 8 mm loops).

Interestingly, despite what was declared at the Kefauver inquest, it was not Klaw's bondage material that the Post Office focused on in their ruling to finally impose a mail block: mentioned more prominently in the hearing report were his cheesecake, high heel, and lingerie pin-ups, and specifically three burlesque shorts: "Voluptuous Body Dance," "G-String Dance" (both featuring Tempest Storm), and "Lilli Dawn, Siren of Tease."

(From *Bound To Please* for Edward Mishkin)

As in defiance of the moral ruling, that year Klaw issued yet another theatrical burlesque themed feature (his third, and most elaborate, produced and distributed by his own film company, Beautiful Productions, Inc.). *Buxom Beautease*, featuring Tempest Storm, Lili St. Cyr, and Blaze Starr, was Klaw's only 1950s big screen production not to include Bettie Page (who was likely fearful after the Kefauver hearings). To what extent Stanton contributed to Klaw's filmmaking output has never been documented. But as with all Klaw productions, this too was a "family" undertaking and listed in the credits, just below Irving's wife, Natalie, was Stanton.

("E. Stanton"—the name Eric used professionally when it was not simply "Stanton.")

## Stanton in Limbo

Like a ghost wandering the terrain of his former, more creative life, Stanton haunted Manhattan on his rare days off. In the months and years following the Kefauver inquest, he seemed to take a special interest in one particular area: Times Square. It was here, following the election of Robert F. Wagner Jr. as mayor in 1953, that changes in the zoning code allowed for a proliferation of certain novelty-friendly bookstores dealing in racy material, not unlike the kind distributed by Irving Klaw. (In fact, a substantial portion of material *was* originally produced by Klaw, but now made available as knockoffs or piracies.)

Discount movie theaters running sensational double or triple features back to back (thus dubbed "grind houses") were also in abundance, attracting thousands. It was here, in the ever chaotic, carnival-like atmosphere of Times Square, that one particular individual caught Stanton's attention: Edward Mishkin. "He had a store, actually four different stores at various times, all in or around Times Square," he recalled years later. By late 1956, those four stores were Kingsley Books (220 West 42nd St.), Times Square Book Bazaar (225 West 42nd St.), Square Book Exchange (584 7th Ave.), and Harmony Book Shop (112 West 49th St.).

Piracy, as both Klaw and Stanton were to understand, would pose a big challenge.

## Stanton Seeks Out Mishkin

Like Irving Klaw, Edward Mishkin was subpoenaed to appear before the Senate subcommittee investigating juvenile delinquency in 1955. Like Klaw, he too was ordered to present certain "books and records," but as he was already being investigated by the IRS (as his lawyer stated) and "all those records" were with them, Mishkin had a convenient out. (Note: this did not prevent the subcommittee from readily estimating his alleged annual earnings as equal to that of Klaw at 1.5 million.)

Like Klaw, Mishkin, under direction of counsel, pled the fifth to nearly all questions posed to him by the Kefauver Subcommittee. In spite of this, at least one revealing (and amusing) exchange transpired [appearing on page 241 of the published transcript]:

**Mr. Chumbris:** Our investigation reveals that you plagiarized material from one Irving Klaw, resulting in serious arguments with said Irving Klaw. Is that true or false?

**Mr. Mishkin:** What was that question again?

**Mr. Chumbris:** Our investigation reveals that you have plagiarized material—

**Mr. Mishkin:** What did I do?

**Mr. Chumbris:** You have stolen material that Mr. Klaw used—Mr. Irving Klaw, resulting in serious arguments with said Irving Klaw.

**Chairman Kefauver:** Plagiarized. Do you know what plagiarized means?

**Mr. Mishkin:** I know what that means now; yes, sir.

**Chairman Kefauver:** Do you want to answer that question?

**Mr. Mishkin:** I refuse to answer under the immunity provisions of the fifth amendment of the Constitution.

Stanton would strike a deal: "I'd go into all the stores and one day I suggested Mishkin buy from me directly."

It marked the beginning of a business relationship that would exceed fifteen years (longer than Stanton's connection to Klaw), and in time, Mishkin proved to be the most easy-going and genial of patrons.

*Bound To Please*, a forty-nine-page, single-panel bondage serial produced in a somewhat hasty Klaw style—which included another nod to Bettie Page (below)—was Stanton's first non-Klaw offering. It was sold in Mishkin's shops (as item #245), as well as through Gargoyle Sales Corp., a mail order business in which Mishkin was a partner.

# Stanton
# Follows Eneg's
# Example

While it is clear that Stanton introduced Gene Bilbrew to the fetish art underground through Irving Klaw, it was actually Bilbrew who branched out first professionally. While maintaining his working relationship with Klaw, it was Bilbrew who had the longest association with Edward Mishkin, starting by some accounts as far back as 1953, and ending with his death in 1974.

Meanwhile, it might be an indication of Stanton's level of naiveté or lack of business acumen at the time that he believed Irving Klaw when Klaw insisted that he alone owned the publishing rights to the name "Stanton." Then again, Klaw was so meticulously efficient as a businessman— even if he was not always truthful—that few disputed any claim he made (below).

For now, Irving Klaw's luck would go from bad to worse. That same year, "Ikay Products, Inc." in Jersey City, New Jersey, was raided by the police. With the first bulletin for Ikay Products appearing in March 1956, only two more advertising bulletins followed.

Furthermore, the Post Office mail block against the name "Irving Klaw" remained until June 23, 1958, while defaming write-ups in the press would persist well into the 1960s, or no less miserably (as we shall see), up until the time of his death.

The trade name "The Pin-Up King" is owned by Irving Klaw and is registered in the United States Patent Office.

# What's in a Name? Stanton and Leonard Burtman

At this stage of his career, it may have been Bilbrew who reminded Stanton that it hardly mattered what pseudonym he used as an artist, as long as he could continue making art. By now Bilbrew had used various aliases apart from Eneg: "Van Rod," "Gilbert," "GB," and "Bondy/J. Bondy."

"Stan"—used on *Bound To Please* for Mishkin (see previous chapter)—would become Stanton's first and most consistent non-Klaw alias. In 1957–58, only briefly he used "Savage." Then there was "Stanten" (with an "e"), his legal name. In fact, it was Bilbrew who had first thrown caution to the wind, signing his real name in working with his newest patron, Leonard Burtman, the man who had followed up the publication of *Exotica* (see chapter eleven) with a new, influential "bizarre" fashion-oriented magazine named *Exotique*.

## Mishkin and Burtman

Like Mishkin, Leonard Burtman had also pirated material from Klaw (specifically targeting Stanton), and it is significant that while both plagiarized material from that one source, neither stole from each other. This is because evidence suggests there was a business alliance between Leonard Burtman and Edward Mishkin, with Mishkin at least initially involved on the distribution end. (It is possible that Mishkin may have originally provided financing

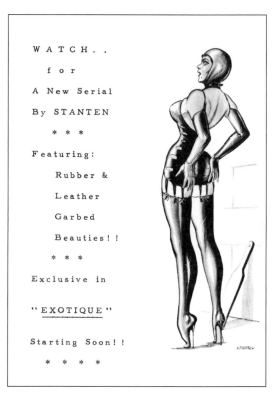

too.) This connection is obvious in the logo shared on the back of Burtman's *Exotica*, which Mishkin sold in his shops—and according to FBI reports out of state—and a similarly dated Mishkin piracy of John Willie's *The Missing Princess*; even the phony publishing imprints were alike: "Exotica Publishing Co." for Burtman and "Erotica Publishing Co." for Mishkin (see p. 76). Unlike Irving Klaw, who admirably appears to have operated with complete autonomy (making him a sure target for others), Leonard Burtman's and Edward Mishkin's associations were always complex, guarded, and certainly shady.

A NEW PUBLICATION OF THE
BIZARRE AND THE UNUSUAL

CATALOG C - 2

THEATRICAL    . . .    MASQUERADE

TANA LOUISE
550 Fifth Avenue
New York 36, N. Y.

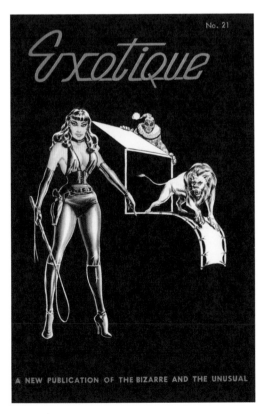

A NEW PUBLICATION OF THE BIZARRE AND THE UNUSUAL

THE BIZARRE & UNUSUAL IN FACT AND IN FICTION.

# Who Was Lenny Burtman?

A former California-based electronics expert who finally met with discredit in his chosen profession, Leonard Burtman relocated to New York City in 1951, to reinvent himself as a pin-up/glamour photographer, magazine editor, and ultimately the most widely distributed and influential "bizarre" fetish art publisher of the 1950s and 1960s.

## Leonard Burtman Timeline: In Brief

1920 (9 August): born in Columbus, Nebraska.

1930–1940: resided (from age nine to nineteen) with his father in the Bronx and Queens, New York.

1940: death of father, Herman, one-time newspaper editor and publisher.

1940s: studied electronics at the California Institute of Technology, the Philco School, Bell Laboratories; lastly employed by a firm handling government/military contracts.

1944 (20 November): arrested for the first time: "theft of government property," for which he received a suspended sentence and two years' probation (1945–1947).

1946 (25 June): second arrest, according to an FBI memo: "Sel. Serv. no Cards"

1949 (26 September): third arrest: for transporting false securities; according to FBI memo: "one year federal prison, Tucson Arizona."

1951: returned to New York City, embarking on a new career as a freelance "glamour" photographer focusing on pin-ups and fetish/sexploitation oriented material.

1954: *Exotica* v. 1 no. 1, first publication (uncredited).

1955: *Exotique* magazine first published, featuring the work of Bilbrew, Bettie Page, Charles Guyette, and finally, Tana Louise and Stanton.

1957–1958: branched out through Burmel Publishing Co., producing other fetish oriented digests/magazines, pulp novellas, and books—many with Stanton art.

(Burtman and "Miss Exotique" depicted by Stanton)

## Tana Louise, Klaw, Harrison, Guyette, Willie, and Himmel

As with his eventual wife, "Tana Louise" Kirby—the future "Miss Exotique" (photo)—Burtman may have had some association with Irving Klaw. Certainly Burtman would take Klaw as a role model (just as Stanton had), and by the late 1950s, engage in selling his own wide assortment of self-generated sexploitation and fetish inclined photo sets and films via mail order.

Historian and sociologist Robert Bienvenu has also suggested that Burtman may have cut his teeth as photographer and editor for Robert Harrison, which would have been during the twilight of his girlie magazine career (1952–1955). Bienvenu also noted an association regarding a similar social circle between Burtman and Charles Guyette (see chapter five), and finally, an uneasy relationship between Burtman and John Coutts (a.k.a. John Willie), who not-so-unreasonably accused Burtman of theft.

It is unknown if Burtman's key business associate was on board with his first publishing venture, *Exotica*, but sometime by 1955, he was certainly present. Benedict "Ben" Himmel, a former union organizer (red flag)—also briefly summoned during the Kefauver hearings—provided further channels of distribution for Burtman, as well as alternate funding (from "undisclosed" sources). Together Burtman and Himmel would forge the first legitimate bizarre publishing imprint: Burmel Publishing Co. Less famously, they also operated a wide assortment of short-lived sham (or unregistered) publishing imprints.

## Stanton vs. Burtman: Round One

Despite remarkably similar interests, the relationship between Stanton and Leonard Burtman was a contentious one, and the artist's involvement with the publisher in the 1950s barely lasted eighteen months. As became apparent during that time, Burtman epitomized all that Stanton would come to hate about publishers: being transparently exploitative, personally insensitive, and above all cheap.

LIMITED-EDITION • • • FULLY-ILLUSTRATED

FIVE DOLLARS

CONQUERING *Goddess*

Stanton's first contributions to *Exotique* did not occur until late 1956 (not long after striptease artist Tana Louise had transformed herself into a fetish model and installed herself in Burtman's life). And why not sooner? Likely, for Stanton, it was due to conflicting interests: his full-time job, plus a toddler at home, combined with what seemed like a reluctance to openly alienate Klaw.

Despite his limited period of involvement with Burtman (as a Sunday artist at best), Stanton's Burmel-era output remains unique and memorable. No longer obliged to draw bondage fantasies as he had for Klaw, he was free to focus on precise sensual elements appealing to the fetishist: the play of textures like satin, silk, leather, latex, and particularly soft female skin tightly encased in these luxurious materials.

First announced in issue #10 of *Exotique*, then offered for sale in full in the back of issue #13 (1957), was his second substantial non-Klaw fetish serial—this time under the name "Stanten"—*Deborah*: "An amazing story of BIZARRE beauties – clad in LEATHER and RUBBER…. All 36 chapters . . . Printed on TOP QUALITY PHOTOGRAPHIC paper . . . @ $25.00."

Aside from *Deborah*, Stanton contributed at least seventy elegantly rendered pieces of artwork—nearly all done using the wash technique he had developed with Klaw (with many produced in color)—that Burtman compulsively reprinted and recycled, as sexploitation/fetish publisher, for the next twenty years. (Of course, the artist would only be paid once.) Stanton also contributed five *Exotique* covers, at least two fashion catalog covers, and eleven "novelette" and digest covers (most published under Burtman's array of phony imprints). Some of the novelettes also included interior illustrations by Stanton. Among the most highly prized by collectors today are *Vixen on the Loose*, *Satan's Mistress*, and *Conquering Goddess* (see p. 78).

Stanton and Burtman's relationship—round one—came to an abrupt halt in early 1958, over a particular serial Burtman had commissioned called *The Sex Switch*: a goofy, comic tale about female dominance and transvestism (one of Burtman's strongest fixations).

Although Burtman had agreed to pay $35.00 a page, upon seeing it completed he could not help but haggle, "This is terrible! I'll give you $5.00 a page for it."

That was it. Stanton collected his artwork, walked over to 42nd Street, and promptly sold it to Edward Mishkin. Burtman later got his revenge by selling Stanton's reprinted art through his bulletins under the name "Eneg."

# 15
# Fathers and Sons

The close of 1956 saw not only Stanton's first involvement with culturally subversive publishers Leonard Burtman and Edward Mishkin, but clear proof that, like it or not, his family was expanding. To Stanton's surprise Grace was again pregnant, and sadly, this fact would only further distance him. Rick clarified:

> Now just imagine, they're married, living together as Catholics, practicing, y'know, the "rhythm method." The rhythm method is a woman's responsibility because she times her periods. My mother, she pulled the wool over Eric's eyes. She said, "Nope, there's my calendar, see I'm good for another three or four days!" So Eric was just getting used to the idea that he had a son when he found out that mom was getting ready to have a second son.

Stanton concealed his anger and his growing distrust of his wife. Meanwhile, Grace's hostility toward his sporadic creative endeavors only intensified as she wondered aloud *when* he would finally put all this nonsense behind him, once and for all, and get serious. Did not his family deserve more of his time? Couldn't he see that the selfish pursuit of art only served to remove him from the world—from "real life?"

When guilt and shame would not produce the desired effect Grace was not above withholding affection, according to what Stanton told his second wife, Britt, who plainly recalled, "She played that game." This of course only drove him deeper into his own fantasy life, where he sought comfort and relief.

The Cold War of the 1950s extended to the Stanten household. More bitter accusations would fly later. The innocent bystanders in all this? Quite obviously the children. Stanton's second son, Guy, was born June 22, 1957. According to Guy Vincel:

> As I was six or seven, I began to ask my mom questions and she was pretty much evasive and just answered: "We didn't get along anymore and his job was something that I disagreed with." And I'd say, "What was it?" She'd say, "Well, he was an artist."

In turn, Stanton later said of Grace: "We met at seaside. I never had sex with her before marriage. We had two sons . . . She was Catholic, didn't like the things I did, thought there was something wrong with me."

## Stanton Seeks Out
## Paternal Guidance

There is no question that fatherhood—at least in theory, if not practice—posed a challenge for Stanton. Maybe it was because he felt he never had a strong role model, or simply because art got in the way? Regardless, at some point after the birth of Guy, at age thirty-one, Stanton sought out the man he had never met, the man who might have altered the direction of his life: his biological father—the mysterious Edward D'Andrea.

As Tom first heard the story: "He'd been waiting all these years to meet him. Finally my dad spotted his name in the paper."

As Britt recalled: "I think he just went to the racetrack one day and found out that's where he worked. Maybe his mother said that she didn't want him to see him, but the first time he met him, looked him up, he was at Belmont Park."

"My dad said he swore he was looking at a split image of himself, with a bigger nose and these really deep blue eyes," according to Tom. "Finally he went over, a little nervous, and said, 'Hey, I just want you to know, I'm your son.'"

Britt: "All his father said back was: 'Hi, son. Do you have any money?' To put on a horse."

Tom: "Basically, he couldn't give a fuck."

Britt: "Eric went to look him up, and it turned out to be a bad thing."

Jim Chambers (family friend):

The last time Eric saw his father, he had his two sons with him from his first wife and his father said: "Listen, I've got this great horse that's really gonna win. I just need some money to put a bet on it, whatever you got. Gonna strike it big on this one!" and Eric said, "Well, we don't really have anything right now. The only money we've got is this change we saved up in a piggy bank for the kids." His father's eyes lit up: "Yeah yeah, gimme that!" Before Eric knew it, his father snatched the kid's money, ran out the door . . . and that was the last time he ever saw his father.

As Britt recalled:

He [Stanton's father] stole their money to put on a horse and that infuriated him [Stanton], and he never forgave him for that, and he never wanted to see him anymore after that. From then on Eric hated his father. But he lived until his nineties. He went from Belmont to Aqueduct. He was thrown out of Belmont because Eric found out he drugged the horses, gave them speed. So he was thrown out. So instead he was training the horses or something at Aqueduct. But Eric said he was just no good. Not a good man.

It was still during this time that Stanton was a parts runner for Pan Am. As Tom heard it: "He would sit in the parts department and basically just get the parts that mechanics needed . . . That's where he said he hurt his back, because he had to lift up heavy things . . ."

Details about the actual event remain elusive, but evidently one day it simply happened: Stanton suddenly found himself in crippling pain, hardly able to walk, let alone do any lifting. As a result he could no longer keep his day job, and this did not sit well with Grace.

Troubles would only intensify, and it was sometime late in 1957, that the two had a falling out over an incident that only underscored their incompatibility.

According to Rick: "Eric was non-confrontational, and my mother was—very much so—a dominant personality."

In Grace's presence Stanton had to watch himself—especially now that he was an easy target. Evidently the only way he could get his art done—as well as indulge in a few harmless fantasies—was to creep down to the basement, where he had set up a little drawing table, just as he had on Lincoln Avenue. According to Rick:

> Eric had hurt his back when my mother—I'm not sure if it was just before or just after she delivered my brother Guy—but according to Eric: my mother never told me any of this—it was a combination of my mother, I guess, just having the baby or getting ready to have the baby and Eric hurting his back that they didn't have sex for several months . . . so Eric's only release at the time—and remember he was a young man in his thirties—was masturbation. And according to Eric, my mother peeked in the basement window of our house on 77th Street and caught him doing that and totally freaked out. 'Cause according to my mother, sex was "just to make babies"—that was it. And this was the last straw for her. In the Catholic Church, y'know, "onanism" is a mortal sin. [Note: "mortal" = damned to eternity.] Because you're wasting a quarter of a million potential Catholics every time you do that. That's what it was . . . My mother—from everything I can remember—she loved you heart and soul until you crossed some line and, once she stopped loving you . . . there was nothing you could do to change that.

Although Stanton later stated that he divorced Grace in 1958, Rick suggested otherwise:

> I believe this story: the story being that my mother stayed married to Eric until I was five. The reason being that she gave him two and a half years. Two and a half years to acknowledge my brother's existence. In that time he never picked Guy up, he never smiled at Guy, he never touched Guy, he never talked to Guy. She told this to Guy. And Guy later asked Eric straight to his face: "Is it true?" And Eric told Guy, "That's nonsense. I'd never do that to one of my sons."

Tom Stanten offered a more obvious explanation: "From what my father told me, my dad at the time—when Guy was born—he had a bad back and he couldn't lift up Guy. It hurt him. 'Cause he hurt himself working at Pan Am."

"My brother," Rick continued, "he was one of the most introverted people you can imagine. Something in my brother's past, in his growing up, had to force him into a box he was afraid to crawl out of. I think it was the fact that he was never shown love by his father." Rick continued:

> So my mother, her grounds for divorce—from Thomas (Vincel, third husband) I heard this—her grounds for divorce were mental cruelty and incompatibility. And the divorce as it went through was that Eric had to give us up, all claim to us, until we were eighteen. And we were not allowed to be brought up in a conversation unless we brought it up. And we were not allowed to be told anything about it until we were eighteen.

According to existing court documents filed in Las Vegas, Nevada, the actual date of the divorce was June 3, 1960. But those same documents also listed Stanton as the plaintiff, not the defendant. In other words, it was he who actively filed for divorce against Grace. The paperwork further stated the cause on his behalf (next page):

There are two sides to every story, and truth is always subjective and prone to distortion, especially when filtered through a mesh of bitterness and anger. But for Stanton, his own well-being—mental and physical—was at stake.

In early 1958, he and Grace were separated. He could no longer go on as things were, no longer tolerate what Rick called his mother's "almost divinely inspired hate." As Stanton recalled in a 1996 interview: "She took the kids, the car, the furniture, and everything. I took off on my own to some crummy place." Because of his severe back pain and anguish at this time, Stanton also developed an addiction to prescription painkillers. After enduring cramped quarters at the YMCA he finally bottomed out, returning to live with his mother—now in South Ozone Park.

For Stanton, so far pursuing his dream and following his own muse had only meant misery, poverty, humiliation, and—always, it seemed—being reduced to the helpless state of a child.

# 16

## Living for the Process

By most accounts it was not selfishness; it was not a deliberate or willful attempt on Stanton's part to be unsocial or stay disengaged. What Grace never seemed to understand about her husband was that the process of making art was necessary. It was not simply a "job" for him.

Something in Stanton's psychological makeup dictated channeling and creating art as a means of attaining a proper balance and some measure of control in his life. The actual art he made—the artifact itself—was always less important than the process. As time would tell, it was the process of making art that Stanton lived for; it was that process of exploration and discovery. And starting in the late 1950s—until the end of his life—he arranged his schedule accordingly, with impressive self-discipline. "He'd be doing art early in the morning," as Amber recalled from her childhood in the 1980s. "Up before all of us. If I

had to go to school I'd probably be getting up at about 7:00 and he'd be up before me. He'd have breakfast ready, freshly squeezed orange juice ready for me and my brother." As she remembered: "He would go to bed at 9:00."

"He was very dedicated to making his art, I know that," recalled family friend from the 1960s, Ed Weiss:

> I used to attend some of his parties because he'd invite me. Before he knew Britt, Eric would have parties once in a while and when the time came, like if it was 11:00 or so, he would say to everybody "Well, the party's over! Time to go!" That would be it. He was tactful, but he would just say, "Look, everybody, it's time to leave. I need to go to bed." And he wasn't joking. He would go to bed! That's the way Eric was. He was very devoted. There's no doubt about it. For him, making art meant everything.

# 17

# 1958: Slow Healing

It would take Stanton some time to recover from the disaster of his marriage with Grace; in truth, a full ten years. The psychological mending began with the unwavering support of one family member in particular, according to Britt:

> Eric said that he was always very proud of his mother, or thankful to his mother. Because all he really wanted to do was draw, and she let him do that. She was the one that gave him space. And that was really the only chance he had. Then finally he started making money. But he was able to do it without money. His mother set him up, allowed him to stay at her house, and said, "You just draw all you want."—and not go to jobs that he hated.

In fact, from that point on, Stanton vowed to earn a living solely as an artist—and an artist of his own choosing—while resolving to never hold a so-called *real* job again.

Meanwhile, his back pain persisted for many years while he managed his dependency as best he could. In a 1996 interview he recalled: "I was a cripple from age twenty-eight to thirty-six years old." Then, in the same interview: "From age twenty-eight to thirty-eight." In fact, it was from 1957–1967/68 (age thirty-one to forty-one). According to Amber, "I knew that he had something, a back injury. And that it got progressively worse. At one point he was in bed all the time . . ."

## Anna's Influence

"She knew what my father did," Amber explained. "She was very open-minded, 'cause I know that—for that time—it probably wasn't very common for parents to be accepting if their son wanted to get into fetish art. It started out obviously more innocently. But she was aware of what he did. And my father wasn't sure if it was a good thing. But she insisted that he carry on, since it meant so much to him . . .

"My family—one of the core values that we have," said Amber, "is that we give each other freedom. Whatever you wanna do, you do it. Love was more important than anything. Love and happiness. So if you wanna do that and that makes you happy—well, we love you and we want you to be happy. And that—that way of thinking—came first from my grandmother, from Anna. She was accepting, very supportive of him. So was my mom. Grace was not very supportive."

# Who Was Anna, Really?

"She was a competitive ballroom dancer," related Amber. "She won a lot of those dances where it was about 'Who can stay on their feet the longest.' Like three days of straight dancing at the Roseland Ballroom in New York City."

She had her share of mundane jobs too. Her daughter Eleanor remembered that she worked at a blouse factory for years. She also moonlighted in a delicatessen, worked as a floor lady in a department store, and as a manicurist "—for *men*. In a barbershop," according to Cathy Hysell.

## Stanton's Love of Outgoing Women

"He said it was in the first grade that he first fell in love. And I think he said that she had red hair. And that she had this sparkling, outgoing personality," said Amber, "And that's something he always seemed to have liked throughout his life. This charming, outgoing type of female. Women that had personality. Y'know, that could wink and tell a joke and keep you engaged. I think, in the beginning, that was his attraction to his first wife. Other than that, there really wasn't any."

As for Anna? "She had a strong personality. My father spoke of her like she was the most beautiful woman in the world," Amber said. "Someone who liked to dance, be social, have boyfriends. Somewhat of a bohemian. Someone who was an open-minded, fun, accepting person. Her focus was enjoying life. Definitely not a wallflower. She was somebody you were gonna remember."

She was that rare person that was always happy, as Eleanor recalled.

"She enjoyed being around people," recollected Cathy. "She had a rebellious streak."

"She was wild," according to Britt. "Very energetic. Brave. Always 'dating.'"

Did Eric at times ever resent her not being home . . . stepping out, so to speak? "I never heard of them not being friendly or fighting," recalled Britt. "Eric was always talking about how beautiful she was and how many boyfriends she had, and what a great figure she had, what a fantastic dancer. That's all I ever heard."

Just as his mother had unconditionally accepted him, obviously he accepted her.

How broad-minded was Anna's view of sexuality? In a story told to family friend Jim Chambers:

When his first marriage went bad, and he was so devastated and depressed as a result that he kinda withdrew from dating and any contact with women . . . next time Eric had sex it was with a prostitute that his *mother* had sent because she was so concerned about him and she didn't want him to give up on women!

By 1958, Stanton's grandmother Sophie had turned to religion, so clearly it was his mother, Anna, who would become the central female force in his life, and in his present physical and mental state, his ballast and confidant. It was she who would consistently engage him, challenge him, and personify the bold, voluptuous, attention-grabbing "Stanton woman" that would dominate his imagination and his art.

# Peerless Sales: Grapplin' Gals and Amazons

Rewinding the clock, other than *Bound To Please* (see chapter thirteen), much of what Stanton contributed to Edward Mishkin early on seemed to include fighting and wrestling women. This may have been material that Stanton had initially created for himself—the kind of escapist work he would always enjoy—or art created for Klaw that Klaw ultimately rejected, possibly for its frequent inclusion of battered men.

All that survive of these early "Stan" wrestling illustrations today are fragments, and these, for the most part, are preserved only for being later reprinted/repackaged by Leonard Burtman, who always seemed eager to relieve Mishkin of any and all Stanton artwork he had—if, of course, he could haggle a low enough price.

## Peerless Sales and Rasslin' Therapy

Starting in 1958 (until circa 1960), Stanton would have a chance to create wrestling/fighting girl comics again—and do it his way—while still using his "Stan" pseudonym.

Peerless Sales, a wrestling fetish and "strong girl" mail order business operated by sports enthusiast and niche fetish aficionado Max Stone, had just begun to supplement its catalog of "feminine muscle" 5 × 7 in. photos and femme wrestling/

jiu-jitsu/judo movies with 8.5 × 11 in. cartoon folders: 11 × 17 in. double-sided printed sheets that folded in half to create four-page narrative booklets. The material centered on hyper-athletic combative women or comic "female dominance" scenarios (still without nudity).

While the first contributors to the Peerless Sales cartoon folders were Phil Miller and the artist known as "Glen," it was not until Stanton came along with installment #7 (see p. 90 top) that the concept took off in any substantial way. In fact, Stanton clearly set a new standard for the niche subgenre—one that would be widely imitated for decades to come.

Following his initial contribution to Stone, Stanton strove to reduce the comic strip style clutter, eliminate the word and thought balloons whenever possible, and once again, as he had with Klaw, simplify the layout by adapting the material to the illustrated story format. In this way, with the majority of the Peerless Sales cartoon folders created in 1958 and '59, the words appear to serve as cinematic voice-over for the images. Stanton also explored the use of the illustrated "real life" letter as a fun means of telling a story—more than once beginning a comic with "Dear S . . ."— a story-telling device he frequently used later with his "Stantoons" starting in the mid-1960s.

Discussing his business dealings with Peerless Sales, Stanton later recalled: "All the pieces I drew for Max Stone were my ideas. He'd pay me by check, twenty-five dollars a page. He'd then sell the copies for $1 a page. He only wanted 'fighting girls.' That was his thing, not bondage like Klaw."

Of course, Irving Klaw had also sold fighting/wrestling girl movies and photo sets since at least the late 1940s (both Peerless and Irving sharing advertising space in Harrison's magazines since 1949), but Klaw soon realized that bondage themed material brought in the greatest return, and so, ever the practical businessman, largely focused his considerable resources and energy in that direction.

## Stone vs. Guyette

Historically speaking, it might be of interest to note that (as with Klaw) a direct line can be traced from Max Stone back to Charles Guyette (see chapter five). Max Stone would, at the very least, take direct inspiration from Guyette, early on even sharing the same business address: 1472 Broadway, room 904, New York—the address of "J. Redwine" and "Yetta," Guyette aliases in the 1930s/'40s.

It may even be possible that Peerless Sales was a direct outgrowth of Guyette's little known wrestling/fighting girl photography side business. In examining Peerless Sales ads and early Guyette ads, even the wording is remarkably similar. The only difference between Guyette and Stone (and even Klaw and Stone) was that Stone was a true specialist. In fact, he was among the very first to exploit the possibilities of a relatively minor and obscure fetish subculture and exclusively make that his business for twenty years.

Being I was in the trimmest of condition
the girls soon found their breaths coming hard
and their strength waning. Sencing this they doubled
their efforts. Peggy scissored my right arm and held my
left tightly with her strong arms. Betty did likewise to my legs and
soon I found myself helplessly spreadeagled on the ground. A second later
Shirley dropped down hard on my stomach with both her knees making me gasp
for air. After repeating this several times until I looked utterly helpless,
Shirley kneeled down, her legs wide spread, and settled herself heavily on
my stomach. I tried to utter a protest but as I started to speak, Shirley
raised her sitter about a foot above me and then came plummeting down landing
solidly on my chest. I thought every ounce of breath was crushed out of me. My
ribs groaned under the impact of Shirley's weight so heavily on me.

2

In the weakened condition I was in now I wasn't even a worthy opponent for one of the girls let alone all three. Shirley, sensing she could control the situation alone, maneuvered me into a full nelson and while on my knees, marched me over to the lakes edge. Strangely I felt like a little kid being man-handled by the neighborhood "BULLY"......

## Stanton and Stone: Kaput

Stanton produced at least thirty-four bestselling cartoon folders before things soured between himself and Max Stone. As with Leonard Burtman, it came down to haggling. Stanton had learned of a commission that paid Stone a hundred dollars a page, while Stone only offered Eric a flat rate of $35.00. After all he'd done for him, essentially inventing a narrative form that established his business and would yield thousands for years to come, wouldn't Stone at least consider splitting this commission 50/50? Stone would not. Stanton packed his things and walked.

It is very hard for me to describe the action that followed because I spent most of the time under water. The only thing I can vividly recall was that every so often my head was raised above water and I made quick gasping attempts to breathe. It was all over. I had been utterly vanquished. Shirley was now sitting on a limp water soaked foe, no longer capable of resistance.
Peggy came over and a little later a thoroughly disheveled Betty.... The three of them stood around me laughing and primping. "That was fun, wasn't it, Georgie?" Shirley giggled.

Well, I really got my lumps that time but it was worth it. The girls know I like a little scrap now and then and they actually enjoy rasslin too. We get together quite often and I have them wear very exotic type of clothing including high heels, corsets, leather boots, soft furs, etc.. It's a long, long story, full of tingling excitement. Would you like to hear about it?
George F. (Instigator)

PEERLESS SALES
BOX 171 CANAL ST. STA.
NEW YORK 13, N. Y.

# The Odd Couple: Stanton and Ditko Share a Studio

By the time Stanton began working for Peerless Sales, Max Stone had switched the address of his brick-and-mortar office from 1472 Broadway to the Kings Tower Building at 276 West 43rd Street. Coincidentally it was here, just two floors below, that Stanton's fellow C&I graduate and friend, Steve Ditko, established a working studio.

The eventful year was 1958. Stanton had separated from his wife, and much like the character Felix Unger from the opening of the classic TV show, we can just imagine Stanton—a sudden bachelor in need of comradeship and psychic shelter—showing up at Ditko's door, dragging his frying pan.

Ditko welcomed Stanton as his studio mate, thus initiating one of the most unique, synergetic, and confounding partnerships in comic art history. In the peculiar way that opposites sometimes attract, the Stanton/Ditko association almost seemed to make sense. Here was Ditko, the unyielding comic artist who was disinclined to draw women; here was Stanton, the mutable fetish artist who was uninterested in depicting men. Ditko's material showed a total unawareness of sex, while Stanton's material conveyed a kooky preoccupation with it. Yet both shared the same ambition of making it as artists; and both, one might say, were earnest and obsessed.

"We had a great working relationship," Stanton recalled in a 1988 interview. "We were the only guys who could have gotten along with each other."

For Stanton, this reunion evoked happier, simpler days at C&I, when he first met Ditko and recalled: "We just hit it off right away. It was a nice friendly thing, just talking about art."

As for the studio they shared? "It was a room about ten feet by twenty. One side was all windows. Steve and my desk faced each other. He lived nearby on 45th Street. I was living in Ozone Park with my mother when I first got started there."

By this time Ditko had suffered a major trauma of his own, contracting tuberculosis in 1954, and nearly losing his life. Following his recovery a year and a half later, Ditko returned to his vocation with renewed determination, contributing to the publisher with whom he had the longest association, Charlton, and later the company that would make his name, Atlas/Marvel.

There is no question that from the beginning Ditko showed signs of being a workhorse, taking almost any project he could get (which would play into their working relationship), as Stanton later recalled, almost with a kind of wonder: "There were times he would spend twenty hours straight doing a comic."

One could only imagine how gratifying Ditko's presence must have been to Stanton after his time with Grace; from being around someone who was repulsed by art to being around someone whose every waking moment was consumed by it. And Ditko was completely accepting of Stanton: "He thought my stuff was funny. We'd laugh a lot," as he fondly remembered years later. "Every experience that I had with Steve was terrific, as far as I was concerned."

## The Return of Klaw

Although the mail block against Irving Klaw remained until summer 1958, Klaw could not—or would not—stand idly by. Following the raid and apparent collapse of his first New Jersey based fetish art branch, Ikay Products, Inc., he soon formed another company, Jani Sales Co., on April Fools' Day in 1957. By 1958, having discarded that business after issuing only one advertising bulletin (April '57), he finally settled on "Nutrix Co."—a company name he had established in New York City earlier and used briefly to sell mail order novelties.

## Nutrix and Stanton

Klaw's first order of business with Nutrix, even before his mail block was lifted, was to reinvent himself as a publisher, and for this he needed the help of his protégé.

By now, Irving Klaw had watched Leonard Burtman gain a foothold in the fetish art business. Like Klaw, he was selling cheesecake and fetish photos, films, and—going beyond what Klaw had done—publishing bound digest-sized magazines. In the process he had borrowed Klaw's star players: Bettie Page, Bilbrew, and last but not least, Stanton.

It was time for Klaw to step up his game. Earlier that year, he had decided that in addition to his usual chapter serials he would also sell bound books that could reach beyond the scope of his mail order business. The model for Klaw's now notoriously famous line of 5 × 7 in. black-and-white Nutrix booklets was inspired by Leonard Burtman's earlier publication, *Exotica* (see chapter eleven). Not only would Klaw compete with Burtman, he would pay him back for his various plagiarisms by building on Burtman's idea. *Vacation in Fetterland*, Vol. One (see p. 227), with art by Stanton, was Klaw's first published Nutrix volume, advertised in March 1958.

For a follow-up, Stanton offered a highly marketable suggestion to Klaw. According to publisher J. B. Rund, "His contribution was the idea for a sort of anthology in this format, which came to be known as *Pleasure Parade*, eventually running to six volumes and containing contributions from all of Klaw's artists." On the cover of several volumes would be Bettie Page, who for unknown reasons in December 1957, had quit New York City and modeling, seemingly for good.

## Stanton + Ditko = Jon Bee

Following their first collaboration for Irving Klaw in 1953 with *Jasmin's Predicament* (as Stanton and Omar), Stanton and Ditko again contributed to Klaw's catalog in 1958. This time, instead of using individual names, they fused together to create just one: Jon Bee.

As advertised in a Klaw bulletin in the spring of that year: "We have employed a new artist named Jon Bee to illustrate a new type of adventure bondage serial about Viking girl plunderers in search of girls for the profitable slave markets. It is titled 'Helga's Search for Slaves.'"

With Book One of *Helga's Search for Slaves* (see p. 96 top) first advertised in March, two other Klaw serials appearing that year (and extending into 1959) also featured Jon Bee: *Bondage Correspondence* (which mysteriously showcased Jon Bee [Stanton/Ditko] + Stanton [apparently solo]) and *Fighting Girl Fracas* (in which the name Jon Bee was ascribed in advertising material while the artwork itself was unsigned).

Why did Stanton and Ditko forge this new identity, Jon Bee? It remains unknown. Aside from it obviously being an indication of how close they had become that the two artists would adopt a single name, Ditko may have been inspired by Stanton's (and Bilbrew's) numerous experimentations with pseudonyms. In 1959, Ditko assumed various aliases of his own, including J. Kodti/Kotdi (an anagram for Ditko, plus the initial of his middle name) and "Space Mann."

In future collaborations with his studio mate extending throughout the 1960s (and early '70s), Steve Ditko would only assume one other pseudonym—though he later disassociated himself from it and any connection with the material.

That alias? "Stanton."

## "BONDAGE CORRESPONDENCE"

(*Bondage Correspondence*, Chapter/page 1, featuring a fusion of Stanton and Ditko.)

# Stanton/Ditko: Partners in Crime

Just as Stanton and Ditko contributed to Klaw, they also collaborated on work for Edward Mishkin.

*The Sex Switch*—the comic originally intended for Leonard Burtman but eventually sold to Mishkin—marked the first in 1958, and set a precedent of sorts for many future collaborations between the two artists, with Stanton rendering the voluptuous femme fatales and Ditko contributing the minor male figures (as with the crying man above). Other Stanton/Ditko collaborations for Mishkin included covers for digest-sized books, among them *Her Highness*, *Smooth and Sassy*, and *Raw Dames* (see p. 98 top).

Again, in each case Ditko drew the lesser male figure while Stanton handled the commanding female. It is worth noting that the material produced for Mishkin was generally of uneven quality for one simple reason: when it came to art, Mishkin seemed to have no critical standards whatsoever, cheerfully accepting "everything and anything," regardless of how irregular or raw. (Especially true in the 1970s.) This might somehow be attributed to the environment Mishkin operated in, which after all was rough and ragged, down-and-dirty 42nd Street, the undying home to misfits and freak shows.

## Stan/Ditko and Max Stone

Stanton/Ditko team-ups included later work done for Max Stone, which in many ways were precursors to the earliest Stantoons both artists would produce starting in the mid-1960s, while Ditko was planning his exodus from Marvel Comics. It is interesting to note that these Peerless collaborations with Ditko were closer in format to what Stanton,

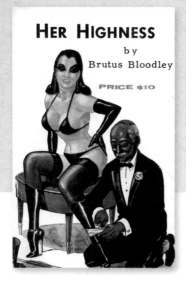

operating solo, generally strayed from—that is, mainstream comics (with standard cartoon panels and word balloons).

Regarding the difference between himself and Ditko, Stanton jested, "I think I always wanted to be a calendar artist." Asked in the same interview if he and Ditko had similar styles, Stanton replied: "No . . . I was into [drawing] girls." And then, quite honestly, he dropped the biggest difference between them: "I really wasn't into comic books."

In other words, unlike Ditko—and much more like Robert Crumb, who would not appear for almost another decade—Stanton saw illustrative art as a means to a subversive end. While Stanton drew "comics," he never considered himself to be a "comic book" artist.

The Stan/Ditko collaborations for Peerless Sales included "A Reel Fight," "Keeping Down The Jones," "Beaten & Bound," and "Battling Bondage Babes," featuring yet another likeness of Bettie Page.

MOMENTS LATER, THE SORCERER AND THE FEMALE WHO TRIED TO AID HIM, ARE BROUGHT BEFORE THE ONE CALLED... *SHAZANA!*

I AM A VISITOR FROM ANOTHER DIMENSION! I COME IN PEACE, SHAZANA! THERE IS MUCH KNOWLEDGE WE MAY EACH LEARN FROM THE OTHER!

YOUR WORDS ARE *EMPTY!!* YOU DO NOT DECEIVE *SHAZANA!* I KNOW THAT MY HALF-SISTER HAS BROUGHT YOU HERE, TO AID HER IN REGAINING HER FORMER THRONE!

## The Two-Way Street

And what of Stanton's contributions to Ditko? While in his lifetime Stanton openly admitted that he sometimes split jobs with his studio mate, can the reverse also be true? Since Ditko has long refused to discuss it, we may never know for sure.

But here and there—apparent to die-hard Stanton aficionados—are recognizable traces of Stanton's hand, going even as far back as 1954 (p. 98 bottom right, detail from "The Payoff": *Strange Suspense Stories* #20) and as late as 1970 (above top, "An Ancient Wrong": *The Many Ghosts of Doctor Graves* #20). And the clue to tracing Stanton's pencil "assists" beneath Ditko's very distinctive inking usually comes down to what Ditko once remarked: "I liked the way he drew women."

## Stanton's Women

While Ditko's characters often seem to float about with a balloon-like lightness, Stanton's figures seemed to be anchored on the ground. His women especially have a certain weight, a fullness of shape—a specific physicality. The character of Shazana (above) from the adventures of Dr. Strange (*Strange Tales* #133, 1965) is a good Stantonesque example.

## Bondage Mischief

And when we note the many claustrophobic enclosures and bizarre bondage devices evident in Ditko's work, particularly in the comics of Dr. Strange, can we suggest who is to blame?

Brendan McCarthy, artist and co-screenwriter of *Mad Max: Fury Road* (2015), in recalling the late Dave Stevens, once wrote: "He introduced me to the work of bondage artist Eric Stanton, which explained to me the elusive 'kink' feel in Ditko's Dr. Strange."

*(Captain Atom # 86, 1967)*

(Above: *Strange Tales* #143, 1966)

(Below: *Strange Tales* #115, 1963.)

## The Use of Wash

While Ditko's specialty was industry standard pen-and-ink, Stanton's strength was his use of wash, a technique he had been perfecting with Irving Klaw since 1953. As explained by Ditko expert Blake Bell:

> Wash is achieved with various degrees of water-and-ink mixtures applied by brush to create a series of tonal values. This allows an artist to achieve painterly affects, but also leaves him without the luxury of making easy corrections. Unlike line art, which can be fixed with white paint and pasted-on drawings—both of which disappear when the art is photographed—wash requires the use of the half-tone photographic process which often reveals smudges and paste-ups. A wash artist has to get it right the first time or start over from the beginning.

Ditko's first published work featuring the use of wash appeared in Charlton's *Mad Monsters* #1 (1961), which clearly showed Stanton's hand (opposite, top). Then, in 1966, following his departure from Marvel Comics, Ditko contributed various illustrated stories to Warren, publisher of the magazines *Eerie* and *Creepy*, which many consider to be among Ditko's best. Many of these were done using the wash technique. According to Blake Bell: "How he developed his expertise in such short order at Warren . . . is unknown."

At this point might we venture a guess?

("Black Magic" [below]; *Eerie* #5, 1966:
Femme [and wash?] by Stanton)

# Stanton/Ditko and the Studio Raid

The year 1959 proved to be rewarding for Steve Ditko, but less so for Stanton, who wavered between bouts of depression following communications with his estranged wife and family and the often unbearable pain from his back injury. Numbing pharmaceuticals helped, but balancing his intake proved another challenge.

In the meantime, during lucid moments he attended to business: the process of making art. Stanton completed several more chapter serials for Irving Klaw, including *Rita's School for Discipline* (January '59) and the rarity, *Captured and Bound by Captain Bonds* ('59: May/June); he also contributed to Klaw's new assortment of Nutrix publications, particularly *Pleasure Parade* (his brainchild), which had five additional volumes published that year. Other Nutrix anthologies inspired by *Pleasure Parade*—*Women In Distress* (volumes One & Two: published March, May '59) and *Bound In Rubber* (March '59)—also included imaginative, sometimes surreal Stanton art (right).

In a new development that year, Klaw also adapted/reissued earlier chapter serials in Nutrix book form. The first of these repackaged works in July '59 (see p. 228), was *Terror at The Bizarre Art Museum* (earlier titled *Bizarre Museum* [see chapter nine]). It was the only volume of rereleased material to which Stanton contributed new art; the remaining Nutrix reissues would simply feature edited and reformatted versions of original Stanton work . . . for which the artist would not be additionally compensated.

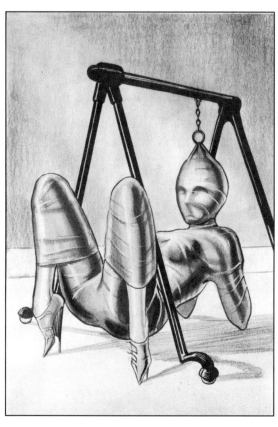

As for Edward Mishkin, Stanton contributed, in addition to the Stanton/Ditko work, at least a dozen covers for digest-sized paperbacks with titles like *Screaming Flesh, Impact, Stud Broad,* and *Touch Me Not.* Other Mishkin commissioned volumes published between 1958 and '59—*Chances Go Round, Masque, Female Sultan, Look at Her Motor Turn Over*—also included interior illustrations.

In what might certainly be called an unexpected turn of events, much of the original artwork for Mishkin (including some of the Stanton/Ditko work)—and everything else of value belonging to Stanton—would be seized in a dramatic police raid on the Ditko/Stanton studio.

At the time of the raid, which occurred on the cusp of the new decade (1959/'60), Stanton was with his Aunt May somewhere in Florida, but the events were recalled by Steve Ditko in response to the question for this book. In Ditko's own handwriting:

Yes. I remember some of the police raid. I was there when the police came in and took Ernie's material.
They looked over my comic book material files on shelves, etc. It was all comic book pages, etc. No interest in it.
Ernie's material was probably in folders, magazine packs, desk drawers, etc. He didn't need much reference material.

Stanton recalled: "Everything that belonged to me—8 mm films, 16 mm films, all my examples of what I did for Klaw, the paperback book covers were confiscated . . . They left behind pencils and blank paper!"

### Yonkers Man Called "Largest" Smut Dealer

According to an article appearing on the front page of the *Herald Statesman*, 10 March 1960:

A man described as "the largest known producer and distributor of pornographic material in the United States" was arrested today.

He is Edward Mishkin, forty-six, of 53 Algonquin Rd., Yonkers, father of three children.

Manhattan Dist. Atty. Frank S. Hogan said Mishkin has published about 80,500 obscene and pornographic books during the last two years, priced to bring in a gross of $563,500 on retail sale.

Police booked him on 198 counts of possessing, publishing, selling, and distributing pornography. Mishkin described his business as "book buyer."

Hogan said Mishkin operates a firm called Publishers Outlet Inc. at 254 W. 42nd St., just off Times Square, which serves as a center for a "nationwide operation."

His dealings, Hogan said, constitute the largest known traffic in pornography in the country . . .

EDWARD MISHKIN

That same day an article appearing in the *Long Island Star-Journal* elaborated: "Hogan said that immunity might be granted to 20 writers, artists, illustrators, printers, distributors and others who worked with Mishkin if they testify against him . . ."

With his material held as collateral by the state, Stanton was among those forced to take the stand.

## Mishkin: How Did It Arrive at This?

As per the *New York Times*, 10 March 1960:

Mishkin's arrest developed from a joint investigation by the police and Mr. Hogan's office that began last October. In December, 350 books were seized at Publishers Outlet, Inc., a bookstore at 254 West Forty-Second Street. This store is controlled by the defendant, according to Mr. Hogan. In January, Mishkin's warehouse was raided and 29,314 books were seized. Mr. Stein (Asst. Dist. Atty.) said that in the last two years, Mishkin had ordered a press run of 80,500 copies that had a retail value of $563,500. Mishkin has a previous record in merchandising pornography and as a second offender, he faces a possible jail sentence up to 159 years and a total fine of $496,500.

Was Mishkin being railroaded? Or were the accusations leveled against him as America's most notorious publisher of pornography correct?

To answer that question accurately, we must go back in time and consider the era: forget that none of the published material entered against him as evidence in the 1960 trial had explicit content, and ignore that most of it would hardly merit the equivalent of a PG-13 rating today. We must overlook the fact that *Playboy* magazine had featured nudity since 1953, and that Tijuana bibles and stag films, which by today's standards, depicted true pornographic (or XXX rated) content, had been produced and distributed in America since the 1920s. All the courts needed legally for Mishkin's published material to be found "obscene" (thus "pornographic") was for that content to appeal to the "prurient"[1] interest of a select few.

Thus framed, the most innocuous risqué material (below) could be found obscene, and in fact was.

## Stanton Stiffs the Prosecution

Of course what the authorities wanted was for Stanton to incriminate his patron by suggesting, as others had done, that Mishkin had specifically given instructions to produce material that in the eyes of the law and public at large might be perceived as deviant (i.e., "sexually morbid, grossly perverse and bizarre"). But in the end, Stanton offered none of that. In spite of being interviewed by the DA earlier that year upon having his artwork seized and providing crumbs regarding his dealings with Mishkin that were later quoted in the *New York Times* while raising expectations of more damaging testimony to come, in court Stanton actually stiffed them, serving up the most thick-headed, useless testimony he could muster while maintaining a straight face.

(*So Firm and So Fully Packed*, 1958)

(*Stud Broad*, 1958)

[1] *prurient*: marked by or arousing an immoderate or unwholesome interest or desire; *especially*: marked by, arousing, or appealing to sexual desire –*Merriam-Webster*

## The People of the State of New York vs. Edward Mishkin

Ernest Stanton [*sic*], having been called as a witness, was first duly sworn and testified as follows:

**Court Officer:** Be seated. Please keep your voice up. What is your name?
**The Witness:** Ernest Stanton.
**Justice Gassman:** What is your second [or middle] name?
**The Witness:** I have no second name. Ernest Stanton.

**Direct Examination by Mr. Stein:**
Q. Do you know the defendant in this case —Mr. Mishkin?
A. Yes, I do.
Q. When was the first time you met him, sir?
A. Oh, I couldn't tell you the exact year, but about '55, '56.
Q. And have you ever done any work for him?
A. Yes, I have.
Q. What type of work, sir?
A. Art work.
Q. I show you People's Exhibit 1A—1A through 1L, a series of twelve drawings; and I ask you, sir, whether you can identify these drawings?
A. Yes. They are mine.

Q. What are they?
A. They are art drawings.
Q. Do you know who drew them?
A. Yes. I did.
Q. For whom, sir?
A. Oh, for Mr. Mishkin.
Q. Now, can you tell us something about these—Did you have a conversation with Mr. Mishkin prior to the time you did these drawings?
A. No. He just gave me a—a book, and I illustrated it.
Q. Well, you spoke to him when he gave you the book, didn't you?
A. Yes.
Q. And what did you—Tell us the conversation that took place?
A. Well, I—I wanted some work; and I asked Mr. Mishkin if he had any work for me. He said he had. He handed me the script; and he said, "Illustrate the script"; and that was the work.

So it went, with Stanton contributing nothing and the Assistant DA getting nowhere.

As Stanton later proudly summarized his testimony: "What I said instead helped the defense." This of course was not appreciated by the DA and his minions. "I remember the court people wouldn't let me stay. I had to leave."

He also recalled the fallout of his decision not to cooperate with the authorities: "When I went to the police to retrieve my stuff they told me everything was burned."

Although the story Stanton related to Ditko was different.

> When Ernie came back from the police station after being questioned, he said the police told he could take back the material. Ernie told them he didn't want any of that material back. No more association with it. So it was probably scrapped.

Why the discrepancy? Although it seems highly unlikely that Stanton would have simply walked away from his confiscated material (i.e., "8 mm films, 16 mm films, all my examples of what I did for Klaw, the paperback book covers . . ."—essentially the only reason he took the stand in the first place), we can assume that he was putting his friend at ease. Keep in mind some of the artwork used as evidence in the trial (e.g., *The Sex Switch*, *Raw Dames*) was also technically Ditko's. And by then Ditko had embarked on his life-changing path with Marvel Comics—which might have been threatened if his involvement with "pornography" became public knowledge.

Vindictiveness on the part of the authorities may not have been something that Ditko wanted to hear. "No more association with it" certainly sounded more comforting.

## Reevaluating the Notorious Pornographer

The truth was, 5 ft. 3 in. Eddie Mishkin (a.k.a. Ed Lantz) was hardly the gangster of tabloid folklore.

### Mishkin Rap Sheet (1936–1959): In Brief

1936 (14 September and 16 September): Arrested on bookmaking charges ("alleged to have accepted bets on horses in a parking space . . .") Receives thirty days, suspended sentence (both times).

1952 (10 June): Charged with possessing obscene material. Charges dropped. ("Accused by Detective Louise Nebb of the 3rd Division of having had suggestive photographs of nude or semi-nude females in a brochure entitled 'The Layman's Manual' in his office at 112 West 49th Street, New York . . .")

1955 (26 May, 31 May): Pleads the fifth at the Senate Subcommittee To Investigate Juvenile Delinquency. Was this a crime? Kefauver and his subcommittee would have the public think so. Thus, the headline in the *Herald Statesman*: "Kefauver Group Charges Mishkin With Contempt," ". . . Three men refused to answer questions about alleged involvement in the sale of pornographic materials. The men were cited

specifically for improper use of the Fifth Amendment to the Constitution, which gives a witness the right to refuse to testify if he believes he might incriminate himself . . . He [Kefauver] added that the three witnesses 'deprived the subcommittee of necessary and pertinent testimony' by resorting to the Fifth Amendment . . ." (Improper use of the Fifth Amendment? In the end, Mishkin [and Irving Klaw] were only "cited" for contempt, never officially "charged." It was just an empty threat [see endnotes].)

1955 (8 June): First investigated by the FBI under the urging of Kefauver and his subcommittee, with an informant providing unsubstantiated information stating: "Mishkin has been able to operate with impunity in New York City because of payoffs to New York City Police Department Detectives at both Precinct and Division levels. They said the payoff reportedly is $1,000 per month to Division Commanders, $500 per month to Precinct Commanders, and $20 per month each to beat officers in pertinent areas where Mishkin operates." This same informant later tipped off the FBI to Mishkin's alleged involvement in a large shipment of "obscene" material from New York to Minneapolis, which after a lengthy investigation turned out to be false.

1959 (29 December): Charged for vagrancy ("when he walked into a bookstore—Publisher's Outlet at 254 W. 42nd Street while a raid was in progress" and "refused to give his address.") Charges dropped.

In retrospect, should we say that "sexploiteer," not pornographer, might best describe Edward Mishkin as publisher at this time?

Or was it simply a case of the authorities specifically targeting material intended for a sexual minority? (As stated in later court documents: "Fifty books are involved in this case. They portray sexuality in many guises. Some depict relatively normal heterosexual relations, but more depict such deviations as sadomasochism, fetishism, and homosexuality.")

In fairness, could not the prurient appeal requirement for obscenity also be applied to *Playboy* magazine, or even mainstream cheesecake pin-ups?

## *"Kingpin" of Smut Gets Stiff Term*

Edward Mishkin, a man described by the District Attorney as "the largest producer and purveyor of pornographic material in the United States," was sentenced yesterday to serve three years in jail and to pay a fine of $12,500.

Guilty.

On 172 criminal counts. Sixty of those related to Stanton.

Most damaging, ironically enough, were Mishkin's piracies of Irving Klaw material: Nutrix publications mentioned at the beginning of this chapter (*Pleasure Parade* [volumes 1 through 4], *Women In Distress*, *Bound In Rubber*, and *Terror at The Bizarre Art Museum*), not to mention several chapter serials, including *Bondage Correspondence* (featuring "Jon Bee").

"Assistant District Attorney Melvin Stein, who prosecuted the case, called Mishkin the 'kingpin in the pornography trade in this country,'" reported the *New York Times*:

Justice Gassman said that the court had been "sickened by reading the books entered into evidence," and added that the availability of the books offered "no assistance to the settling of unsettled lives in our troubled times."

What else could Mishkin do but shrug and appeal the verdict?

In the meantime, finished with Max Stone and still cross with sexploitation/fetish publisher Leonard Burtman, Stanton was again forced to rely on Irving Klaw.

# Stanton's Dominating Women: Three Narratives

## Flashback: The People of the State of New York vs. Edward Mishkin

Cross Examination by Mr. Kern [the defense]:

Q. Mr. Stanton, you are still drawing these same type of covers and illustrations, aren't you?

A. Yes, I am.

Q. As a matter of fact, you're working right now on—on drawings for Newtrix [*sic*] Publishing Company?

A. That's correct.

Q. And the drawings which you are making are the very same kind of drawings which you made in connection with these books, isn't that correct?

A. That's correct.

As suggested by defense attorney Michael Kern during the trial, it may be asked why Mishkin was being tried and not Irving Klaw?

No doubt that same question had already crossed Klaw's mind. And by 1960, well aware that all eyes were on him, Klaw was taking even greater precautions in censoring artwork and photos repackaged in his Nutrix publications. This meant cleavage was diminished; midriffs were eradicated (as with the Bettie Page staircase ornament above); and photo re-touching/amending—another Stanton specialty under Klaw—became obsessive, with black undergarments lengthened and transformed into velvety skirts and white lingerie and slips altered into shimmering silken dresses.

Yet there was no disguising the fact that these were still bondage fantasies.

By mid-1960, Irving Klaw's sponsorship of chapter serials came to an end. Stanton's *Bettina In Jeopardy* (April/August '60), complete in fifteen chapters/episodes and featuring yet another incarnation of Bettie Page ("Bettina Pagette"), would be the last.

## "CAPTURED AND BOUND BY CAPTAIN BONDS"

## *  BETTINA  IN  JEOPARDY  *

## From Amazons to Tame-Azons

"Dominating women," did you say?—If ever there was a subgenre waiting to be reinvented by a particular artist, this was it for Stanton.

Keep in mind that before he was obliged to illustrate bondage fantasies for Klaw, Stanton's real interest was in drawing fighting gals and Amazon fetish comics (even if his Amazons in 1950 wore tiny Roman helmets [below]).

In time he admitted, "The word 'Amazon' became a key to my fantasies."

What is likely Stanton's most subversive creation, the Prinkazons, would evolve out of his unique concept of Amazons, but first to arrive in 1960, were his "Tame-Azons."

## Tame-Azons Subdue and Subjugate Man

A Nutrix-era success spawning four sequels, *Tame-Azons Subdue and Subjugate Man* incorporated elements of Amazon fantasy, mixed wrestling/fighting, bondage, and forced feminization while actually being a tale of marital strife—not the first by Stanton. Initially advertised in Nutrix Bulletin #30 in fall of that year, it marked a thematic tipping point in Stanton's evolution as a cult artist. It also exemplified Stanton's eccentric and often amusing fixation with proportionately large women.

## New Sub-genres of the Nutrix Era

While Klaw's fetish material had influenced publisher Leonard Burtman early on, Burtman in turn would influence Klaw, and by 1960, content relating to dominating women and fantasies of male subjugation and transvestism—frequently featured in Burtman material—received special attention in their own unique Nutrix publications.

In Burtman's case, such fetish subcategories related directly to his own fixations and fantasies, and narratives of forced dress-up "transformation" in particular seemed to occupy a great deal of his attention; in Klaw's case (as with Mishkin), it was purely business: the market seemed to support such material now, so it seemed a worthy commercial investment.

I'M NOT GONNA DIE, AND I DON'T INTEND TO BE A SLAVE!! — The two girls roll over and over on the beach and into the water~

**"DAWN BATTLES THE AMAZONS"**

The first installment of this series begins with an unhappy wife who, eager to get to the bottom of her husband's resentfulness and disinterest of late, enlists the services of "Tame-Azons Inc.," a marital overhaul agency. Two "Amazonic" operators of mythic proportions, Portia and Potentia, are soon dispatched to her home and waste no time in zeroing in on the errant husband and making a corrective attitude adjustment.

The structure of the narrative is of a story-within-a-story, and so once forced into constrictive bondage and overwhelmed by the Tame-Azons, the subdued husband passes out, falling straight into a dream in which he wakes up on a remote island "inhabited only by Amazon type girls and no men"—much like that of Wonder Woman lore. Here, forcefully captured and humbled by an Amazon with Potentia's features, he is dragged before the island queen, Portia, who regards him with disdain, insisting his former, troublesome gender identity be stripped at once:

Roughly throwing her captive man to the floor, Potentia slipped a rubber sheath skirt around Paul's chest and waist and told him to shed his trousers, which he did very reluctantly. Then seizing a pair of tweezers and scissors, Potentia began plucking Paul's eyebrows after snipping off some of his hair to make way for a wig hanging from a stand nearby.

While Portia was slipping a pair of sheer black nylon stockings on his legs, Potentia sat astride Paul's chest, pinning him down with her body weight and applying lipstick.

Paul suffered in silence, for he knew by this time that it would be useless to object to his conquerors' tactics.

Slowly but surely Paul was being transformed into a woman.

Not content to stop there, the Amazons proceed to the next phase of his subjugation: he is bound with rope while a "spring steel clamp gag" is inserted in his mouth, bizarrely kept in place by chains fastened to his newly pierced earlobes.

Next he is ordered to bow down before Portia and "swear allegiance to her cause by kissing her spurred boots," which the husband refuses to do, despite his agony, and then the story takes an interesting narrative twist:

Paul heard Portia's words of warning and in his dazed dream, his mind wandered to thoughts of his wife, Michelle, and how he had mistreated her. As his thoughts swung over to his wife, while still in a light sleep, the girl threatening him with dire punishment seemed to take the face and form of Michelle in place of Portia.

This was quite strange, as formerly Michelle had been a meek and submissive wife.

Clad in feminine garments, Paul was extremely reluctant to kiss anyone's boots, let alone those of his own wife. Then someone came from behind who looked like Portia and stuck a high-heeled foot between his bound ankles and tripped Paul.

Paul fell with a loud thud on the floor and the girl behind him propped him up on his knees. Then he saw that it was Portia who was forcing him to bend forward.

He tried to pull his head back, but Portia's strong hands on his head made it impossible. His efforts to avoid kissing Michelle's boot were all in vain. His unwilling lips now touched Michelle's boot as a symbol of obedience and the thoroughly subdued man was now completely under the command and wishes of his wife.

For the first time in their many years of marital strife Michelle had the look of mastery on her beautiful face. The Amazon type costume that Michelle was wearing brought out every luscious curve of her sensuous body and Paul now began to regret having been tempted to cheat on this most desirable woman.

Paul woke up from his troubled dream to find that he was still bound onto the bench on which Potentia and Portia had tied him before he fell asleep. Everything that had transpired had been a figment of his imagination and he was no longer dressed in female attire . . .

"You had better give in now," Portia went on, "and save yourself a lot of punishment, for we Tame-Azons mean to earn our fee . . ."

"I'll be good from now on," Paul continued. "I love my wife and will never need your services again. But, for goodness sakes, get me out of this bondage before I go out of my mind. I know when I'm licked."

Michelle was delighted with this sudden change in Paul's attitude towards her and most pleased that it had not taken weeks or months to make Paul change his behavior.

While Potentia was releasing the thoroughly chastised and chagrined Paul from his enforced bondage, Portia took Michelle aside and gave her some hints on how to handle Paul in the future in case he went back on his promise.

After Potentia and Portia had departed, Paul related the full details of his dream to Michelle. Whereupon Michelle told Paul that the possible reason why Paul had dreamed up this bizarre dream was that in his subconscious mind he really desired to be overpowered by a woman.

Michelle suggested that they try out her theory and when Paul agreed, they began a short trial period of letting Michelle dominate Paul. They rented an Amazon type costume from the Tame-Azon office, along with a brown leather bondage costume for Paul to wear.

As the preceding illustrations indicate, at times it may be of great value to see Stanton's art alongside the original text to fully appreciate his work. His work—and lifelong ambition—not simply being that of comic artist, but of interpreter of psychosexual fantasy. (Some might suggest interpreter of maladies.) And Stanton's audacious contributions often convey an extra dimension of disturbing edginess and wit barely hinted at in the original writing.

## Tame-Azon Sequels

The next two Tame-Azon installments are likewise noteworthy.

In *Men Tamed to Submission by Tame-Azons*, Portia and Potentia are called into action by a mysterious agent to "subdue and vanquish" a thoroughly obnoxious "he-man" TV actor. Targeting their mark at a party, they soon chloroform him and spirit him away to Tame-Azon headquarters, where they swiftly set out to administer their own hands-on brand of radical therapy.

Step one: subdue the client and make him more amenable to change through the magic of ritual bondage. (Keep in mind Wonder Woman had her magic lasso too.) Step two: as issues of hyper-masculinity seemed at the root of his personality imbalance, some corrective feminization was in order.

Waking to discover his arms sheathed into a pair of laced leather opera gloves and his pants symbolically shredded, the he-man TV actor might have informed the Tame-Azons—if not for the gag in his mouth—that *he* actually was their anonymous employer, and that he had intended this whole episode, including the kidnapping, as part of a publicity stunt.

Too late for that, as a constricting corset and brace are fixed on his chest, and thigh-length boots—then bracing rods—are applied to his legs and his gag is quickly replaced by a horse bridle bit (p. 115 top).

When Michelle donned her Tame-Azon costume, an amazing change came over her, and from a meek mousey type woman, she immediately became a strong domineering type of person. This transformation was amazing to observe! Her whole attitude towards Paul seemed to change and she no longer was afraid of him. Strangely enough, even Paul felt this new air of domination and confidence in Michelle and he dared not disobey his wife's commands.

This was a complete reversal of his character and Michelle's astute analysis had hit the nail on the head. This was what he had really wanted all along. That had been the reason why Paul had sought the attention of other females in a vain attempt to rid himself of his frustrated inhibitions.

Instead of being grumpy, mean and uncooperative to his wife, he was now madly in love with her . . .

This time Potentia was determined to break down Dan's will by binding his gloved hands underneath his thighs. Placing her sturdy legs around Dan's back, Potentia pushed Dan's head down between his booted knees while she tied a rope through slots in the rods that had been attached to his boots. This put a great deal of strain and stress on Dan's bowed head.

The tedious bent-over position in which he was now placed caused his body to ache all over but there was no relief in sight for him from Potentia, who was intent in subduing him.

As with most sessions involving S&M, the scene ends not in sexual gratification, but emotional catharsis. With intense restraint, the futility of struggle, and the eradication of ego came humility and a letting go—peace and a chance to be reborn.

Part of the deal was that the mysterious employer of the Tame-Azons promised to pay an additional large fee if they could reform Dan Marlo into becoming a quiet, modest and pleasant person, instead of the loud-mouthed overbearing braggart that he presently was.

"Sadomasochism," according to Dr. Roy Beumeister, professor of psychology, "is a way people can forget themselves . . . Masochism is a set of techniques for helping people temporarily lose their normal identity." This would be significant if the adopted identity was a wellspring of stress. The concept of gender as a performance (also known to theorists as "gender performativity") might come into play here. For that reason, it may be fitting that the protagonist of the story is an "actor." By the end, he is greatly relieved to put this he-man role behind him by becoming someone else—albeit in women's clothing. The story concludes with the actor's self-hating and boastful ways—"his one-time air of braggadocio"—vanquished forever.

## Stanton's Wide View of Fantasy

Stanton was well aware of the undercurrents of his material, though he argued against labels that only served to create prejudice:

> You know, this whole area of fantasy in our field is considered by people who don't understand it to be sadism or masochism. It isn't that at all. You don't have to be a sadist to love to see something; you don't have to commit a crime . . . All kinds of people like a kind of excitement that other people sometimes think is sadistic or masochistic, yet both groups go to the movies oftimes for just this thing . . . but they don't lose control of themselves over it. I really don't like to relate these things to sadism or masochism. I think, more accurately, they are just in the fantasy field.

## Stanton and the Heart of Darkness

What Stanton may not have discussed was why he was attracted to such dark, sexually charged material to begin with.

It might be argued that he was simply "being paid" to do such work, but if we trace his career from the start, we clearly see that his choices were deliberate: to seek out Klaw, Burtman, and Mishkin. Unlike what has been suggested of other artists

(Joe Shuster and Bill Ward, to name a few), Stanton did not gravitate toward such material "out of desperation," but genuine curiosity and interest.

And why? Tom offered a clue: "He said sex is the bottom line of the psychology of people."

Sexploitation, particularly fetish art, became a means of exploring the human psyche. He saw these stories—many of them—not simply as "porn," but as journeys of self-discovery. Sex was just the key that unlocked the door.

Tom added: "I think my dad was a psychologist for a lot of people . . ."

And why were the stories often so dark? It might be suggested that the deeper and darker the secret, the closer you arrived at the truth. Wasn't this also the goal of psychoanalysis? Wasn't Sigmund Freud also an interpreter of dreams?

Often in assessing the value of sexploitation culture, we—as custodians of history and art—must be aware of our cultural bias, which assumes the material *must* be of lesser value and not worthy of our attention because it is sexually oriented.

### *Bondage Artist Dominated by Tame-Azon*

Just as we are underscoring the more weighty aspects of sexploitation narratives, we arrive at the third and final Stanton Tame-Azon installment (as the last two were contributed by the artist known as "H." [Harry]). Clearly this time out the objective was a little different, being far less an exploration of identity and gender and far more a romp involving kinky slapstick comedy.

Contrary to what may be assumed from the title—that Stanton was working out some potential guilt over being a fetish artist for Klaw—this is much more about his guilt over not producing *more* fetish work in a timely fashion. Irving Klaw is never mentioned directly in the story, but the Nutrix Company is, and it is the publisher who, fed up with the ridiculous excuses and unreliability of his "popular artist," hires Potentia (this time suspiciously resembling Bettie Page) to set him straight. As an investigation reveals, the artist was too busy breaking the "Klaw Cardinal Rule": carousing with bondage models after work, then "going to nightclubs and drinking most of the night. He would then be sleeping most of the next day, which accounted for the delay in handing in the artwork to meet the publisher's publication deadline."

There is no ego-busting feminization in this particular Tame-Azon sequel, but plenty of comeuppance, where the irresponsible and perpetually hung-over artist receives a solid taste of Tame-Azon-style remedial therapy and bondage before ending up wrapped in tape like a mummy.

The story concludes with the artist, "crestfallen and embarrassed," promising to be more self-disciplined.

So we might ask: where was Portia—Potentia's mate—during all of this? In Latin America, the story tells us, where she was busy establishing a Tame-Azons Inc. franchise. And this with the global revolution of Women's Lib still many years away and hardly yet imagined.

## Stanton's Dominating Women

Before there was Xena ("Warrior Princess"), before there was Varla (from *Faster Pussycat, Kill!... Kill!*), and before there was Emma Peel (from *The Avengers*), there was Stanton's bad-ass women. These were rampant transgressors, gender outlaws, and cultural rule breakers. Call them paranoiac male projections, call them avenging proto-feminist goddesses: no artist at the time undermined

traditional notions of male and female roles and responsibilities like Stanton.

Progressing from John Willie inspired bondage scenarios, it was finally with his "dominating women" that Stanton found his own unique direction, and one might say his own signature.

# Satellite and Stanley Malkin

As Stanton was redefining a specialty that would set him apart from other artists and even bring him a certain notoriety and cult fame, he met one of the most important patrons of his life—although the relationship got off to a bumpy start.

"I met Stanley through Mishkin," Stanton later remembered, referring to Stanley Malkin, Times Square bookstore owner and operator.

As Stanton recalled, he, Malkin, and Mishkin formed Satellite Publishing Co., a business venture at first centered on a fetish digest-sized magazine named *Bound*. With Stanton serving as creative director and primary artist, Eneg was also brought in.

Perhaps as Leonard Burtman had established Burmel Publishing Co. through *Exotique*, eventually branching out with his own satellite assortment of products (i.e., fetish-inclined photo sets, one-shot specialty digests/magazines, etc.), Stanley Malkin hoped to do the same. His primary concern, evident from the start, was obtaining subscribers, and so each issue of *Bound*—as well as every other Satellite publication—included a prominent subscription page through which it appears the publisher intended to grow an audience. It is unknown to what extent he was successful.

Stanton's initial involvement with Satellite hardly lasted beyond a year and issue #4. "We printed some things. I did some good work for them," as Stanton recalled:

BOND

No. 1

BONDAGE HOTEL - VIXEN'S VENDETTA - THE CAPTIVE
PHOTOS - ILLUSTRATIONS

They were to get manuscripts and I was to illustrate and they would handle the publishing. Well they found out they could do photographs cheaper than illustrations, but books with photo covers did not sell as well, so they wanted me to just do covers suggesting that there were drawings inside. I didn't like that and eventually they forced me out.

Before long another shadowy associate became involved who would carry the company without Malkin into the 1970s: Pasquale Giordano (a.k.a. Pat Martin, a.k.a. Pat Martini). However, in the year Satellite was incorporated (1961), Stanton contributed some unique work, including the kinky comic serial *Vixen's Vendetta*, the classic *Have Leather . . . Will Fashion* (featuring what is likely the first appearance of the word "dominatrix" in a fetish context), and *Suzanne's Punishment School* (next page), which included some attention-grabbing graphite work and a vibrant watercolor cover, setting the tone for the stand-out digest-sized booklet covers he would shortly produce in the '60s. Stanton also directed Satellite's first fetish photo sessions, which included, much as he had done for Klaw, posing and rigging of the models (see following pages). His "B" set photos, comprised of 128 prints, featured dark-haired Peggy Evans, who would soon work with Leonard Burtman, most notably appearing as the cover girl for *High Heels* #1.

ALL BOOKS OF SATELLITE PUBLICATIONS ARE MADE UP OF NEW AND ORIGINAL MATERIAL AND SELL FOR $5.00 EACH.   ALL BOOKS SOLD ONLY BY MAIL.

HAVE LEATHER WILL FASHION...A beautiful young bride tries to regain her husband's waning love by wearing leather bondage costumes, but finds the exotic garments should be worn by him.  All happens under the masterful direction of a girl bondage expert. Vividly illustrated by STANTON.

HOW TO TAME A ROOMATE...A fighting girls story at its best, as two girl roommates struggle for the love of a handsome man with the loser forced into leather bondage. Excitingly described and dramatically illustrated by STANTON.

CORRESPONDENCE ISSUE NO. 1...Contains sensational letters on all subjects such as Dominant Women; A Bondage Party; Fighting Femmes; Fashions etc. and are presented to you with dramatic photographs and vivid illustrations by STANTON.

In an FBI memo dated 15 December 1961—unknown to Stanton at the time—*Have Leather . . . Will Fashion*, the illustrated novella *How to Tame A Roommate*, and *Bound* #3 were targeted by the agency to determine their suitability for prosecution. After an FBI lab analysis and recommendation to a local US Attorney the case was dropped (4 April 1962).

Likewise, in a separate, earlier FBI investigation (8 May 1961), issue #1 of *Bound* was targeted when Mishkin tried to distribute it in Philadelphia. ". . . It appears that the magazine is designed to appeal to a perverted female mind," noted one FBI agent (3 July 1961), possibly perplexed by themes of dominating women. That investigation was also discontinued after further review.

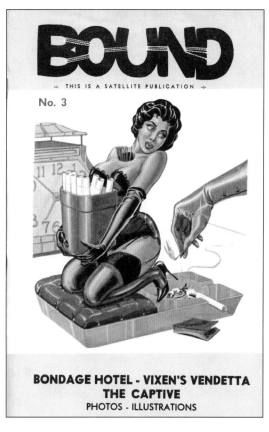

Victoria withdrew a pocket-knife from her waist-belt and with a sudden quick thrust severed the rope that held him aloft. He crashed to the floor and lay motionless as Victoria stalked over to Valerie and slapped her cheek smartly.

Silently, desperately, the Duke attempted to work loose, but the knots had been set while he was unconscious and had imposed no muscle tension or resistance. His struggles weakened, he knew it was useless. Victoria surveyed the captive and placed her heel gently upon his chest. She increased the pressure gradually as she spoke..

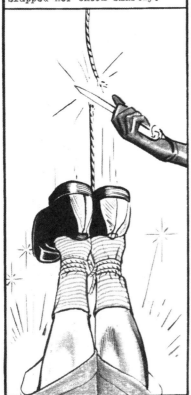

(*Vixen's Vendetta*, 1961)

SET # B-1

SET # B-2

SET # B-3

SET # B-4

There are eight photos in each set. Each set sells for Three Dollars. Mark which set or sets you wish by number plus 20¢ for postage and handling.

We have new numbers coming out every week, photos and drawings. We have been very fortunate to obtain one of America's foremost artists in this field—STANTON.

# Stanton and Selbee Associates

In 1962, Stanton's productivity for Irving Klaw would grind to a halt. Infrequently commissioning new work from his name artists at this point, Klaw had settled into an unfortunate pattern of recycling modified material from his glory days and otherwise producing dreary, luridly titled photo bondage booklets for easy profit.

Apprehension perhaps played a part in his reluctance to invest too heavily in the future of Nutrix, but the enterprising spirit was obviously gone. Enter Lenny Burtman, whose creative ambition was soaring just as Klaw's was waning.

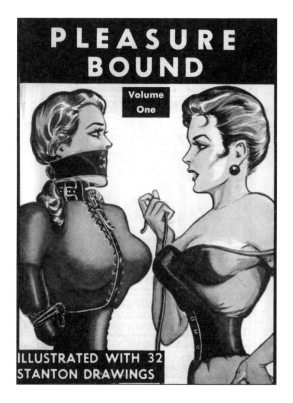

## The Trials of Leonard Burtman

Much happened to Burtman after his falling out with Stanton in 1958. While he would continue to produce and distribute *Exotique* and a wide assortment of fetish related material, the authorities were closing in. That same year Burtman became aware that he was under surveillance by the FBI, the US Postal Inspection Service (a federal law enforcement agency within the Post Office), and last but not least, local law enforcement (who then functioned in coordination with postal inspectors).

While being tracked by the police, Burtman claimed the FBI was conducting illegal searches; it was not paranoia. By 1959, the offices of

Burmel Publishing Co., the warehouse of Pigalle Imports (distributors of Burmel material), and even Burtman's home had been raided. Leonard Burtman and partner Benedict Himmel were subjected to multiple overlapping court battles, the first of which involved charges of obscenity and resulted in the demise of Burmel. Kaysey Sales, his next publishing imprint, also fell under legal attack. Finally in 1960, approximately one month after his divorce from Tana Louise (same month, same year as Stanton divorced Grace: June 1960), Leonard Burtman re-invented himself most famously with Selbee Associates, Inc.

## Stanton and Selbee

Under the imprint Selbee Associates, Burtman first published the digest-sized magazine *Masque*, a half-hearted continuation of *Exotique*, which folded with Burmel; and the *New Exotique*, which folded with the Kaysey Sales imprint. Although Bilbrew remained primary artist for its short run, each issue contained at least one illustration by "Stan," an indication it was Stanton art produced for someone other than Burtman. Regardless, by 1962, Burtman had officially extended an olive branch and openly employed "Stanton" as a regular contributor to his new line of full-sized magazines: *Pepper*, *Paris-Taboo*, *Diabolique*, *Orbit*, *Nocturne*, *Exotica* (reinvented), and *High Heels*. As part of the deal perhaps (we do not know what promises Burtman made in reconciliation), Stanton replaced Bilbrew as titled "art director" (e.g., *Orbit*, listing "G. Bilbrew" in the masthead in 1961, listed "E. Stanton" in 1962). Bilbrew, unfazed, picked up the slack at Satellite Publishing Co., becoming the primary artist for *Bound* and other Malkin related publications.

## Selbee and the New Sexploitation Era

Following the huge success of magazines like *Playboy* and *Modern Man* (*Playboy*'s strongest competitor), the late 1950s and early 1960s saw an explosion of full-size slicks featuring topless nudity. Some, backed with big money, were sold in broad daylight on newsstand racks and published monthly (like *Playboy* and *Modern Man*), while others, funded with less money, were passed under the counter in poorly lit liquor and tobacco stores and published irregularly. Selbee magazines were of the latter.

While *Playboy* projected sanitary yearnings of the girl next door, Selbee magazines featured hard strippers and B-girls who looked like they had been around the block. Selbee slicks were not "lifestyle" magazines promoting upward mobility or the "sporting life," but sordid, low-rent affairs. Yet oddly enough, this very quality seemed to contribute to their unique charm and certainly their wide collectability today as disreputable, politically incorrect relics.

THERE WAS NO OTHER NAME FOR IT, THAT DANGEROUS DESIRE TO CARESS, TO KISS, TO LOVE THE FEMININE FLESH...

*a short story...*

*by*

*Lee Garamond*

Straying from strictly fetish oriented material that appeared in *Exotique* (and digests Burtman continued to publish on the side), these full-size sexploitation magazines adhered more closely to the conventions of leg and "heel and hose" periodicals, which were then in their heyday. Likewise, the artwork provided for these magazines was appropriate for this audience, featuring larger-than-life, balloon-boobed femmes and burlesque humor of the kind that inspired influential sexploiteers like filmmaker/"glamour" photographer Russ Meyer and producer/writer David F. Friedman.

Stanton's work from this period is largely noted for its inspired use of pencil and charcoal

(see following pages), which during the early '60s mostly seemed to have replaced his reliance on the technique of wash. As always in his art (and well suited to Selbee magazines), women were center stage, poised, and projecting sexual power, while the men—what few appear—were generally on the sidelines: dull, unattractive, and forgettable.

## Stanton/Ditko and Selbee

Just as Lenny Burtman lured back Stanton, Stanton reeled in Ditko, with whom more often than not he split the more "comic book" inclined pen-and-ink commissions. Under the umbrella of "Stanton," both he and Ditko produced a series of filler cartoon serials and one-shot gag comics. These Stanton/Ditko serials included: "Cherie" for *Paris-Taboo*, "Spies in Spikes" for *High Heels*, v. 1, "Space Dolls" for *Orbit*, "Miss Patience" for *Pepper*, "Midnight Maiden" for *Nocturne*, "Black Widow Sorority" for *Diabolique*, and the longest-running "The Savage Sisters" for *Exotica* (with the serial later continued in the rebooted *High Heels*, v. 2).

Using charcoal/pencil only, Stanton also contributed solo serials, which included "Satana" for the magazine *Satana*, "Stormy The Stripper" for *Striparama*, v. 2, and "Case of the Lost Legs" for *Leg Show* (all three magazines beginning in 1962). Along the lines of earlier collaborations with Ditko, Stanton illustrated the voluptuous femmes while leaving the lesser, often generic male figures to Steve.

It has been widely noted that Ditko's inking at times seems to overpower Stanton's pencils in these cartoons, but close examination clearly reveals the contributions from each artist. As for Ditko's heavy reliance on pen and ink over pencil, it was driven, in part, by his need to produce volume for Charlton and Marvel Comics, which meant creating most of the finished product during the inking process while spending less time on penciling. Being the yin to Ditko's yang and adamantly oddball, Stanton focused entirely on the penciling process, sometimes to his detriment (commercially speaking), and eschewed inking, perhaps making the case for why he never directly worked for Charlton or Marvel Comics—subject matter aside.

"ISN'T IT DISGUSTING WHAT SOME
GIRLS WILL WEAR TO ATTRACT A MAN!"

*From out of the medieval past, returns a forbidden female sport . . . sword dueling in secret European college sororities . . .*

## Female Sword Dueling Returns

by
Carlson Wade

(More often than not, Stanton's art pieces were used to introduce
one of Burtman's self-penned efforts.)

# SATANA

by Stanton

(Stanton serial without Ditko)

(Bottom: "Case of the Lost Legs" for *Leg Show*.
Stanton sans Ditko, underscoring his singular fixation with
creating tone and depth using pencil/charcoal.)

# The Savage Sisters

# An Idol's Passing

*John Coutts was dead;* at least that was the word that reached Stanton in the early months of '62. Transmitting this rumor, which had spread through "bizarre" social circles (like those connecting Coutts to the likes of Charles Guyette), was current publisher, Leonard Burtman.

As it turned out, Burtman got it half right: diagnosed with an inoperable brain tumor in April 1961, John Coutts (a.k.a. John Willie) was not dead, but certainly dying.

Upon hearing the news, Stanton toyed with the idea of creating an affectionate homage to his idol. And where else to begin but with his iconic creation *Sweet Gwendoline*? Thus the concept of "Sweeter Gwen" was born.

With typical resolve, Stanton got right to work. "I roughed out 30 pages and took them over to Burtman and he said 'great,'" Stanton recalled. Then, back at the studio: "I went and did tight, tight penciling, but then I got another commission and I had to stop on 'Sweeter Gwen.' I asked Steve Ditko to ink it for me and we'd split the money 50% / 50% . . . We came up with a very beautiful story and we finished it and took it over to Burtman. He loved it and that was it."

The first installment, signed "J. W. Stanton" (John Willie Stanton), appeared in a one-shot publication, *Exotique Quarterly* (see following pages), released that April. The full narrative appeared for sale in a Burtman catalog that summer (coincidentally, August: the same month of Coutts's passing). Like Stanton's Burmel-era serial *Deborah*, it was first printed on photo paper and only made available to mail order customers—and not cheaply: "3 Chapters for $5.00 per chapter / $12.00 complete." (This in an era when a full thirty-two-page comic book cost 12¢.) As pointed out by publisher J. B. Rund: "It can be assumed that the publisher knew he had a good 'item' and was going to milk it."

Stanton was no less ecstatic about what he rightly perceived as an instant classic, and in a manic fit and rare lapse of modesty earlier that year declared in a letter to Paul H. Gebhard of the Kinsey Institute: "I am now completing the GREATEST THING I OR ANYONE ELSE HAS EVER DONE including John Willie . . ."

In the end, not only was *Sweeter Gwen* a tribute to his creative predecessor, it was also, somewhat ironically, Stanton's most mainstream comic: at once an acknowledgement—as far as layout and progressive storytelling design—of the influence of his former Cartoonist and Illustrator's school instructor, Jerry Robinson, and an abiding guilty pleasure, *Mad* magazine—a double-fondness Ditko also shared (note close-up of the shelf in their studio: right).

As for Ditko's one illustrative contribution to this crossover undertaking? Quite obviously, it was the somewhat incongruous character Teddy Truehart (top right), the Faithful Frederick/ Hairbreadth Harry/ Dudley Do-Right stock hero/ clod character that John Willie initially intended to include in the narrative of *Sweet Gwendoline*, but somehow never found room.

It might be worth noting that for his take on Gwendoline, Stanton was far more successful at integrating characters and plot points than Willie. From the moment the story begins the narrative machine of *Sweeter Gwen* is off and running, with not a single panel wasted in driving the sequential storytelling arc to its tightly worked conclusion. Willie, it should be said, had some difficulty with sequential continuity, and in correspondence expressed his dissatisfaction with the original *Gwendoline* serial (which he later revised), as well as with *The Missing Princess* (later renamed *New Adventures of Sweet Gwendoline* by Klaw).

For his 1962 updating of Willie's *Gwendoline*, Stanton also modernized the female characters, making them, like the Nyoka model of his adolescence, strong-willed "women of action"— unafraid to be physical. Gwen, for instance, is transformed from the Victorian model of demure, ultra-femme "lady" into an earthy, 'rasslin-friendly country gal—in fact, not far from *Babe, Darling of the Hills* (bottom).

And just as John Willie/Coutts cast himself as the melodrama's bungling mustachio-twisting villain Sir Dystic d'Arcy, Stanton did likewise, but in a typically self-deprecating light as a prideful, overly excitable gnome, Sir D'Astard D'Astardly, an alter ego he would reference in the future.

Last but not least, Stanton managed to work Bettie Page into it, recasting a buxom, playful version of her in the role of stylish secret agent U89. (In *Sweeter Gwen*: "YU-69.")

Stanton and Ditko meshed so well creatively that to many they seemed like a single artist. This even led skeptics to question Stanton's physical existence. And by 1971, because of *Sweeter Gwen* specifically, it would appear in print—stated as fact—that "Stanton" was none other than Steve Ditko. For Stanton, such was the price of dwelling in the shadows.

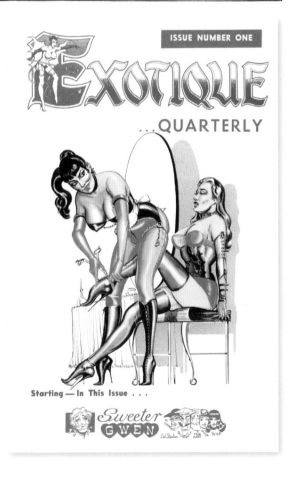

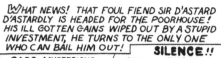

(First installment of three pages as it appeared in *Exotique Quarterly*.
Note the compact storytelling, the efficient composition of each panel, and how effectively
Stanton works in the fetish elements: shoes, ankles, stockings, and legs.)

FORTUNATELY, CLOSE BY IS OUR HERO, TEDDY TRUEHART...

HARK! DO I HEAR THE SWEET VOICE OF MY SWEETER GWEN? GREAT SCOTT! SHE IS IN DISTRESS!

HAVE NO FEAR, SWEETER GWEN I AM COMING TO YOUR AID!

I, TEDDY TRUEHART, WILL SAVE YOU SWEETER GWEN!

HEE HEE OLE D'ASTARDLY SCORES AGAIN! $ $ $

WITH HEAD HELD HIGH, CHIN OUT, OUR FEARLESS HERO CHARGES FORWARD! SINCE HE FAILS TO SEE GAGA'S SLEEK SILKEN CLAD LEG IN HIS PATH, HE IS AMAZED THAT THE GROUND SHOULD RISE UP AND STRIKE HIM ON THE BACK OF THE HEAD.

OH! HE CAUSED A RUN!

I'M COMING GWEN! WAIT FOR ME!

WE GOT HER! NOW WE'LL SEARCH HER SHACK. WE'LL FIND THE MAP OR WE'LL MAKE HER TELL US WHERE IT IS! THEN WE'LL LOCATE THE SECRET MINE AND I'LL BE RICH!! HEE HEE HEE HEE

THAT SLY WEASEL IS UP TO SOMETHING!

OH, DEAR! WHAT WILL BECOME OF MY DAISIES? "SOB!"

WILL SIR D'ASTARDLY SUCCEED IN HIS FOUL SCHEME? WHAT HORRIBLE FATE AWAITS OUR SWEETER GWEN?? to be Cont'...

# 26

## The Kinky Origins of Spider-Man

That same spring 1962, while Stanton was penciling the concluding pages of what would become *Sweeter Gwen,* Ditko embarked on the most important project of his career. "For me," recalled Ditko, "the Spider-Man saga began when Stan called me into his office and told me I would be inking Jack Kirby's pencils on a new Marvel hero, Spider-Man. I still don't know whose idea was Spider-Man."

As fate would have it, editor/writer Stan Lee rejected the Kirby test pages and proposed that Ditko take a crack at it.

In 2002, addressing the memory of that first, ill-fated version of the superhero, Ditko wrote:

Kirby had penciled five pages of his Spider-Man . . . The splash [page] was the only one with a drawing of Spider-Man. A typical Kirby hero/action shot . . . Kirby's Spider-Man had a web-gun, never seen in use. The only connection to the spider theme was the name. The other four pages showed a teenager living with his aunt and uncle. The aunt was a kindly old woman, the uncle was a retired police captain, hard, gruff, the General Thunderbolt Ross type [from *The Hulk*], and he was down on the teenager. Next door or somewhere in the neighborhood there was a whiskered scientist-type involved in some kind of experiment or project. The end of the five pages depicted the kid going toward the scientist's darkened house. That was the Spider-Man "given" to me. That is the total of Kirby's Spider-Man "creation" . . . five unused penciled pages of an unfinished story.

In the rejected Kirby test, the character evidently resembled Captain America (formerly co-created by Kirby), complete with swashbuckler boots and gloves, and most significantly, a half-face superhero mask; instead of the Captain America shield, he had a holstered web gun.

that Stan Lee alone was the creator, as he had the "idea," and this was accepted as truth. But of course this is false.

Jack Kirby also stated in print: "I created the character. I created the costume."

Again, false.

Fact: the costumed hero known today as "Spider-Man" was not designed at Marvel Comics, but at the West 43rd Street studio shared by two collaborating artists, who at this time were practically joined at the hip: Stanton and Ditko.

Neither Jack Kirby nor Stan Lee was present at the creation of this costumed icon.

The mystery that remains is at least two-fold:

a) Did the secret world of bizarre culture that Stanton embodied in the studio inspire the creation of the greatest superhero of all time?
b) To what extent did Stanton personally contribute or help shape the creation? Or, we might ask, would his absence from the studio at that time alter the character as we know it today?

Let us examine the first question, which, in some way, also relates to the second.

According to Ditko expert Greg Theakston: "The first thing Ditko did was to redesign the costume. His new version featured a mask that covered the entire face, a ploy that immediately set the character apart from heroes appearing at that time. Prior to Spider-Man, heroes had open faces (like Superman) or half-faces (like Batman)." According to Ditko, "I did it because it hid an obviously boyish face. It would also add mystery to the character and allow the reader/viewer the opportunity to visualize, to 'draw,' his own preferred expression on Peter Parker's face and, perhaps, become the personality behind the mask."

So from where did Ditko draw his inspiration for the full face mask if not (according to Theakston) from the world of comic books? Would it be fair to say from bizarre culture? Or specifically from Stanton, since he had been creating hooded characters for almost as long as he had been a fetish artist? (Note the Stanton example drawn for Klaw in 1953, p. 143.) As Amber Stanton has noted: "It is interesting that Spider-Man more than all the other popular comic book superheroes has an erotic S&M quality. He wears a full body suit covering every inch including his entire head and face; much

"Stan never told me who came up with the idea for Spider-Man, or for the Spider-Man story Kirby was penciling. Stan did tell me Spider-Man was a teenager who had a magic ring that transformed him into an adult hero . . ."

As Ditko pointed out: "Almost all the bits of this 'creation' (the scientist, magic ring, etc.) were discarded/never used. So what is left of the 'original creation?' A name, a teenager, an aunt and uncle."

In recounting the history of Spider-Man's invention, this is where things get complicated, as it deals more with shifting memory and personal pride than recorded fact. For years, it was assumed

In fact, touted as the bondage scenes are in *Wonder Woman*, there may be *more* submerged variations of bondage play in *Spider-Man*. The only difference is that comic books convey a boy's world, which unlike the material Stanton contributed to Irving Klaw, Leonard Burtman, and Edward Mishkin, is largely asexual and devoid of women.

like a fetish latex body suit." Would it be fair to say that Stanton had been drawing full-body fetish suits at least as long as he had been drawing full-face masks? According to Amber: "Spider-Man is into bondage. He captures villains and binds them with his webs." Is this an exaggeration or a truth? According to Tom: "My dad explained his idea of the web coming out and showed me the fingers *like that*." Amber also mentioned: "the idea of the web shooting out of Spider-Man's wrist and the movement which he made with his hands to release the web." According to Tom: "He said it would be a web shooting out and he said his take on it was that the web goes around someone as if it was bondage and it was a fishnet stocking." According to what Stanton told Rick Vincel: "Eric came up with the 'bondage' part of it. Y'know, shoot your web and they're 'entrapped.'"

Now one might argue that Kirby had also designed a web gun with the same purpose of "entrapping" bad guys, but close examination of many of the cartoon panels in Spider-Man conveys an idea closer to what Tom explained: webbing that *encircles* and binds, much like in fetish fantasies.

(Artwork by Eneg)

# Spring 1962

Let us step back and recreate the scene at 276 W. 43rd Street. The magazine (*Exotique Quarterly* #1) containing the first installment of *Sweeter Gwen* is published and likely sitting on Stanton's desk, and sometime later Ditko arrives at the studio from the Madison Avenue office of Marvel Comics with his new assignment: "a 1 or 2 page synopsis" plus rejected art for a fantasy involving the origin of a teenage superhero and a simple demand from Stan Lee: "Draw me a Spider-Man!"

Hoisting himself to his feet, back throbbing with pain, Stanton sidles up to Steve's desk, "Whatcha got there?"

**Ditko:** Some crap from Kirby. (Spreading out the rejected Spider-Man pages.)

**Stanton:** Looks like Captain America with a web gun.

**Ditko:** Tell me about it. It stinks. And now I'm supposed to turn this into an immortal masterpiece, like my career depends on it.

**Stanton:** Maybe it does.

(*Note:* although Ditko had created Captain Atom for Charlton comics, this was his first superhero assignment for Marvel Comics.)

**Ditko:** Uh, maybe I need to do some research. Stuff to do with spiders, going back through the ages.

**Stanton:** Maybe you can start with this old copy of *Exotique*. (Flops it on his desk.)

**Ditko:** (Examining it.) You did that? It stinks.

**Stanton:** No, Eneg.

**Ditko:** Anyway, this character—he's supposed to shoot a web, I dunno how. The web gun idea is old.

**Stanton:** Maybe it spews from his wrist, like when he touches himself.

**Ditko:** Touches himself?

**Stanton:** Like that. (Shows the motion with his fingers.)

**Ditko:** Spews?

**Stanton:** Spews like sperm.

**Ditko:** Nice, Ernie. Take it to Mishkin.

The previous is just speculative, but there is no doubt that Stanton and Ditko were both involved in "spider" brainstorming.

Ditko later wrote: "There have been earlier uses of the spider 'idea' in comics: Paul Gustavson's Alias the Spider, DC's Tarantula with his web gun, and certainly many other heroes, heroines, villains, and villainesses (such as, in this last category, the earlier Black Widow, before Simon or Kirby or Lee)."

This accounts for the Selbee filler strip "Black Widow Sorority" (next page) published in 1962, coughed up by Stanton/Ditko, likely during the heat of research for Spider-Man or during the penciling and inking of the first eleven-page comic, which saw print early that summer.

We might wonder if "Black Widow Sorority," aside from being a playful exploration of Spider-Man motifs, was also Stanton's reflection (expressed in a female context) of Ditko joining the boy's club ("fraternity") at Marvel? Certainly this assignment was, in effect, an initiation for Ditko from "backup features" fantasy artist to "lead story" front man, after which he would attain equal footing in that famed bullpen.

Returning to the copy of *Exotique Quarterly* #1 mentioned previously, and likely sitting on Stanton's desk, we might wonder: was this item also a part of the discussion regarding Spider-Man that spring? (Certainly the publication would have been something shared with Ditko, since it contained the work on *Sweeter Gwen*, and Ditko likely would have been curious to see how the strip looked in print.) Now, in flipping the magazine over and examining the back cover (see p. 148), several possibilities stand out.

The first thing that seems odd are the colors of the lettering. Why aren't they black? Second, is it only a coincidence that these colors are the same that Ditko recommended for his new superhero, Spider-Man? Ultimately, the choices were made by the colorist at Marvel (Stan Goldberg), who chose cherry-red and dark cobalt. But colors that you see here are suggestive of the very ones Ditko had personally recommended. (As he stated: "My original color combination was a warm red orange on the webbing section and a cool blue on the body parts.")

# BLACK WIDOW Sorority

by Stanton

cont....

The second thing that stands out regarding this back cover is the figure of the woman and what she is wearing. No, not just the cape and the kinky lion tamer jumpsuit, but her eye mask. Or, more precisely, the distinctive shape of her eye mask that calls to mind the shape of the eye mask worn by Spider-Man. Which suddenly makes us realize that the design behind Spider-Man's unique look may be doubly kinky. Not only does he wear a full face mask, but an eye mask on that full-face mask. The eye mask is of course black, which explains why the rest of the mask could not be black, since that would render the eye mask indistinguishable. Finally, this absence of black (beyond the eye mask) would allow for the webbing design ("the use of the spider theme," as Ditko put it), which was one of Ditko's most inspired touches.

(Detail: kinky lion tamer [transparency from original art].
Eliminating the eyes would simply make it faster to draw.)

We might ask: How else did Stanton help shape the creation? According to Craig Theakston: "by suggesting the Spider signal, which could be flashed on buildings and on crooks, much like the famous Bat signal." According to Tom, "Aunt May was my dad's aunt, his babysitter from childhood, when he was sick a lot. That was put into character." Again, Theakston—who wrote that Stanton did admit to contributing "to the flow of action of the stories" and that, "Together he and Ditko would have 'skull sessions' and choreograph many of the great action sequences throughout the books." All this, yet in a 1988 interview (with Theakston)— which Stanton prefaced by saying, "Steve doesn't like me to talk about him"—Stanton insisted: "My contribution to Spider-Man was almost nil." True, he mentioned: "When we worked on storyboards together, I added a few ideas." Then quickly again, as if to not offend his old pal: "But the whole thing was created by Steve on his own . . . The whole thing was Steve Ditko."

"In fact," Theakston wrote, "many of the issues suggest Stanton's hand in the mix."

Photo by Steve Ditko

## The Invisible Man

According to Rick, "Eric purposely underplayed his role and contributions to the comic." Amber also supported this claim, even clearly suggesting why: that openly admitting to any involvement over the years would have brought too much unwanted attention to an artist who needed to operate in anonymity.

"My dad explained," said Amber, "that he wanted to protect the family by keeping a low profile." And as she vividly recalled from her childhood (in the 1980s): "He even declined most interviews with famous shows such as *Donahue* because we were children and in school, fearing that it could negatively affect our lives if people knew he was an erotic fetish artist." In a separate interview, family friend Jim Chambers likewise affirmed:

> I don't think he really liked being the center of attention. He liked to be a sort of behind the scenes type of person. He could've gotten media attention as an artist because he was fairly well known. He could've been on TV or radio, could've done newspaper interviews or stuff like that. But he kinda shunned the spotlight."

Aunt May, 1957

## So What about Peter Parker?

According to Tom: "I think there were a lot of similar characteristics between my dad and Steve Ditko. I think there was a lot of feeling like an outsider. I think that's what Peter Parker was . . . And I think it was a mix between my dad and Steve Ditko."

At the time, Stanton was as physically vulnerable as pre-Spider-Man Peter Parker and just as predisposed to bouts of misery and self-doubt. Like Ditko, Stanton wore glasses too (though rarely in photos). "Gwen," as in *Sweeter Gwen* and Gwen Stacy was a shared interest . . . if not an inside joke.

It might also be remembered that while Ditko became a life-long resident of Manhattan and Stan Lee and Jack Kirby both resided on Long Island, it was Stanton who lived in the borough depicted in Spider-Man comics. More specifically, although the neighborhood mentioned in the comic is Forrest Hills, Queens—which then was the upscale Greenwich Village of that borough—we can recognize Ditko's depiction of Stanton's less affluent, less artsy Ozone Park neighborhood. Did Stanton take his friend on a few exploratory/research excursions through that part of New York to pick up the local color? We can well imagine it.

## Superheroes vs. Fetishists

Regarding the question of character and dual identities, much has been made of the parallels between fetish culture and superhero culture as it exists in the fantasy world of comic books. Like superheroes, people in the fetish underground also have secret personas that they must protect at the cost of harm to their loved ones. By day they are obliged to fly under the radar, appearing "normal" or inconspicuous, while at night or during select occasions, they reveal shadow identities and even fit into costumes—these often form-fitting—made of latex or leather (material which to them might have a charged or magical property).

Often masks, calf-high boots—even capes—are a part of these fetish costumes, just like in the superhero world.

What can we make of this?

## Who Created Spider-Man?

Nothing can be taken away from Ditko and all that he contributed to the costume and the comic, and obviously this is the way Stanton wanted it documented for posterity: ". . . the whole thing was created by Steve on his own . . . The whole thing was Steve Ditko."

But as always, there is something that Stanton is not telling.

"This is why people loved Eric," remarked Britt, his second wife. "He could be trusted to *keep secrets*."

# Burtman's Transformations, Plus Steve Ditko

Not all of Leonard Burtman's titles would succeed. By 1963, his first line of Selbee magazines: *Pepper, Paris-Taboo, Diabolique, Orbit, Nocturne,* and *Exotica* would fall by the wayside, while four central titles (*Satana, Striparama, Leg Show,* and *High Heels* [v. 2]) emerged as his primary line. New titles in which Stanton was listed as art director included *Female Mimics* and *Focus On.*

Of enormous interest to collectors is the premier issue of *Focus On* showcasing Bettie Page (her name at last spelled correctly), which contains an impressive array of Page photographs by Burtman, the filler strip (p. 154) "Cartoon on Bette Page," revealing Stanton's memory of the model's regional accent (once described as "real Smoky Mountain Tennessee"), and playful line art by Stanton/Ditko (above).

Also of cultural importance, and likely closer to Burtman's heart, was *Female Mimics*, the first full-size, nationally distributed magazine dedicated to transvestism, and by association gay culture, with the title obviously inspired by the Irving Klaw book *Femme Mimics*. The powerful half-face image of the Klaw book (p. 155) that perfectly depicted the coexistence of alternate, if not contradictory identities even found its way into *Spider-Man*, after a variation of the idea (by Eneg) appeared on the cover of the 1962 Satellite publication *Bound and Transformed.*

For the publication *Female Mimics*, Stanton contributed several original strips and line art that Burtman recycled into the 1980s. As usual Stanton dragged in Ditko, with interesting (and often fun) results.

For certain transmutations (see p. 155 bottom), it is fascinating to see Stanton and Ditko operating artistically as two halves of one whole: Stanton: female; Steve: male . . . or is that Steve: female?

One thing is for certain; the nature of the work Ditko was doing with Stanton was like nothing he was doing for Marvel or Charlton comics.

(Most sought-after Selbee magazine *Focus On:
Bettie Page*, 1963, with "E. Stanton" listed as art director and containing Stanton art.
Highest-grade vintage copies are wildly priced.)

# Stanton on
# LGBT Material:

"The first time somebody approached me to do a homosexual story," Stanton later recalled:

I thought at first, "This is not for me. I don't want to do this." However, I read the story, and in the reading of it I could tell it was very beautiful to the man who wrote it. There was a lot of feeling and sensitivity there. After I'd illustrated it, this fellow (he's dead now, a great shame) and I had some long talks about transvestites he knew, and he clearly explained why they were the way they were then, and are now. And we talked of many things. I miss his educated conversations and wonderful personality. Anyway, I've learned from him and others that there are any number of sexual eccentricities—things I may not care for and you may think are disgusting—but to the people who have them, they're very lovely and important. A lot of these people are very lonely because they think that no one else shares their fantasies. I've drawn things for them that made them say, "How did you know this is how I felt? I thought no one else understood this. Or me."

# The Girls

by Stanton

Although Burmel Publishing Co. and the Kaysey Sales imprint that briefly followed were crushed by the authorities, the spirit of Burtman's labor of love fetish magazine, *Exotique*, survived into the 1960s in various incarnations.

Previously mentioned was *Masque*, Burtman's attempt to continue *Exotique*, which ran for four issues. Issue number 5 of *Masque* would morph into the magazine *Connoisseur* ("C-1"), shifting after the second issue into a series of *Exotique*-like transformation "photo fiction" digests/magazines until reaching C-17, at which point the series again included art.

In 1963, it was Stanton who contributed the impressive cover paintings for these booklets, in addition to select interior illustrations. These precisely rendered watercolor covers and graphite

sketches for the *Connoisseur* series, among other similar non-Selbee Burtman publications issued that year, would showcase Stanton's development as an artist, and in years to come, earn him the respect and following of such illustrative greats as Olivia De Berardinis and Dave Stevens.

Early 1963 also saw the first appearance of *Sweeter Gwen* in book form, for which Stanton also provided a watercolor cover. Adding to his deep bitterness regarding Burtman in later years was that Stanton was only paid a flat rate of $35.00 for each of these illustrative paintings, which also meant surrendering the original art. *Sweeter Gwen* proved a tremendous success for Burtman, running through countless reprintings throughout the 1960s, 1970s, and beyond. A "flat rate" meant that Stanton never saw another nickel from his work.

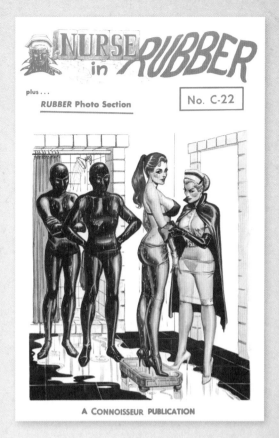

# BOUND AND SPANKED

ILLUSTRATED

LIMITED EDITION

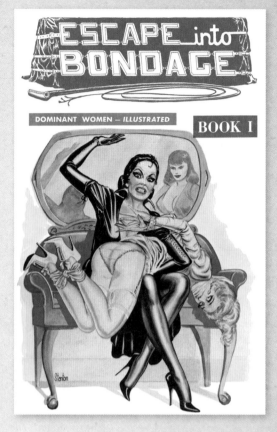

ESCAPE into BONDAGE

DOMINANT WOMEN — ILLUSTRATED

BOOK I

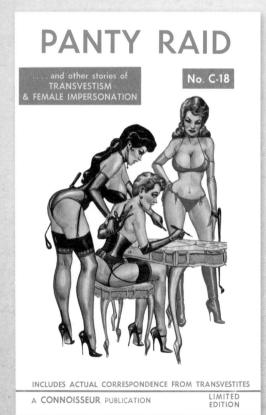

# PANTY RAID

.... and other stories of
TRANSVESTISM
& FEMALE IMPERSONATION

No. C-18

INCLUDES ACTUAL CORRESPONDENCE FROM TRANSVESTITES

A CONNOISSEUR PUBLICATION

LIMITED EDITION

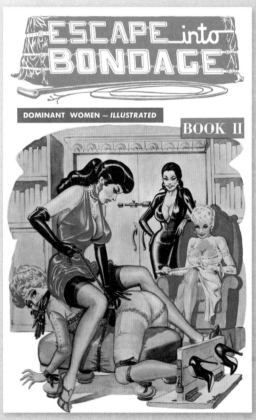

ESCAPE into BONDAGE

DOMINANT WOMEN — ILLUSTRATED

BOOK II

# 28

# Sexploitation Pulp Artist

Stanton's reconciliation with publisher/entrepreneur Stanley Malkin began at the tail end of 1962, when Malkin tracked down Stanton at his mother's house in Queens to make amends. *Bound,* Malkin's attempt to replicate the publishing success that Burtman had experienced with *Exotique*, had proven a disappointment, and it may have been at this time that Malkin pitched a new venture—one in which Stanton's participation was central: a full line of pulp fetish paperbacks with far greater distribution potential than Malkin's former publications, for which Stanton would be hired as primary cover artist.

Malkin was proposing a salaried position, plus an all-bills-paid bachelor pad on the Upper East Side of Manhattan, on the simple agreement that he produce four modest pulp covers a month (which Stanton might produce in a week). And what could he say to that?

In later years, Stanton recalled Malkin's generosity with fondness: "He was the best I ever worked for . . . He even furnished my small apartment on East 87th Street. I'm talking about a television, curtains, everything . . . He'd say 'do whatever you want . . .'"

As a token of renewed understanding, Stanton would agree to contribute to the final (farewell) issue of *Bound*, #9. As it turned out, it was an "all-Stanton" edition.

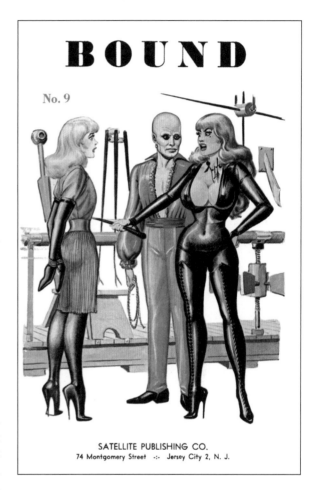

**BOUND**

No. 9

SATELLITE PUBLISHING CO.
74 Montgomery Street  -:-  Jersey City 2, N. J.

## First Niter and After Hours Books

In mid-1963, while maintaining employment with Burtman, Stanton moved to his new digs at 531 East 87th Street and produced his first oddball cover paintings for Stanley Malkin. The first book to appear in print, likely in fall of that year, was *Strange Hungers* (see p. 167). More than likely, for Malkin this book was just to test the waters,

as it was a mishmash of "exotic" short stories (two curiously attributed to a pen name Burtman had used, "Carlson Wade"), and not, by definition, a pulp novel. The back cover read, "Another Original First Niter Book," even though it was the very first volume. Additionally, it was numbered #101, rather than #1—another attempt at appearing like an established line, which might help in promoting consumer confidence, attracting potential distribution, and even confusing authorities.

As Malkin had proposed the job of pulp cover artist to Stanton, he likewise offered a similar position to Bilbrew, for whom he created an alternate imprint: Nitey-Nite Books, a line that lasted for only four titles. Chris Eckhoff, a vintage paperback bookseller and expert, is correct in asserting that Bilbrew was "notorious for ignoring the rules about the degree of acceptable nudity." Proof of this appeared on the cover of the first Nitey-Nite book, *The Love Cult*, which featured topless nudity—a big no-no in the book business at that time (even today).

Malkin was legally liable, as he had incorporated the company ("Nitey-Nite Books Inc.") under his own name and that of his wife, Loretta (in addition to a third partner in Buffalo New York, William J. Smith). With the collapse of the Nitey-Nite imprint, Bilbrew contributed cover art for the fifth book of the First Niter series before fading into a period of obvious creative decline and absence—possibly linked to substance abuse problems—which extended throughout 1964, before resurfacing again at full strength in 1965, largely with the sexploitation pulp imprints attributed to the Sturman brothers based in Cleveland, Ohio.

Stanton (who was no stranger to addiction and dysfunctional coping methods) pulled it together to produce forty-six playful gouache paintings for the First Niter line and forty-three more that appeared on Malkin's next line of books, "After Hours," incorporated in 1964, by Malkin legal operative William J. Smith. More book imprints would follow, with Stanton art in tow.

These "adult" paperback covers for Malkin stand in sharp contrast to Stanton's earlier, darker netherworld explorations for Irving Klaw. In general they reflect a droll, mildly twisted (yet progressive) understanding of sexual politics and top/bottom dynamics, which have made the pulps, as artifacts, endearing, if not valuable, to liberal-minded collectors. Being female-centric in spirit, a great many of the covers convey lesbian themes. Then there is the comedy arising from a reversal of gender roles, where women are generally cast as physical aggressors while men are shown as compliant and fragile creatures. The vibrant, sometimes oversaturated "comic book" color choices of the covers, in part attributed to Stanton's admitted color blindness, are another factor in their cult appeal.

Largely for their humor and quirky charm, it is for these sexploitation paperback covers that Stanton is best remembered today.

Madame Butch

by

Edward Marshall

95c

AH 131

ADULT

READING

AH

AN ORIGINAL AFTER HOURS BOOK

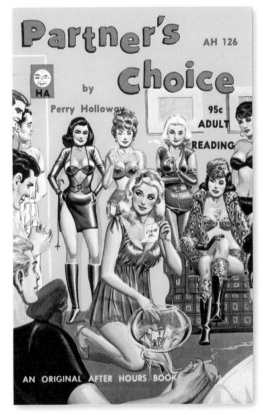

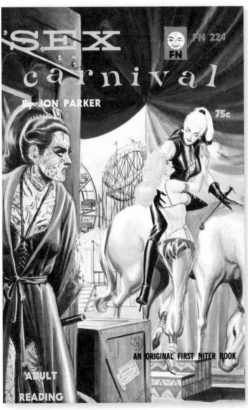

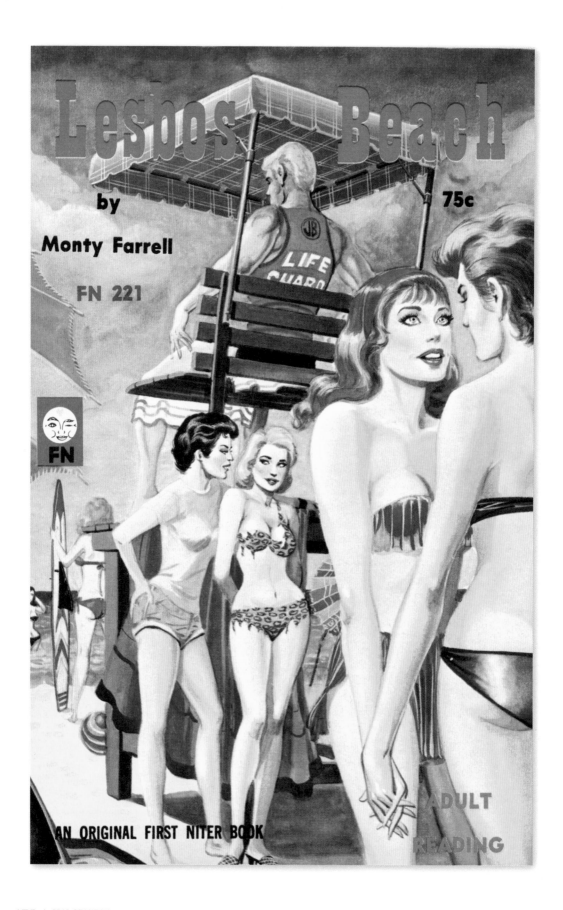

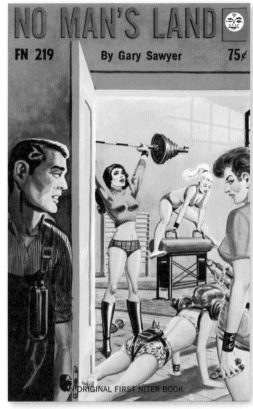

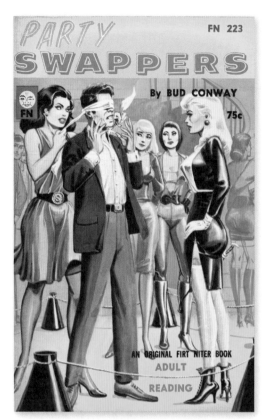

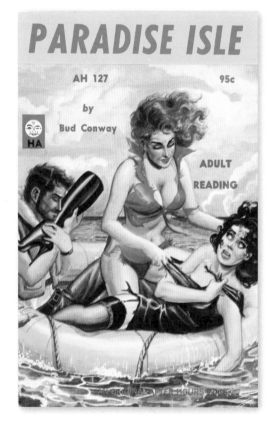

**FRUIT TOWN**

75¢
FN 112A  An Original Book by **Monty Farrell**

**ADULT READING**

AFTER HOURS
AH 106
75¢

**RENT PARTY**

**An Original Book**      by Jon Parker

**ADULT READING**

75¢

# DIAL "P" FOR PLEASURE

FN 110

BY MYRON KOSLOFF

AFTER HOURS
75¢
AH 108

# THREE'S A CROWD

An Original Book by Bud Conway

**ADULT READING**

(Stanton's goof on Ditko.
The banner [left] declares "Spiderwoman." We
might imagine the two artists shared a laugh.)

# 29
## The End of Selbee

LIMITED EDITION . . . NUMBER ONE

Evidently Leonard Burtman did not deliver on many of the early promises made to Stanton, and by 1964, their relationship was beginning to show signs of strain. When Stanton finally pointed out that he was being underpaid for his contributions to Selbee Associates and suggested even the most modest raise, Burtman flatly refused under the pretext that "he couldn't afford it."

As it turned out, Burtman's claim of his company's insolvency may not have been entirely exaggerated. By 1964, Selbee Associates Inc. was heading toward a financial crisis, largely due to non-payment from a secondary distributor, Chicago-based All-States News Co.

And there were also legal troubles stemming from a city-wide anti-smut campaign kicked into high gear by Catholic priest and moral entrepreneur Father Morton A. Hill, who after dramatically staging a hunger strike to protest indecent literature had managed to direct particular scorn on Selbee publications. On January 28, 1964, a sixty-six count indictment was filed in federal court against Selbee and other corporate titles owned by Burtman and partner, Benedict Himmel. As a result of all this counterproductive activity, in 1964, only three full-sized Selbee magazines were published, as opposed to seventeen the previous year. Of these, Stanton's name as art director appeared inside two of them, and they would be the last.

S-K Books, a sham imprint, was evidently fabricated to counteract the many problems the publisher was having with full-size slicks. It seemed Burtman went back to basics to reconstitute himself.

## Bizarre Life

Although initially lasting only two issues as a digest-sized periodical, and likely self-distributed, *Bizarre Life* represented a reaffirmation of Burtman's fetishist pedigree. The title alone may have been a combination of John Willie's *Bizarre* and its British predecessor, *London Life*. Beyond the uncredited John Willie, Charles Guyette, Irving Klaw, and Stanley Malkin photographs, there were Burtman's own contributions to the history of the bizarre and unusual—repackaged Burmel/Kaysey Sales/Selbee-era spreads—not to mention random examples of the new fetish-inspired "mod" stylings from London (already sported by Honor Blackman on TV's *The Avengers*). There was also art by Eneg

(recycled, as he was currently AWOL) and old and new work by Stanton.

As for other S-K Book publications? They featured some of Stanton's most widely collected gender-bending covers (next page).

As it turned out, it was during this period (1964/65) that Stanton provided his final 1960s artwork for Burtman. Even as Burtman navigated financial and legal troubles, found new ways to reinvent himself under a series of corporate veils, and relied on "package deals" offered by secondary distributors to produce his magazines, all Stanton art appearing in Burtman's publications from this point on—at least until the early 1970s—would be repackaged material. And Burtman would recycle often.

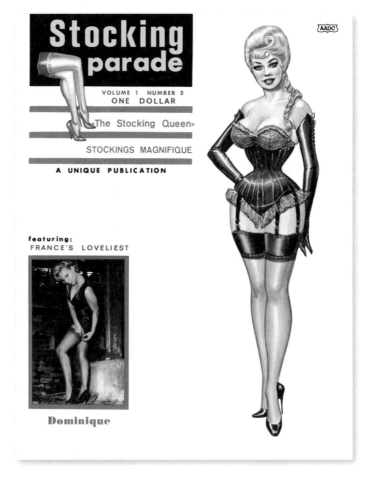

(*Stocking Parade* V. 1 no. 5, 1966, Unique Publications, featuring recycled Stanton art: one of two color paintings relating to Burtman's only feature-length sexploitation film produced in the early '60s, *Satan In High-Heels.*)

**LIMITED EDITION** · NUMBER TWO

Photos, Fiction, Articles, Drawings & Letters

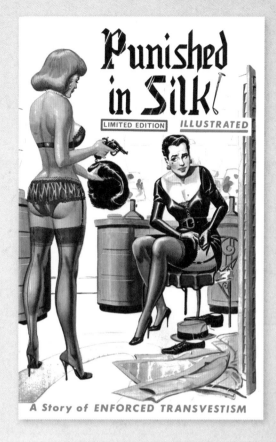

**LIMITED EDITION** · **ILLUSTRATED**

A Story of ENFORCED TRANSVESTISM

**LIMITED EDITION** · **ILLUSTRATED**

Featuring: America's Leading FEMALE MIMICS

LIMITED EDITION . . . NUMBER ONE

# The End of Nutrix and the Return of Gwendoline

There would be no hope of Stanton rekindling a working relationship with Irving Klaw, because by late March 1964, Nutrix Co. was forced out of business by federal authorities.

The nightmare for Klaw began on June 27, 1963. That afternoon, postal inspectors and a US marshal descended on 35 Montgomery Street in Jersey City (the business premises of Nutrix) and promptly arrested Klaw's brother-in-law and acting manager of Nutrix, Jack Kramer, soon after confiscating material in the warehouse.

Simultaneously, in Manhattan, no less than three postal inspectors and two deputy marshals appeared at 212 East 14th Street bearing a warrant for Irving Klaw's arrest. As stated in court documents:

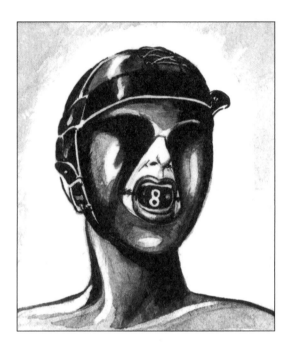

> Klaw was in an office there at a desk. The officers were admitted; [Deputy Marshal] Caffrey went up to the desk, showed Klaw the warrant and arrested him. The office was of substantial size. There were racks and shelves with some pictures and other items on them and also a quantity of similar items on the floor. The postal inspectors and at least one of the marshals looked at the material in the area generally between the door of entry and Klaw's desk, material visible from the place where Klaw was arrested. They took away a substantial quantity of this material . . . No consent of Klaw was asked or given.

On March 18, 1964, Irving Klaw was convicted, according to court documents, of "having knowingly used the mails to distribute . . . printed circulars, pamphlets, booklets, drawings, photographs and motion picture films, which were non-mailable in that they were obscene, lewd, lascivious, indecent, filthy and vile." He received a $5,000.00 fine and was sentenced to two years in prison. For his part as manager of Nutrix, his brother-in-law was fined $2,500.00.

Both would appeal.

Stanton's final work for Klaw—unintended though it may have been at the time—was the short psychosexual fantasy "Domination Conservatory," which had appeared as part of a Nutrix anthology in June 1962.

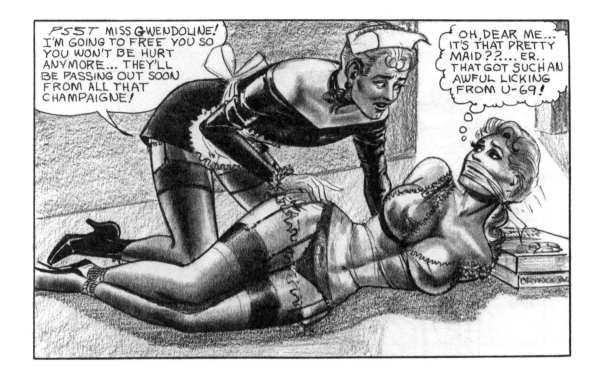

## Mishkin vs. the Authorities

Meanwhile, Edward Mishkin had been waging battles of his own.

Following Mishkin's well-publicized arrest and subsequent conviction in 1960, local and federal law enforcement agencies were unrelenting in applying heat, and raids on Times Square bookshops became so frequent that even newspapers grew weary of reporting it. (The *New York Times* went from listing store names to simply cataloging numbers: "Striking simultaneously at various locations yesterday morning . . . Nos. 105, 117, 130, 227, 228, 251, 254, and 259 . . .")

In 1962, while still appealing the 1960 decision, Mishkin was tried and convicted on a separate charge, this time, according to tabloids, for "conspiring to import from England pornographic books and pictures." In truth, the circumstances were much less dramatic, involving a waiter from the *Queen Mary* who, operating with federal authorities, had personally sought out Mishkin to deliver a subway locker key (". . . a present from

the boys in England"). The subway locker was under surveillance and the store clerk sent on Mishkin's behalf was promptly arrested. (The package from England contained a dozen copies of a single illustrated pamphlet, *Thrashed In Many Ways*.) For his involvement Mishkin was sentenced to six months in federal prison. As Assistant US Attorney Thomas F. Shea pitched it to the media: "Mishkin tried to set up a smuggling operation through an English seaman."

Two weeks after his sentencing, the State Supreme Court upheld his first case—his 1960 conviction—on all but thirty-two counts.

What could Mishkin do? What else, but again appeal his 1960 conviction, as well as his new 1962 conviction.

And keep on appealing: 1963, 1964, 1965 . . . !

Meantime, amid ballooning legal bills, Edward Mishkin continued to run his book shops, which for him also meant publishing.

## The Return of Gwendoline

Following the success of *Sweeter Gwen*, Mishkin pitched a sequel to Stanton. With several modifications. As a shop owner in Times Square, Mishkin had noted the brisk sales of cross-dressing material, with Burtman's transvestite publications being consistent bestsellers. So why not include a transvestite in the Gwendoline follow-up?

One might ask: what did this have to do with John Willie's original concept?

Nothing, of course.

But Stanton obliged, wedging in the character of the sensitive male maid, "Eustace" (p. 181).

First sales of the serial were through Mishkin's mail order business.

Initially (see p. 182 top) it was **broken into three-chapter** installments and printed on photo paper, as with *Sweeter Gwen*. Two more chapters were added later, despite the final page of the third chapter declaring "Fini."

Although not as well-conceived narratively as *Sweeter Gwen*, *The Return of Gwendoline* featured some of Stanton's best 1960s sex-ploitation art—and unquestionably the best graphite work he ever did for Mishkin.

## Boone Enterprise

Much as Burtman fabricated S-K Books as a below-the-radar publishing entity, Mishkin devised "Boone Enterprise" as a means of reinventing himself.

Under the imprint Mishkin took a stab at repackaging '50s Gargoyle Sales material with *French Maid* ("The Saga of a Woman Who Was Dominating"), commissioning Stanton to draw the cover (see p. 259). When sales of that item proved only moderate, Mishkin progressed to what seemed like a more marketable idea—mostly repackaging Peerless Sales material. By this time, likely, Max Stone's business was on its last legs. It may even be possible that Mishkin had acquired original Stanton and Eneg material directly from Stone.

In any event, Mishkin cut up the Peerless material as Klaw had cut up Golden Age serial chapters for his Nutrix booklets and produced a series of digests comprising the first bound collections of the Peerless Sales narratives: *Cartoon and Serial Classics*—all with new Stanton covers. Stanton created at least five such color covers, although Mishkin abandoned the series for unknown reasons after the third volume.

Next up was Mishkin's attempt to enter Stanley Malkin territory by testing his luck with sexploitation paperbacks. In this case, "the unexpurgated French Edition" of the Frank Harris memoir, *My Life and Loves* (actually a copyright-free reprint of the original one-volume 1931 edition), with cover design (front and back [p. 259]) by Stanton. *My Love Life*, as it was redubbed, marked the publisher's only known attempt to enter the mass market paperback field, and we can assume that sales were only middling, because soon enough Mishkin returned to more cutting-edge—and less wordy—material with the illustrated publications he would cook up with Stanton and Ditko.

Not to be outdone by Leonard Burtman, Mishkin lastly reproduced *The Return of Gwendoline* in book form, cutting up the panels in perfect imitation of Burtman's *Sweeter Gwen* and even commissioning Stanton to do a watercolor painting for the cover. Payment this time was modestly improved at $100.00 cash.

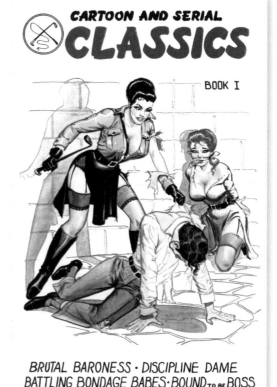

BRUTAL BARONESS · DISCIPLINE DAME
BATTLING BONDAGE BABES · BOUND TO BE BOSS

Plus: An exciting 2nd serial, Gwen's cousin Ann

# Stanton/Ditko and the Birth of Stantoons

While Stanton continued to produce his eccentric cover art for Stanley Malkin's various lines of pulp paperbacks, by the mid-'60s he had also engaged in a publishing venture that marked a milestone in his life. By now, Stanton's name had become so identified with certain themes in the bizarre underground (i.e., "dominating women," "fighting femmes," "bondage capers," "gender-bending tales") that he was able to launch his own brand of cartoon.

Incorporated in September 1965, by Malkin intermediary William Smith (as a proposed partnership between Malkin and Stanton), "Stantoons Inc." was not complete autonomy yet for Stanton, but certainly a step in the right direction, foreshadowing things to come.

Along for the test run of this enterprise—perhaps with an eye toward forging a similar endeavor of his own—was studio mate Steve Ditko, who had been plotting his escape from Marvel Comics. Evidently at odds with Marvel publisher Martin Goodman over royalties and his recent work on Spider-Man, and no longer on speaking terms with editor and compulsive self-promoter Stan Lee, Steve was fast reaching the breaking point and ready to jump ship.

The first advertisement for Stantoons Inc. appeared in back of the early 1966 sexploitation paperback *Mask Of Evil*—First Niter #226 (coincidentally written by cult filmmaker Edward D. Wood Jr. under the pen name "Charlene White"). By then Ditko had dropped notice at Marvel and thrown caution to the wind. Soon enough Ditko yielded some of his most inspired art for Warren, publisher of the magazines *Eerie* and *Creepy*, alternately producing drudge work and his most uncompromising comic heroes for Charlton. All the while, back at the studio—which had always been Ditko's one true home—he could rely on his brother-in-arms, "Ernie," for a bit of comic relief. Case in point: these irreverent Stantoons!

First up and setting the tone was the dominant wife howler, "My Husband, The Loser," followed by the epic fighting-girl scenario, "A Dull Day in the Neighborhood." There followed "My Friend, The Enemy" and "Broken Engagement—Part A." Some were straight comics, others illustrated stories. Ditko would ink, but under the umbrella of "Stanton" also contribute original art. Soon, the errant team of Stanton/Ditko rattled off more than a dozen installments, producing various classics along the way such as "On A Kinky Hook," which eventually vied for popularity with *Sweeter Gwen*, and "Correspondence Letter A" (a.k.a. "No Holds Barred"). As the following examples attest (pgs. 188–193), Ditko took his involvement with Stantoons Inc. quite seriously. In fact, it might be suggested that these earliest Stantoons marked the collaborative high point between these two artists.

"Stantoons Inc.," as it was originally conceived, continued for as long as Malkin's First Niter and After Hours books kept the Prudential Bldg., Buffalo, address (often embedded in the comics, like a running joke [see p. 186]), after which Malkin eventually passed his end of the business over to Mishkin, as Mishkin marked his second attempt to market/distribute repackaged Peerless Sales material with "Stantoons Inc. *Collectors Cartoon Classics*." These 5.5 × 7 in. booklets (p. 193) would finally be replaced by more conventional-sized works, which Mishkin evidently felt more comfortable in producing and were likely more marketable. Stanton and Ditko again teamed up on these, cheerfully venturing into exploitation territory ("exploitation" as it is often used to define movies), with Stanton lastly producing far more deviant work on his own, perhaps anticipating the direction his art would need to take beyond the 1960s.

("Correspondence Letter A" [a.k.a. "No Holds Barred"];
note the weight of the female form.)

("Broken Engagement": tight penciling from Stanton, brilliant inking from Ditko.
A fight that accentuates not only the physicality of the women,
but the fetish aspects of legs and stockings.)

-44-

(Ditko's original artwork is easy to spot: only the femme is Stanton's, with everything else Ditko.)

## ON A KINKY HOOK
by Stanton

LATER:
DOUBLE O-44? O-35 HERE! I'VE GOT TO SEE YOU AT ONCE!

OH, OH LOOK.

WE FOUND THAT SNOOPER AGAIN! THIS TIME, ULYA, DO YOUR SPECIALTY ON HER!

MY... PLEASURE, ..HOOK!

STANTOON # 5: This serial may become an all-time classic. It describes the exotic adventures of secret agent DOUBLE O-44. In this first chapter she investigates the KINKY CULTS. You will be bound in suspense. This is sure to be a collectors item.

ON A KINKY HOOK—CHAP. 1 ......$2.00

1

SHOW-TIME, OO-1'! SWEET SUZIE'S PERFORMANCE WILL GET YOU TO SING FOR US!

I'LL NEVER TALK! BUT I'LL GLADLY SING...WHAT WOULD YOU LIKE TO HEAR??

THERE'S NO BUSINESS LIKE SHOW BUSINESS..

SHUT UP AND TALK! HEY! WHAT'S THAT NOISE?

I'LL NEVER TELL YOU! ASK ANOTHER QUESTION!

♂ THERE

STATOON # 6: Double o-44's continue. Trapped, bound and tor Kinky Hook, things do look hope favorite agent. Fortunately, her and stamina carry her through vicious brawl with the Queen of

ON A KINKY HOOK—CHAP. 2
(Completed)

STANTOONS INC.

# COLLECTORS CARTOON CLASSICS

BOOK 3

8 CARTOON FEATURES By STATON & GLEN

TOUGH DAME • FEMALE RUMBLE • STING OF DEATH • BRAWL WITH A BLACKMAILER • JUNGLE QUEEN • PERFECT SECRETARY • CREOLE CAPERS • ADVENTURES OF SASSY •

# Stanton and Ditko Go Grindhouse

We might do well to remember that Stanton and Ditko's studio was in the vicinity of Times Square, and that there had always been a relationship—one might say a progressive interplay—between the area's aberrant film culture and the bookshops. Past the mid-1960s, it was only inevitable that the increasingly lurid, almost psychotic energy of the place would inform the art.

Such was the case with a series of titles both artists collaborated on for wayward bookstore operator Edward Mishkin. *Pressure Sale* (books One and Two), *The Case of The V-Pants*, *Maid Secured*, and *Horror Pillory* all hinge on wildly over-the-top "violence and revenge" themes at that time lining up audiences at local grindhouse theaters. The only twist, since Stanton was involved, was that these stories usually involved womanly revenge and some kind of macho man comeuppance—often a literal "stripping of the pants"—in which the usual power dynamics, obviously based on gender, were subverted.

For instance, in the Evelyn Handleman narrative *The Case of The V-Pants*, the story concludes with the male abuser's trousers literally held upside down—"up and outward by the cuffs"—to form a "V" as "a new symbol of victory for democracy." As with most Stanton related material, it is the bold, headstrong, independently minded women who are triumphant in the end . . . while the men (and their unliberated lackeys) limp off to lick their wounds.

## From Pro-Femme to Pro Femme-Domme

Also emerging from the 1960s grindhouse inspired heyday and produced for Mishkin (sans Ditko) was a popular series of Stanton digest-sized illustrated booklets tapping more psychological sub-currents.

Femme-Domme (or fem-dom) themed narratives involving explorations of male vulnerability, definitions of gender roles, and boundary play would begin to define and sometimes even limit Stanton's creative output.

Viewed objectively, these sexploitation scenarios offered an alternate reality: a dream-like dimension where female characters function symbolically, and are thus allowed to be physically dynamic in unlikely and fun ways.

In *Grip of Fear* (another grindhouse-style title), a playful tussle over a nude photograph devolves into a slippery slope horror story of domination, humiliation, and abject surrender. For the male character that is.

As the story begins, a blind date between the protagonist Jim and Paula—an attractive woman Jim's cousin had set him up with—is going well. The date has progressed to her apartment and she is showing him her portfolio of modeling work when a single nude shot surfaces and Jim, trying to be funny, snatches it and refuses to give it back. A wrestling match ensues, and before long this lady proves she is no push-over. Not only does she forcefully retrieve the photo, she handles him "like a baby," leaving him gasping in amazement. "*What gives*, he thought.*"

What gives is that he is trapped in a twilight zone fantasy of power reversal, revealing a host of deeply conditioned male fears (i.e., loss of control, loss of masculinity, of not being "on top").

Like most fem-dom fantasies, this is an erotized exploration of male terrors.

What is a boy's greatest dread? Being called a sissy. The greatest fear for a straight adult male? Ineffectualness. Impotence. Being seen as "less than a man."

As this nightmare unfolds, a rematch proves Paula's earlier victory was no fluke; she is the boss. And after she is through flaunting her physical superiority, making him say "Auntie," he tries to flee her apartment, but she grabs him and ties him up. As far as she is concerned her ownership is complete. Then she cheerfully phones her friend, Audrey (Jim's cousin), her voice sounding "bell-like, girlish," thanking her for the introduction. "Come on over, Audrey, dear. We can have some fun with Jim. And be sure to bring your camera."

Conspiring women? And what is this about a camera?

As it turns out, this entire paranoiac evening has been pre-arranged, and this, in part, is a story of revenge.

> "Now, Paula, I want you to take the next few of these shots. I want to see my 'beloved' cousin struggling to escape real pain."

Jim found himself in a cold sweat from the deadly quality in Audrey's voice. So he'd tattled on her some when they were kids and she'd gotten spanked for it. So he'd stolen a few things and she'd been blamed. So he'd lied to an early date of hers that she was pregnant and gotten her talked about. That was long ago when they were kids. She surely didn't intend to carry this revenge through to today now that they were both adults! How wrong he was!

Not only does Audrey taunt him, accuse him outright "of being puny, a sissy, a push-over for a pretty girl and then not man enough to handle her"—she bunches up some coat hangers and administers the first real corporal punishment of the night and has it all recorded for posterity on film. After which he is chained to a desk and forced to write a detailed confession of childhood wrongs.

By the end, satisfied with her cousin's reparation, Audrey leaves. And now Jim, "exhausted, emotionally shattered," begs Paula to be unchained. She agrees on one condition: that he confront his masculine fear of commitment. How so? By putting a guarantee in writing, making out "a bill of sale," signing over his life to her, his heart and soul.

In this light Paula is suddenly transformed (proving that this—like many fem-dom fantasies—is also a story of romantic surrender):

> She was dressed again, freshly made-up, perfumed, gowned, and bejeweled. Never had he seen anyone more beautiful in all his life.
>
> "And if I refuse?" Jim asked.
>
> "Then, when I release you, you may never see me, phone me, or hear from me again as long as you live."
>
> "Now may I make one more request concerning this document?"
>
> "Yes," Paula replied. Her fingers were walking across his bare shoulder. Her perfume assailed his senses. He felt the pressure of her thigh against his arm.

> "May I also write into this assignment of my person to you a stipulation that it is contingent on your giving serious consideration to—" Jim turned scarlet and tried again. "Oh, hell, Paula," he blurted. "May I say that I am doing this in consideration of your agreeing to at least think over marrying me?"
>
> Paula smiled prettily, "Why, yes, Jim. I think that would be very nice."

Typical of these scenarios, there is no profanity, no explicitness, no obvious sexual gratification, but an emotional release—a catharsis, referenced in his being "exhausted, emotionally shattered." *Grip of Fear* ends happily with Jim's "submission"—the renunciation of his male ego, his former self, to mark a new beginning. In the course of this intense psychosexual session the protagonist has overcome his terror of ownership, which no longer has a hold on him. In the process, he understands he is no less of a man for being conquered—especially by this seductive, intelligent, and (lest we forget) strong woman.

soon she targets the emblem of his masculinity—his trousers—stripping them not with the idea of sex, but emasculation: "Let's see how much fight you have without your pants." Sure enough, as if by magic, he is rendered powerless.

As the other roommate joins in, his mortification is magnified with a ritual that Stanton would represent here for the first time. "Since he likes my panties so much, I'll give him a first-hand view of the pair I have on." Queening, as it is known in fetish parlance, represents more than a bit of goofy sex play, but a ritual of ownership, implying both submission and a humiliating renunciation of status for the male (depending on the context). And as we have seen so far with Stanton related material, the trappings of femininity—particularly stockings, garters, and panties—work like kryptonite, making men weak. "She hitched up her skirt and with a rustle of silk and nylon began to sit down on his face."

But the passive peeper's humiliation is just beginning. Just as the ladies grant him mercy, allowing him to rise to collect his things, he unwisely snaps around and insults them both. This of course ignites further womanly rage—and beguiling sexual power. At last, as one of the women strips down to her lingerie to brawl, our fateful peeper swallows

## The Passive Peeper

In what might be Stanton's most polished and psychologically acute post-mid-'60s work for Mishkin, we have another eroticized male horror story, this time again involving a loss of control and the potential danger of being caught not "wearing the trousers."

Pity the passive peeper, who is too timid to ask pretty young gals on dates and resigns himself to sneaking longing glances through open windows and occasionally stealing their feminine underthings.

"Don't look now, June, but our peeping tom is at the back door again," one female character remarks to her roommate.

"Apparently he's going to keep on bothering us unless we do something."

Stanton fantasy femmes are anything but passive: "Suppose we could lure him into the house on some pretext . . . then work him over . . ."

Before long, as proposed, one of the roommates baits him into the house. Next thing the unsuspecting peeper knows he is being thrown to the couch, and

hard, knowing somehow he has already lost this fight. Before he realizes what is happening he is being dragged into the next room: "C'mon to bed with me . . . There are a few things I want to try with you"—but again the promise of consummation is just a mockery. Before long corrective bondage is applied using nylon stockings, which of course—as only a true fetishist might understand—have a magical property akin to Wonder Woman's lasso, thereby rendering him completely helpless.

After tormenting him a bit more—putting a bar of soap in his mouth (to cure him of his "vile tongue") and then gagging him with another feminine article: a rubber "falsie"—out comes the camera (a convention we have seen before), highlighting and recording his ignominious defeat.

Not content to let it end there—and proving that this is purely a male-scripted power exchange horror story—the ladies next don riding boots, leather gloves, and last but not least spurs with the intention of further taming him. (Typical of Stanton fantasy femmes, the ladies look incredibly graceful and beautiful—even as they indulge in the most unladylike behavior.)

With his former identity at last stripped away and now fully subdued (i.e., domesticated), the peeper has become their property—theirs to do with as they please, and to prove it they make him swear an oath, make him wear female underthings, and even apply a little lipstick to boot. With the threat of blackmail hanging over his head and his boundaries completely breached, he declares, "I'll do anything, but let's keep this just between us."

They finally allow him to leave, "a sore-muscled, pained, and rueful man," but not without some nylons dangling out of his pocket—"a flag of victory to the girls" and a reminder of their power over him.

### Hampered By Heather

Also concocted for Mishkin and closely related in publication date, theme, and artistic technique (i.e., the free use of wash) is *Hampered by Heather*—another bid to establish a running series like that of super-secretary Evelyn Handleman, but which never progressed beyond the first installment for unknown reasons.

The somewhat disjointed text accompanying Stanton's inspired art tells another tale of a secretary who really runs things—in this case not only a department store, but the most innovative and

profitable boutique within it called the "Leather Domain." Assisting Heather in running this shop while also providing original "bizarre" creations is her own personal corsetiere and kinky worshiper: a leather craftsman/artist named "Luther," who Stanton depicts in his own likeness.

The story begins in melodramatic style, with the Leather Domain in danger of being shut down and the artist replaced. At fault is the spoiled and chauvinistic boss's son, who intends to install his young mistress, a naïve leather sandal maker, in the department for highly selfish reasons: so that she might be more readily available to him for the occasional midday quickie.

Of course, Heather swiftly takes matters into her own hands, arranging an ambush that results in an elaborate form of bondage in which the son is brought face-to-face with his mistress and is made to confess—in Wonder Woman magic lasso style—his less than honorable intentions toward

her. Heather succeeds in not only proving the man's superficiality and total lack of integrity, but in awakening a vengeful dominant streak in his mistress. With Heather as her guide the mistress then takes control, putting the boss's son through the wringer, and the long last act of the narrative, which is full of hallucinatory incongruities, is one of feminine fury and retribution (not to mention stern corrective discipline).

By the end, the mistress assumes full command of the relationship—and this broken, former "ladies man"—as his wife. His ownership complete, he ends up working for her—zombie-like—at her privately owned business—making sandals.

## The Genius of Fem-Dom

As we have seen, fem-dom sexploitation fantasies reveal a great deal about male psychology, male vulnerability, and the preoccupation—or love/hate relationship—men have with status and power. The fascination—and horror—with male submission in these narratives may arise from the conflict of eroticized fear that some men feel being transposed over deeply rooted, shame-based masculine conditioning. For Stanton, whose unique gift was an unparalleled understanding and appreciation of such psychology, this was how such storylines were endlessly provocative.

# Jail Time for Mishkin

For Stanton employer Edward Mishkin, the 1960s would represent a blur of arrests and appeals. His "smuggling" conviction of 1962 was affirmed in '63, and while conducting appeals in 1964, he was arrested again. By December 1965, his major case—the 1960 conviction—rose to the US Supreme Court, and on March 21, 1966, the highly publicized decision was upheld, six to three.

With a final request for a retrial at last denied in May of that year—after yet another, almost comical bookstore arrest while on bail in April—Mishkin had no recourse but to begin serving his three-year prison sentence.

In 1967, while incarcerated, Mishkin hired a new legal team, arguing—not without merit—that his 1960 conviction had been based on illegally obtained evidence. Although this first attempt proved unsuccessful, the following year Mishkin was back again, and this time the argument was presented with greater effect—as phrased in court documents:

> Late in 1959 and early in 1960, New York City police conducted some four or five searches and seizures—one ostensibly with a warrant, the others allegedly incidental to lawful arrests—by which they gathered a substantial quantity of books and cartoons claimed to be obscene . . .

In light of more recent, overturned court cases, this legal strategy was successful, and on April 2, 1968, short of his full sentence, Mishkin was released.

## Mishkin's Pain Trilogy

If the authorities assumed that jailing Mishkin would put an end to his publishing endeavors and presence on Times Square, they were wrong. If anything, he emerged from prison even more determined to push a few boundaries. Straightaway, he commissioned a series of illustrated narratives featuring more extreme content to be sold via his shops and underworld network, and for this he called on Stanton.

Mishkin's Pain Trilogy introduced a series of transgressive, grindhouse-style "fantasy island" themed titles that ultimately included *Legacy of Pain*, *Isle of Agony*, *Citadel of Suffering*, and what seemed like an aborted attempt at another trilogy, *Grotto of The Tortured*. In all of these stories, the reader is transported to a realm where bizarre culture is a way of life.

In the first fantasy, *Legacy of Pain*, a pair of renegade kink-friendly lesbians forcibly take siblings hostage and whisk them away to a faraway isle where they are auctioned off as personal slaves. *Isle of Agony* follows the adventures of the brother and sister as they make their escape from captivity and rally other "slaves" to take up arms against the despotic lesbian rulers of the island (the same who had kidnapped them). *Isle of Agony* ends in an ironic twist, with the other so-called slaves admitting they were quite happy playing their roles—in other words, this was their consensual fantasy/vacation and they even paid for it!

*Citadel of Suffering*, the third part of the series, introduces vampires who purchase a share of the island from the ruling lesbian queens, who then quickly depart to cash the check. As the brother and sister duo are forced to endure a series of grueling kinky predicaments at the hands of the vampires, including some bloodletting, the lesbian rulers at last return to the island, claiming the vampire check has bounced and that now there will be hell to pay. Typical of all of Stanton's showdowns, the female characters are victorious while the male characters (even the vampiric ones) are trounced physically and mentally. By the end of *Citadel of Suffering*, the female sibling experiences an empowering coming-of-age while the male half is reduced—in what might be a kind of dark wish fulfillment—to yielding his identity and personal freedom.

Legacy Of PAIN

❧ FULLY ILLUSTRATED ❧

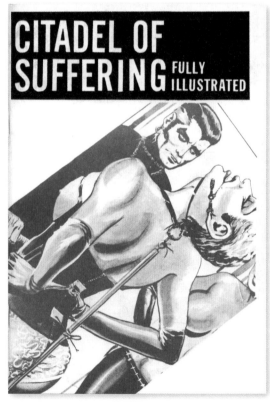

CITADEL OF SUFFERING FULLY ILLUSTRATED

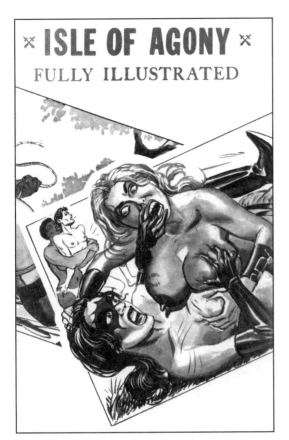

# ✕ ISLE OF AGONY ✕
## FULLY ILLUSTRATED

# 34

## Klaw's Tragic Fate

And what of Stanton employer Irving Klaw? While he successfully challenged his 1964 conviction and won on appeal in July 1965, he paid a terrible price: most of his catalog of photographic negatives and prints, including those originally obtained from John Willie and Charles Guyette—plus original artwork—would be obliterated in arbitrary fashion some time prior to the jury's verdict.

Irving Klaw allowed it as disillusionment and fear took hold of him. As Paula, Irving's sister, recalled in a 1976 interview:

> Irving's attorney thought it might make a good impression during his trial if Irving destroyed all the merchandise he was being prosecuted for selling. He had me take it all over to our office in New Jersey and do away with it. We used a paper shredder, and I just stood there and watched, tears running down my face. All that work; all those years. What a waste.

A full decade of unrelenting harassment, negative publicity, and social ostracism also took its toll on Klaw's family. His most fragile son succumbed to drug addiction. In 1965, his wife of twenty-four years, Natalie, would die of a sudden heart attack. Less than twelve months later, an undiagnosed—or willfully ignored—case of peritonitis would result in the death of Irving Klaw. "His whole life was in his business," Paula reflected. "It really wasn't fair to his wife because he spent very little time at home. He wasn't, I would say,

the best husband in the world, but he was the best brother in the world."

As execututrix of the estate of Irving Klaw, Paula continued Movie Star News, but not without difficulty. By 1968, she failed to settle Irving Klaw's debts and ran into legal trouble. Her own nephew, Jeffrey Klaw, sued her to recover the bank-absorbed sum of $18,094.36 from a trust Irving had set up in his name in August 1966, just fifteen days prior to his death. If nothing else, this might indicate several things. That the personal animosity between Irving's children and Irving's dearest family relation—Paula—had deepened over the years. (". . . his wife was a little jealous of me since we worked together all the time.") It also underscored that the vast sums of money Irving Klaw allegedly made during his many years in operation, variously quoted in the media as one million or 1.5 million annually, was largely the stuff of yellow journalism—i.e., fiction.

With rare exceptions, all that exists today of original Klaw era artwork are photo reproductions. In a 1978 interview, Stanton was resigned to the fate of his scarcest art: "I think whatever Klaw hadn't sold probably was part of the material he destroyed during the trial back in the 1960s."

# 35

# Malkin's Incidental Undoing

The beginning of the end for Stanley Malkin occurred on October 10, 1967. It was then that an officer for the NYPD, while on routine patrol, caught sight of what appeared to be incriminating evidence outside a warehouse at 44–43 Purvis Street, in Queens. As stated in court documents:

> he had observed a quantity of partially burned photographic film and certain remnants of theatrical props in a garbage container outside a building at the said address and concluded that the premises were being used for the purpose of manufacturing and distributing obscene movies and stills in violation of law.

The resulting raid yielded no hard evidence of illicit photography or filmmaking, but instead exposed cartons of paperback books bearing "lurid titles." Thus, another search warrant was sought by officers. Court documents described in dramatic detail what happened next:

> Armed with this second warrant, the next day the police again raided the warehouse, literally cleaning it out of at least 277,000 copies of books, and seized a truck parked outside the premises bearing perhaps another 4,000 or more additional books. While the exact numbers and titles may be subject to some difference between the parties, from a reading of the sworn inventory of Patrolman Schlipf dated November 8, 1967 it would appear that but 60,600 copies of the seized books were of five of the nine titles designated in the affidavits supporting the second warrant and that, in addition thereto, the seizure encompassed at least 236,500 copies of seven or more titles (defense counsel claims over 100 titles) of other books as well as miscellaneous office records, supplies and equipment nowhere named or referred to in the warrant or in the supporting affidavits.

## EMD
## (Eastern Magazine
## Distributors)

In fact, the raid had not been conducted on what was legally the property of Stanley Malkin, nor was Malkin mentioned anywhere in the subsequent legal documents or court proceedings. Instead, the action was taken against his book distributor, known then as "Eastern Magazine Distributors" (a.k.a. EMD), and a man named Albert Bosco—one of two individuals accountable for Stanley Malkin's entire paperback publishing enterprise (which, by 1967, included five imprints: First Nite [a.k.a. First Niter], After Hours, Unique Books, Wee Hours, and the more obscure Victorian Classics). The other individual behind Malkin's paperback trade? We might recall the name William Smith, a.k.a. William J. Smith (see chapters twenty-eight, thirty-one).

## Tracking
## Malkin's Ghostly
## Presence

We already know that Stanley Malkin started out as a Times Square bookstore operator/owner. In 1957, his name appeared on business registration for The Little Book Exchange, a bookshop at 228 W. 42nd Street. By the early 1960s, according to Times Square/publishing historian Jay Gertzman, Malkin's base of operation moved to Seventh Avenue, a store named The Liberty Gift Shop—in 1964, renamed Forsythe Books.

Although Gertzman cited Malkin as "Liberty's owner," by then Malkin's direct involvement with his business interests (i.e., bookshops and paperback publishing imprints) would be legally untraceable. As former Malkin employee—the late paperback author, Gil Fox—bluntly described Malkin (a.k.a. "Stanley Malcolm"): "He owned a bookstore on Times Square. It was Mafia connected. He paid cash, no records, no receipts."

## Buffalo, New York,
## and William J. Smith

So who was William Smith? Was he a mobster, or working on behalf of mobsters? There is no evidence either way. What we know of William Smith is that in late 1962, he was mentioned in connection with a police raid in Buffalo, New York. In the legal action (37 Misc.2d 947) he was described as "the manager and operator" of Main Street Book Shop, when on December 5, 1962, a team of police officers stormed in and confiscated "79 cartons of magazines, books, periodicals and other publications."

Impounded in that haul was an impressive amount of material published by Satellite Publishing Co. (in fact a full—if not complete—catalog of Malkin published material until then). William Smith, as we know, also incorporated various companies on behalf of Stanley Malkin—most importantly After Hours Books, Inc., and Stantoons, Inc., and the address of his store, "626 Main Street," would also appear under the heading "After Hours Books, Inc."—rubber stamped inside select Malkin paperbacks. But Smith's involvement did not end there, as evidence from a future legal case revealed: Smith also co-signed all of the printer's checks for Malkin's later book imprints, such as "Unique Books, Inc." and "Wee Hours, Inc.," even as Malkin's more obvious cover (the other co-signer) was his final distributor—the "president" of EMD (as well as Boro Magazine Distributors, Inc.)—Albert Bosco.

## The Lawsuit
## That Uncovered Malkin's
## Operation

It finally boiled down to Malkin not paying his bills. Or his source of revenue/funding being cut off.

But in late 1967, following the raid on the Queens warehouse, Malkin was sued by his printer, and in the course of that trial—"Articolor Graphic Co., Ltd., against After Hours Books, Inc., et al., and Stanley Malkin"—testimony shed light on how Malkin operated.

As the corporate secretary of Articolor Graphic Co. stated in his sworn affidavit:

> • We are sure that Stanley Malkin individually had a reason to attempt to hide behind all of these corporations for various other reasons, other than his business relationship with us. In our instance, the entire course of business was with him personally and he, in each instance, did designate various corporate entities to be indicated as the publishers of the books . . .
>
> • At his direction, the bills would be made out to Wee Hours Books or Unique Books but as can be clearly shown, that covered also a series of other corporate defendants which he claimed to own and control . . .
>
> • The initials on the billing indicates the book by number with the book initials indicating the publishing corporation designated by Stanley Malkin . . . The statement of December 13, 1966 made out to Unique Books, Inc. indicated on the lower part that four separate books were designated as A. H., again pursuant to Stanley Malkin's direction, this being After Hours Books, Inc., one of the named defendants . . .
>
> • The statement of January 10, 1967 though made out to Wee Hours Books, Inc. shows F. N. on the statement, this meaning that on those particular books, defendant First Nite Books, Inc. was shown as the publisher by direction of Stanley Malkin . . .
>
> • Stanley Malkin made all the payments on this account by personally paying cash or personally delivering checks with a total of sixty-nine payments being made to and including the October 30, 1967 payment. When the premises were raided by the police and District Attorney on October 30, 1967, these payments ceased through no fault of the plaintiff herein . . .

> • The fact is that the Defendant, Stanley Malkin, seeks to hide himself from various public authorities through these corporations vaguely described as being in Buffalo, when in fact they are in business in Queens County and as can be readily seen their banking connections and accounts are in Queens County or in Manhattan . . .
>
> • Albert Bosco was never considered by either us or Stanley Malkin as anything other than a front for Stanley Malkin, as was the Corporations. Stanley Malkin's relationship was personal and direct and the fact that he sought to hide from public authority by subterfuge was never a part of his dealings with us . . .
>
> • He indicated that all of these corporations were his and the fact of a "dummy" set of officers, stockholders and/or directors to shield him from prosecution is not binding upon us . . .

On behalf of Stanley Malkin:

> **Bosco:** Stanley Malkin is not now, nor has he ever been an officer, director, or stockholder of any of the defendant corporations . . .
>
> **Seymour L. Shuller (attorney):** Stanley Malkin states that there was never any discussion about his being personally liable for any of the work that was always billed to the corporation. There is no writing or documentation to support this contention . . .
>
> . . . there is no writing sufficient to indicate that a contract for sale has been made and signed by the corporate defendants or their authorized agents, and that the corporate defendants have not admitted in their pleadings, testimony or otherwise, that the alleged agreement for sale was made.
>
> **Stanley Malkin:** I am not and never have been an officer, director, or shareholder in any of the defendant corporations . . .

In short: without anything in writing, and without proof of Malkin's connection to any of the listed corporations (or any written agreement of sale), the printer had no case. Malkin was not legally liable or responsible, as he left no paper trail. The only evidence the printer could produce were invoices and signed checks—these co-signed by Albert Bosco and William Smith, individuals with whom the printer had no business relationship or agreement.

In the end, what did all this have to do with Stanton? Certainly it would bring an end to the most comfortable—and incidentally longest—salaried position of his life (1963–68). By mid-1968, despite attempts to hang on, Malkin was put out of business. This evidently coincided with a decline in the sexploitation paperback industry as a whole—possibly the aftershock of a major decision in the US Supreme Court ("Massachusetts vs. Memoirs of a Woman of Pleasure") that would pave the way for more sexually explicit material, and within several more years, bring on the birth of XXX hardcore. As for Stanton's final contributions to his favorite patron? They were a series of ink drawings described as "Daliesque." What followed after that were cheaper paper covers that had no illustrations at all.

In the case of the raided Queens warehouse (56 Misc.2d 1080), the books were eventually returned, "involving as it did"—in the words of the court—"a massive seizure of constitutionally protected matter clearly outside the scope of the warrant."

But by then the damage was done.

How many paintings did Stanton ultimately produce for Malkin: *300*, as he later estimated? The original paintings mostly went unaccounted for, and no catalog of them was ever made.

# 36

# The Unbearable Blues

By 1968, Stanton had undergone a few ordeals of his own, including possibly the greatest indignity of his life: the final loss of his sons, Rick and Guy, to their adopted father, Thomas Vincel.

In 1997, two years before his death, Stanton finally reunited with the children of his first marriage, but in 1967, according to Rick, his adoptive father, Thomas, would legally "take over" as full guardian. "My mother had met Thomas," related Rick, "after she'd divorced her second husband, who had gone to jail after being involved in a liquor store robbery." At this time Stanton was still relying on—and often abusing—prescription pain medication to deal with his back pain, which on some days left him almost completely incapacitated. And there was still open hostility between himself and his ex-wife, Grace—another source of anguish and pain for the boys. It was finally Thomas Vincel who suggested that it might be best if he "stepped down" legally. "Which killed Eric—y'know, when I was conversing with him later," said Rick, "he had tears in his eyes when he was telling me . . . but for our sanity, our sake, he agreed: Okay I'll sign my children away."

The legal—and clearly symbolic—procedure common in those days meant having the name of the biological father literally erased from the birth certificate of the child. As Guy explained: "When my father Tom Vincel adopted me, he said, 'Guy, I want you to know I met your birth father Ernie Stanten, and he's fine with me adopting you. You're

not going to see him, and legally he has no right to see you until you're 18 years old . . . but if you want me to be your dad, your name is gonna change from Stanten to Vincel.—I'm going to be listed as your father on your birth certificate. So 'Ernie Stanten' will be gone. Are you okay with that?' I said, 'Yeah, you're my dad.'"

According to Rick Vincel, "My mother spent the rest of my life telling me that Eric moved to Chicago."

To say this decision weighed heavily on Stanton is to make no small claim. In fact, he was plunged into such a wretched state that his sanity would be tested, as Amber recalled her father telling her: "It was during the Christmas season, and he was driving over a bridge and thinking of his sons, and suddenly he thought of turning the wheel, crashing straight through the guard rail. But then, over the radio, he heard—or thought he heard—what sounded like bells . . . like tolling church bells. He wasn't religious at all, but somehow that saved him. Made him stop."

## Stanton Regains Control

Stanton discovered an alternative to prescription drugs by accident:

> It was 7:30 in the morning and I was watching television with my remote, and I turned to Richard Hittleman's yoga program. They were reading a letter from an eighty-seven-year-old woman that couldn't raise her arm above her head until she followed his program. I started doing yoga every morning and after two months I could touch the floor.

"Yoga. Thank God for yoga," he said in a 1978 interview. "Once I started, I went from 189 down to 148, from a thirty-six-inch waistline to a twenty-eight . . . Every day, as much yoga as I could take. Great pain, but without it, I probably would have killed myself."

Stanton's renewal, as it turned out, would not only be physical, but spiritual. From that point on he practiced yoga faithfully, and even absorbed aspects of Eastern thought into his life.

It was a discipline and a way of thinking that he passed on to Amber, who also became an artist and a life-long practitioner of yoga. "I started by going alongside my dad when I was little," she recalled. "He used to do headstands all the time . . . I'm still able to do headstands today because I started doing them with him when I was little."

As family friend Jim Chambers recalled: "He used to say, 'I believe that I'm God. And you're God. And you're God. And everybody's God.'"

In this Stanton may have paraphrased Hittleman, who would teach that "self" is another word for God and that this divine selfhood was present in all people.

## "Ernie" Becomes "Eric"

This brings us to an event that has never been adequately explained. Of those that knew him best, including Britt; children, Tom and Amber; and dear friends Paul Quant, Jim Chambers, Ed Weiss, and even Steve Ditko, no one can shed light on this rite of passage. But as it happened, circa 1967/68, as dramatically as a butterfly sheds its past life in emerging from a cocoon, "Ernie" became "Eric." This name change, although never legally registered (just as with "Stanton"), was highly symbolic and personal in nature, and it was permanent. From that point on Stanton would be known to everyone—with the conspicuous exception of Ditko—as "Eric."

Coincidentally, in early 1968, "Eric" also stopped sharing studio space with Steve Ditko.

"He always hated the name 'Ernie,'" Britt recalled. "He told me, 'I'm Eric—Eric Stanton.' So I said, 'That's fine.' That's who he was."

# Enter Britt

Staying at the Webster House for Young Women in spring 1968 was twenty-year-old Britt Strømsted. Just the year before, she had become engaged to her Norwegian boyfriend, Knut. This was before he was called up to the military. As Britt explained it:

Everybody in Norway—all men—have to go to the military, even if there is no war. They have to go for eighteen months to the north of Norway, and while he was up north I had a girlfriend—an American girlfriend—named Penny, who told me, "Why not visit America while Knut is in the service?" So I really came here to visit Penny. I stayed at Webster House in Manhattan, where I met another girl, "Natasha." And she took me to visit Eric. She just happened to meet him a few weeks earlier and she said, "I'm going over to see an artist, to learn how to draw. Wanna come?" So I went over there with Natasha to his apartment. We sat at his bar, had a couple gin tonics, and he pulled out a camera, took pictures of us. It was a film, a movie film, but it got lost when we moved. And that was the first day I ever saw him. Eric filmed me and Natasha waving to him, just sitting on the bar stools...

A few days later he called me. He knew I lived at Webster and the phone was in the hall. I went and picked it up. It was Eric. "Do you remember me? I'm the guy with the beard, Eric Stanton?" He said, "Would you like to go out with me? Go out for dinner?" I said, "Okay." And he said, "When?" I said, "Well, anytime." Finally he said, "How about right now?" I said, "Okay." So I met him at his apartment. He was waiting many hours because I walked. I walked all the way to his apartment, and I thought that was normal, to walk 'cause in Norway we walk a lot.

So I walked from 34th Street and 11th Avenue to 87th Street. He thought I wouldn't come. He laughed, "You should've just taken a cab." I said, "I didn't think of that." And then he just took me out for dinner. We went to the Bavarian Inn, a German restaurant . . . And then we went to his apartment, I think. And we talked and talked. And he asked me things, like if I wanted to do modeling for him. He would pay me and everything. And I said, "Yeah."

And then he called me up and asked me to come over and he would take pictures of me in wrestling positions. He went and bought me underwear—or we went together. He said, "You gotta have black lace underwear and white lace underwear." And it didn't bother me in any way. I didn't think it was dirty.

And then he said, "Do you want to do wrestling scenes with Natasha?" I said, "Okay." So she came over another day and we did modeling holds, wrestling holds. He told us the holds. And we just did what he told us to do. He said, "pretend you're pulling her hair," and I had to pull her hair. We pretended we were pulling each other's hair out. [Laughing] And he took lots of pictures of it. I guess he sold them or something, I don't know. But he paid us . . .

So I kept meeting him off and on, taking pictures. Then I went to visit Penny in Boston. Then I went to Oklahoma to see a girlfriend, and Eric asked me to come up before I went back to Norway. I visited him for about a month and I stayed in his apartment. And we went to Jones Beach. We went out at night to bars and nightclubs. Just had a lot of fun. And then I went back to Norway. And then we wrote letters to each other. And I called Eric and asked him, "What are you doing?" He said, "I'm here, lying in bed, waiting for you to come back." Then I thought I had to go back to America one more time, I have to find out. I still loved

Knut, but I belonged with Eric. I just felt it in my soul. And I said, "I want to come back." So I came back. It was September or October. Eric was so happy, oh boy. He was at the airport, waiting . . . I lost Knut and my mother was so mad, saying "How can you do this?"

## Malkin's Parting Gift

By 1969, Stanley Malkin had remaindered what was left of his paperback trade. But before retiring to Florida, he turned over all his mailing lists to Stanton—some 20,000 names. These accumulated not only from Stantoons Inc. but Satellite Publishing Co., which was now under the control of Pasquale Giordano (a.k.a. Pat Martin/Martini). As a token of friendship Malkin also returned fifteen original paintings to Stanton, along with whatever else remained of his ruined business, which amounted to eight original pieces by Eneg, six by artist Bill Alexander, and one by Bill Ward.

Although Stanton remained on warm terms with his surviving publisher, Edward Mishkin, contributing stray art and occasional serials, it was through Malkin's mailing lists that Stanton would most radically reinvent himself—this time as an entrepreneur—embarking on a mail order business eventually named "The Stanton Archives" and finally gaining autonomy.

By 1969, Stanton had also acquired his most devoted supporter, a mysterious, wealthy customer/enthusiast from the Bronx who went by the name "Charlie Mitchell." (According to Bélier Press publisher J. B. Rund: "All of the material in the later 1990s Taschen books, except for the Klaw, Mishkin, Burtman, Malkin, and Peerless stuff, was done for C. M., who became a major patron.")

Leonard Burtman circa 1968

## Burtman Brought Down

Finally, just outside the orbit of Stanton's renewed life, it was former employer Leonard Burtman's turn to face disaster. On May 21, 1969, according to the *New York Times*, Burtman, business partner Benedict Himmel, Pasquale Giordano (of Satellite Publishing Co.), and alleged "high lieutenant of the Genovese Mafia family"—Charles Tourine— were indicted "on charges of conspiring to pay a bribe to a customs agent to pass pornographic literature into the United States."

While the courts were unable to reach a verdict regarding Tourine and Giordano, Burtman and Himmel were found guilty as charged and both received a fine of $5,000.00 and were sentenced to a year in prison . . . after which their partnership dissolved.

# 37
# My Britt

It was with Britt Strømsted that Stanton started a new life. They married twice. The first time—a symbolic union, in which they exchanged heartfelt devotions—occurred in Norway in June 1971. The second marriage, which was somewhat more conventional—"to make it legal, American legal," as Britt explained—transpired in December 1980, at Immanuel Lutheran Church in Manhattan.

As far as Eric was concerned they were married the moment Britt returned to him from Norway. From then on, as Britt recalled: "It was just me all the way. He called me 'My Britt.' And I was his and that was it—forever. He never looked at other women. I don't know why he loved me so much . . . I don't know what it was."

According to family friend, Ed Weiss, "I never saw Eric really get attached to anybody until he met Britt. That's when he really got attached."

Recalled family friend, Tim McDevitt, "He told me how thrilled he was when he met Britt. He told me what a wonderful romance and marriage that was . . . when he met her. She just lit him up, gave him energy."

## Dispelling Ghosts

Not only did Britt offer Eric renewed hope, she also gave him the opportunity to redeem himself as a father, putting to rest the specter of failure that would have haunted him the rest of his life. But it was not easy for him, as she recalled:

> When he met me, he didn't trust anybody. He never wanted to have children again . . . after he had his own and lost them. I didn't want to have kids right away, 'cause I was young. But when I got pregnant later he said, "What are we going to do about it?" I said, "Well, I'm gonna keep it," and he looked worried. Maybe he was worried about his age too, I don't know. But when Tommy was born he was crazy about Tommy. And Amber. And he loved his kids. Because it was different. It wasn't like with Grace.

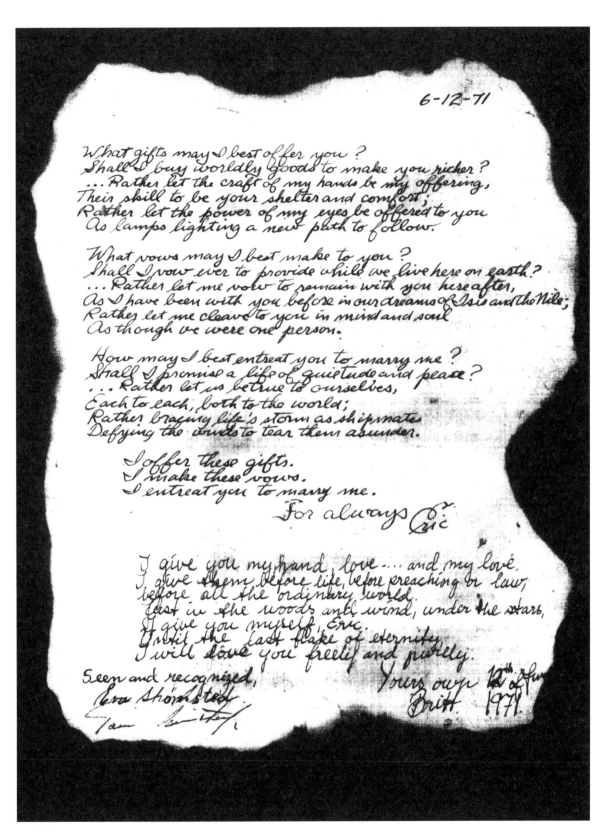

6-12-71

What gifts may I best offer you?
Shall I buy worldly goods to make you richer?
... Rather let the craft of my hands be my offering,
Their skill to be your shelter and comfort;
Rather let the power of my eyes be offered to you
As lamps lighting a new path to follow.

What vows may I best make to you?
Shall I vow ever to provide while we live here on earth?
... Rather let me vow to remain with you here after,
As I have been with you before in our dreams of Isis and the Nile;
Rather let me cleave to you in mind and soul
As though we were one person.

How may I best entreat you to marry me?
Shall I promise a life of quietude and peace?
... Rather let us be true to ourselves,
Each to each, both to the world;
Rather bracing life's storm as shipmates
Defying the winds to tear them asunder.

I offer these gifts.
I make these vows.
I entreat you to marry me.
                    For always Eric

I give you my hand, love ... and my love.
I give them before life, before preaching or law,
before all the ordinary world.
Last in the woods and wind, under the stars,
I give you myself, Eric.
Until the last flake of eternity
I will love you freely and purely.

Seen and recognized,                    Yours own 12th of June
Eva Shönstedt                           Britt 1971
Jan Lewitsky

(Wedding vows, first marriage to Britt)

# Enduring as an Artist

By the 1970s, with the end of the sexploitation/soft core era at hand, Stanton survived through reinvention. Using Malkin's mailing lists as a starting point, he groomed and maintained an active, international customer base. Private commissions from loyal fans in turn became the back catalog of his mail order business, as he retained originals and only sold printed and xeroxed copies of the illustrated narratives.

This would lead up to the idea of repackaging selected commissions in staple-bound booklets named (naturally) Stantoons, which he first produced in offset printed form in 1982. Following the example of Irving Klaw, he also published and promoted other artists, in addition to offering fan-inspired films and photo sets, through his "Stanton Archives."

In time he would purchase a house in Connecticut, raise two children while maintaining his privacy, run his mail order business successfully, and never stop drawing. As what was known as "bizarre" gave way to more mainstream fetish culture in the 1990s, Eric Stanton would become the most famous fetish artist in the world.

*Eric Stanton*
September 30, 1926 – March 17, 1999

# Acknowledgments

Special thanks to:
Amber Stanton/Stanten
Britt Strømsted Stanten
Tom Stanten
Rick Vincel
Guy Vincel
Eleanor Kochengin Giardelli
Cathy Giardelli Hysell
Paul Quant/Flanagan
Jim Chambers

The author would also like to thank:
J. B. Rund
Steve Ditko
Chuck Majewski
Robert Bienvenu/Robert V. Bienvenu II
Ed Weiss
Tim McDevitt
Jeffrey A. Kurland
Carole Jean
Chris Eckhoff
Kent Akselsen
Andrew Rolfes

# ERIC STANTON COLLECTOR'S GUIDE

## "The Underground Years"
### (1949–c. 1970)

### Irving Klaw: Serials/ Novellas/Nutrix Booklets

(Special research credit and thanks to J. B. Rund)
*Note*: chapter serials were sets of unbound photo prints. They could be purchased in complete sets or individual episodes/pages. The dates appearing below are the best approximation for when the material was issued based on a nearly complete set of recovered Klaw advertising bulletins and their respective postmarked envelopes.

**Fighting/Wrestling Girls Chapter Serials:**

*Battling Women* (May 1949–April 1950): 20 episodes/pages. "VJP" appears as artist of the first three episodes/pages. Stanton contributed episodes/pages 4–20. (Episode/page #4 is likely the sample page that Klaw paid Stanton $8.00 for; see chapter four.)

*Fighting Femmes* (Nov./Dec. 1949–June 1950): 12 episodes/pages. Stanton completed eleven of the twelve, the first contributed by an unknown artist.

*Juanita Lady Wrestler* (July 1950): 20 episodes/ pages.

*Dawn's Fighting Adventures* (Feb./March–June 1950): 18 episodes/pages.

*Dawn Battles The Amazons* (June/Sept. 1950): 15 episodes/pages.

*Diary Of A Lady Wrestler* (Sept./Oct. 1956 ["Lovelies Inc." advertising bulletin #3, #4]): 12 single panel episodes/pages.

**Miscellaneous Bondage Klaw-era Art:**

Untitled (June 1950: Cartoon and Model Parade, 31st Edition, p. 10): "4 new drawings by Stanton" marked "A, B, C, D" (available as 8 × 10 in. or 4 × 5 in. size prints).

*School of Bondage* (June/July 1953): 4 fetish bondage illustrations (8 × 10 in. size only).

**Fetish Bondage (Comic Format) Chapter Serials:**

*Jill, Undercover Girl* (July/Oct. 1950): 20 episodes/pages – Stanton's first "damsel in distress" serial.

*Poor Pamela* (April/May 1950): first 5 pages by "G." (Oct. 1950–Jan. 1951) – remaining 19 episodes/pages by Stanton for a total of twenty-four serial episodes/pages.

*Diana's Ordeal* (Feb./June 1951): 30 episodes/pages.

*Perils of Diana* (June/Sept. 1951): 30 episodes/pages.

*Sheba, The Slave Girl* (Oct. 1951–Feb. 1952): 24 episodes/pages.

*Phyllis In Peril* (Sept./Dec. 1952): 20 episodes/pages.

*Bizarre Museum* (Jan./June 1952): 20 episodes/pages.

*Priscilla, Queen of Escapes* (July/Aug. 1952): 30 episodes/pages.

*Duchess of the Bastille* (Feb./June 1953): 30 episodes/pages.

*Jasmin's Predicament* (July–Oct./Nov. 1953): 30 episodes/pages with Steve Ditko.

**Bondage (Illustrated Novella Format) Chapter Serials:**

*Bound in Leather* (Aug./Nov. 1953): 30 episodes/pages.

*Mrs. Tyrant's Finishing School* (Oct./Nov. 1953–Feb. 1954): 20 episodes/pages.

*Bound in Leather, Book II* (Dec. 1953–June 1954): 30 episodes/pages.

*Leather Boot Club* (Nov. 1954–Feb. 1955): 30 episodes/pages.

*Pleasure Bound* (Jan./Aug. 1954): 30 episodes/pages.

*A Hazardous Journey* (July/Oct. 1954): 30 episodes/pages.

*Pleasure Bound, Book II* (Nov. 1954–May 1955): 30 episodes/pages.

*Madame Discipline* (Feb./May 1955): 30 episodes/pages. Last completed serial before the Kefauver inquiry (see chapter twelve).

**"DIARY OF A LADY WRESTLER"**

Having had several requests for an illustrated fighting girl serial, we have commissioned popular artist Stanton to draw some new illustrations on the entertaining sport of lady wrestlers. This new serial is titled "Diary of a Lady Wrestler" and tells the story of how Betty, an amateur lady wrestler battles her way into the professional ranks by pinning down one of the best lady wrestlers in this rough sport. Only the first 12 episodes, each size 8 x 10 are available at present at price of 60 cents each episode or all 12 episodes for $6.00 plus postage.

*Scenes from "Diary of a Lady Wrestler" drawn by Stanton*

*Girls' Figure Training Academy*
(June 1955): 22 episodes/pages
(advertised in Klaw's "Ikay"
catalog, NJ).

*Marie's Unique Adventure* (April
1956–April 1957–Oct. 1958):
30 episodes/pages.

*Fifi Chastises Her Maids* (May
1956–April 1957–June 1958):
20 episodes/pages.

*Rita's School for Discipline* (Nov.
1958–Jan. 1959): 15 episodes/
pages.

*Helga's Search for Slaves* (March
1958–Jan. 1959): 30 episodes/
pages by "Jon Bee" with Steve
Ditko.

*Captured and Bound by Captain
Bonds* (May/June 1959): 10
episodes/pages.

*Bettina In Jeopardy* (April/Aug.
1960): 15 episodes/pages; the
last of the unbound chapter
serials. Another Stanton nod to
Bettie Page.

### Chapter Serials with Various Artists, including Stanton:

*Fighting Girl Fracas* (Sept. 1958–March 1959):
25 episodes/pages (various artists, including
"Jon Bee," twenty-one related to Stanton).

*Bondage Correspondence* (Nov. 1958–July
1959): 30 episodes/pages (various artists,
including "Jon Bee," twelve related to
Stanton).

*Set #41* (Nov./Dec. 1949: Cartoon and Pin-Up
Parade, 30th Edition, pp. 26–27):
miscellaneous artists, twenty-six in total,
including two by Stanton (first appearance
of the name "Stanton" in print).

### Nutrix Booklets (* indicates new work):

*Note*: after the post office mail block following
the Kefauver inquiry (see chapter thirteen),
Irving Klaw separated his more obvious fetish
art from his Hollywood/celebrity/cheesecake
pin-up business and established a presence
in New Jersey.

*Pleasure Parade*, Vol. 1 (May or Dec. 1958), Vol. 2 (Jan. 1959), Vol. 3 (Feb 1959), Vol. 4 (April 1959), and Vol. 5 (May 1959): various artists, including Stanton* (final *Pleasure Parade*, Vol. 6, does not include Stanton art).

*Bound In Rubber* (March 1959): various artists, including Stanton.*

*Women In Distress*, Vol. 1 and Vol. 2 (March and May 1959): various artists, including Stanton.*

*Terror at The Bizarre Art Museum* (July 1959): edited and cropped version of *Bizarre Museum* (1952) with new text and eight additional drawings.*

*Beautiful Fighting Girls*, Vol. 1 (March 1960): various artists, including Stanton.*

*Tame-Azons Subdue and Subjugate Man* (Sept. 1960): with 20 original illustrations by Stanton.*

*Men Tamed To Submission by Tame-Azons* (Nov. 1960): with 20 original illustrations by Stanton.*

*Girls Tied Up In Leather and Rubber* (Dec. 1960): with 18 original illustrations by Stanton.*

*Bondage Artist Dominated by Tame-Azon* (Feb. 1961): with 21 original illustrations by Stanton.*

*Women Of History Dominating Males* (Jan. 1961): various artists, including Stanton.*

First, in 1956, was Ikay Products, Inc., which was raided by the police (May 31, 1956), then Jani Sales Co. in 1957. Finally, Nutrix Co. in 1958 (see chapter nineteen), through which he released a series of unique, visually distinctive bound booklets. Publisher's address on these: 35 Montgomery Street, Jersey City 2, NJ.

*Vacation in Fetterland*, Vol. 1 (May 1958): with ten original illustrations by Stanton.*

REVISED
BULLETIN
#15

# NUTRIX CO.

35 Montgomery Street     Jersey City 2, N. J.

PRICE

25 CENTS

### NEW BONDAGE STORY BOOK!     NOW ONLY $3.75

## "TERROR AT THE BIZARRE ART MUSEUM"

*Illustrated With 22 Drawings By Stanton*

We have received many requests from bondage enthusiasts for longer books about bondage experiences. In compliance with your letters, we have just published a brand new complete bondage novel titled "TERROR AT THE BIZARRE ART MUSEUM" which is illustrated with 22 full-page drawings by Stanton. Price is only $3.75 plus 15 cents for postage and handling.

"TERROR AT THE BIZARRE ART MUSEUM" tells about the fantastic and harrowing experience that a male reporter and his female photographer assistant come in contact with when they are sent to interview Bonnie Dage, owner of the Dage Art Museum. The reporter is amazed at the life-like wax dummies in the wax works museum which are in bondage displays illustrating famous crimes of horror and terror. Some of the bound figures illustrate scenes from horror atrocities such as "Murders in the Rue Morgue," "Blood Thirsty Bats of Dracula," "Girl in the Medieval Iron Mask," "Women Cut in Half By Saw" and other blood chilling displays.

The wax figures representing the crimes are clothed in reproductions of their apparel worn and items used to perpetrate their heinous crimes. They were made life-like by adding color to the dummies' faces so that they looked almost human in appearance. The reporter-artist discovers some of the dummies were wet and sticky to his touch and upon investigating further he found that some of the supposedly wax dummies were really human girls covered with plastic material.

Before he can report his astounding discovery, he is captured and beaten by the female owner of the museum. He is later rescued from his hazardous plight and the crazed art museum proprietor placed in jail. SEND ONLY $3.75 plus 15 cents postage for your copy of "TERROR AT THE BIZARRE ART MUSEUM" now to Nutrix Co., 35 Montgomery Street, Jersey City 2, New Jersey. All enthusiasts for a leather costumed high heeled booted woman, bondage, high heel patent leather shoes, bizarre bondage apparatus, will find something to their liking in this 64-Page well-illustrated book, we are sure.

*Illustrations From "Terror At the Art Museum"*

*Pleasure Bound*, Vol. 1 and Vol. 2 (March 1961): edited and cropped version of *Pleasure Bound* (1954).

*Women In Distress*, Vol. 1 (March 1959), Vol. 2 (May 1959), and Vol. 3 (March 1961): various artists, including Stanton.*

*Bondage Enthusiasts Bound in Leather*, Vol. 1 and Vol. 2 (Oct. 1961), Vol. 3 (Nov. 1961), and Vol. 4 (Dec. 1961): edited and cropped version of *Bound in Leather* (1953) formatted to fill four volumes.

*Cruel Duchess of The Bastille*, Vol. 1 and Vol. 2 (Feb. 1962): edited and cropped version of *Duchess of the Bastille* (1953) formatted to fill two volumes.

*Perilous Bondage Escape Artistes*, Vol. 1 and Vol. 2 (March 1962): edited and cropped version of *Priscilla, Queen of Escapes* (1952) formatted to fill two volumes.

*Jasmin's Predicament*, Vol. 1 (March 1962) and Vol. 2 (April 1962): edited/cropped version of *Jasmin's Predicament* (1953) formatted to fill two volumes.

*Cruel Mrs. Tyrant's Bondage School*, Vol. 1 (June 1962): edited and cropped version of *Mrs. Tyrant's Finishing School* (1953/54). No second volume.

*Tales of Female Domination over Man*, Vol. 5 (June, 1962): various artists, including Stanton.* His final contribution for Klaw (see chapter thirty).

# Leonard Burtman: Burmel Era Art, 1950s*

(* See chapter fourteen)

*Exotique* Stanton ("Stanten") appearances: more than one hundred digest/magazine illustrations (if we include the serial *Deborah* and the five *Exotique* covers). All art between issues #10 and #27 (from late 1956 through early 1958), with the Stanton/Burtman falling out occurring circa issue #25, if not earlier (all else—including the thirty-six chapters/pages of the serial *Deborah*—produced prior). All published Burmel art past mid-1958 was recycled Stanton material.

**Stanton Burtman contributions, other than *Deborah* or *Exotique*:**

*Slave-Mistress* by H. Zucca (cover and the same image repeated inside): T.L. Publishing Co. NYC, 1957. First Stanton "book" cover for Burtman (other than *Exotique*). A 1966 re-issue of this book featured a Bilbrew cover with "Stan" color art on the back cover.

*Dominant Desires* by Harold Arllen (cover and interior illustrations, with the cover illustration repeated): T.L. Publishing Co. NYC, 1957.

*Vixen on the Loose* by Carlson Wade (cover and interior illustrations): T.L. Publishing Co. NYC, 1957.

*Confessions of a Transvestite* by Carlson Wade (cover and the same image repeated inside): B. & L. Publishing, NYC, 1957.

*Passion Party* by Helene Wilmont (interior illustrations): No publisher listed, Burtman attribution, 1957.

*Pushover*, no author listed on the cover (interior illustrations): No publisher listed, Burtman attribution, c. 1957.

*Virgins Come High* by H. Tennob (cover and interior illustrations): No publisher listed, Burtman attribution, 1957. This publication also played into Burtman's obscenity trial: New York v. Benedict Himmel and Leonard Burtman (1959).

*Woman of Evil*, no author listed on the cover (cover and excellent interior illustrations): No publisher listed, but similar in appearance to *Virgins Come High*, Burtman attribution, c. 1957.

*Come-On Girl*, no author listed on the cover (interior illustrations): No publisher listed, Burtman attribution, c. 1957. This publication also played into Burtman's obscenity trial: New York v. Benedict Himmel and Leonard Burtman (1959).

*Photo Album*, no.6 (back cover art re-used from *Dominant Desires*): Burmel Publishing Co. NYC, 1957.

*Submission*, no author listed on the cover (cover art): Raven Publishing Co. NYC, 1958.

*Conquering Goddess* by Carlson Wade (cover and interior illustrations): B. and B. Press, Brooklyn, NY, 1958.

*Satan's Mistress* by Gloria Campbell (cover and interior illustrations): P.B. Publishing Co. NYC, 1958.

GIRLS TIED UP
IN LEATHER AND RUBBER

ILLUSTRATED WITH 18 DRAWINGS BY STANTON

AND 6 ACTUAL BONDAGE PHOTOS

GASP--- I MUST HURRY---- NADINE WILL BE HERE ANY --UH-- MINUTE.!

OOOHH!

HOLD STILL!

*Bizarre Desires* by Edith Reynolds (cover): Burmel Publishing Co. NYC, 1958.

*Correspondence Digest*, no.1 (cover): Burmel Publishing Co. NYC, 1958.

*Myrna Learns The Ropes* by Joss Conrad (alternate cover): Burmel Publishing Co. NYC, 1958.

*Submission In Leather* by Betty Sanders (cover and the same image repeated inside): Burmel Publishing Co. NYC, 1958.

*The Initiation of Pauline* by Joss Conrad (cover and the same image repeated inside): Burmel Publishing Co. NYC, 1958.

Fashion catalogs: C-1 (interior illustrations), C-2 (cover and interior illustrations): Tana Louise, NYC, 1958.

C-4 (cover, interior illustrations) pamphlet, saddle-stitched: Burmel Publishing Co. NYC, 1958.

*Bloomer Boy* by Evelyn Adams (cover recycled art from *Exotique*): Hudson Press, NYC, 1958.

*The Wicked Three* (cover recycled art from *Deborah*): Burmel Publishing Co. NYC, 1958.

**Burtman Recycled Stanton Art:**

*Correspondence Quarterly*–magazine (interior illustrations): Kaysey Sales Co. Inc. NYC, 1959.

*Costume Catalog*–magazine (interior illustrations, one as "Stan"): Kaysey Sales Co. Inc. NYC, 1959.

*Correspondence Annual*–magazine (interior illustrations): Pigalle Imports, NYC, 1959.

*The Triumph of Elaine*, Part I by Beth Hilliard (cover): Pigalle Imports, NYC, 1959.

*The Triumph of Elaine*, Part II by Beth Hilliard (cover and interior illustrations): Pigalle Imports, NYC, 1959.

*Note*: because of the legal climate of the time, various Burtman publishing imprints, as with those of Edward Mishkin, were not legally registered businesses, but undocumented "hit and run" ventures. B. & L. Publishing, B. and B. Press, Hudson Press, P.B. Publishing, Raven Publishing Co., T.L. Publishing, and Tana Louise (the imprint) were all unregistered.

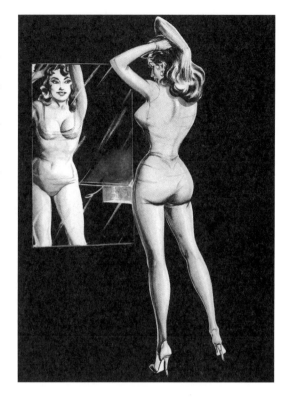

# Peerless Sales*
# Presented with Original Peerless Sales Catalog Numbers and Descriptions:

(* Stanton as "Stan," see chapter eighteen)

P-7, "She Loves To Wrestle": Val Savage is a beautiful but vicious female. A boy who taunted her got into a pickle he will never forget.

P-11, "Sally, June & Joan": Three girls share an apartment. The wrestling match they put on is told in letter and picture.

P-13, "Little Man, You've Had a Busy Day": Sally, June, and Jean are horsing around. The boys drop in and George talks himself into a fight.

P-14, "Well Beaten! Well Bound!": The Sassy French maid lets her grudge explode on her mistress, leaving her trussed and gagged.

P-21, "Taking Her Down a Peg": Helen thought herself a Mildred Burke. Karol figures she needs taking down, but is pinned down and dunked in the surf.

P-22, "The Instigator": George lures his two dates into the woods and gets them into a murderous fight.

P-23, "Mayhem Meeting": Robert, slugged in an alley, is saved by Fran, who really can fight. He is introduced to her club.

P-24, "Learning the Ropes": Bob goes to the club for a lesson and he gets it.

P-25, "Grudge Fight": Lisa and Fran get into a murderous fight.

P-26, "Free For All": Fran's engagement party ends in a free-for-all.

P-27, "Conquered & Enslaved": Bob marries Fran and is enslaved.

P-33, "The Instigator Gets His Lumps": George is surrounded by the three girls he lured into a fight. All three pile on him.

P-34, "The Dancer & The Wrestler": Lynn is peeved at her roommate's secrecy. She tries to beat it out of her and catches a tartar.

P-35, "Blonde Nemesis": Vera cares nothing for women wrestling and Paul loves it. They see Joan the Blonde champion beat 220-lb. Tiny Jane in a murderous match and the attraction of Joan is too much for him.

P-38, "Gossip & The Brawl": Redhead Marvella gossips to Vera and gets herself the fight of her life.

P-37, "Fight For Survival": Vera goes to Jack Lane's gym and gets into a do-or-die fight with Giantess Mary.

P-38, "Vicious Vera": The name fits her. In her first pro fight she crushes Tiny Jane.

P-39, "Winner Take All": Vera takes on Joan and wins the belt and Paul.

P-40, "The Cat Girl": Vera tangles with a high-heeled intruder. Alter a savage fight she discovers it is a boy.

P-59, "Private Eye": Lois Carver is the only woman in the business. A big blonde tries to steal her client and ends up crushed and bound.

P-60, "Female Rumble": Lois is attacked on her client's estate and almost dies twice: by gun and by drowning.

P-61, "Sting of Death": Lois fights a murderer and hurls him to his doom.

P-82, "Brawl With a Blackmailer": Lois beats the blackmailer to a pulp.

P-63, "Jungle Queen": Lois follows the boss to the jungle hideout, smashes his racket, and ties him up for the police.

P-67, "The Lady Cop & The Punk": Joe and his girl think the lady cops are a push over.

P-68, "Black Fury": Hannah, the colored maid, can't take her master's abuse and he ends up beaten and bound.

P-69, "Barroom Hassle": The buxom barmaid shows a souse of the female persuasion how she can be handled.

P-86, "A Reel Fight": A "scene" turns into a furious bare fist slug test.

P-115, "Rosaria": Carmen and Rosaria get into a fight that comes close to murder.

P-116, "Keeping Down The Jones": Tattletale starts a four-way mother and daughters fight that rages all over the floor.

P-136, "Beaten & Bound": Billy thinks he has it on Sis, but ends up at the dirty end.

P-137, "Brutal Baroness": She gives "Our Man" a murderous workout, but gets nowhere.

P-155, "Battling Bondage Babes": Roped and gagged, she manages to turn the tables on her attacker.

P-156, "Ordeal at the Office": The office snitch gets hers from tough Sheila, who does a double tie-up job with the office boy.

* Also attributed to Peerless Sales: P-supplemental, "Whipped Woman": 16 cartoon panels. Two women, both circus performers, engage in a fight for dominance. One woman wields a whip.

Dear Sir;

My husband has been receiving material on women wrestlers from you for several years now and this is the first time either of us have ventured to correspond. The letters that have been your latest item are indeed the best in the field. Perhaps your artist will find my letter interesting enough to use as an illustrated series. You certainly have my permission to do so and I will try to be as brief and to the point as I can.

I think it might be wise to tell you first that I am an attractive raven haired full breasted woman with the following measurements, height 5ft. 7in. weight 130., chest 38 somtimes 40, forearm 10 in., biceps 10 to 11in., thigh 19in., wrist 6in.

A year ago, before I married Bill, I was living in a fashionable estate in New Hampshire. One morning, our maid, who seemed to resent our positions, made some sort of remark under her breath and I asked her what it was. Knowing we were alone in the house she decided it was a good time to tell me what she thought of me. I slapped her face and told her to get out but she stood her grounds daring me to try that again. I raised my hand to slap her again but before I could she leaped at me and grabbed two fists full of my crowning glory and said not before she showed me a thing or two. I realized that I was in for the fight of my life because she was bigger than I and at least 10lbs. heavier.

"Pig," she hissed through clenched teeth. There was lightning in her eyes as she dug deeper and yanked harder at my hair till I screeched and fell forward, twisting, hurting, blinded by tears. I felt her teeth in my forearm and pain as her long red nails clawed at my negligee. Desperately I tried to reason with her, but she slashed at my shins with her sharp heels, her head thudded against mine, stunning me.

1

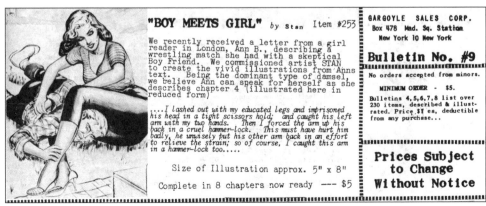

## Edward Mishkin-Associated Stanton Material, 1950s:

(See chapters thirteen, twenty, and twenty-one)

Gargoyle Sales Corp. (Stanton as "Stan") serials/art thus far recovered:

*Bound to Please*, Item #245, a Klaw-like fantasy (c. 1956): 48 episodes/pages, later published by Satellite Publishing Co. as *Bound Series B*, volumes 1 and 2, and B.S.F. Publishers (Leonard Burtman) as *Bound to Please*.

"Boy Meets Girl," Item #253, a mixed wrestling fantasy (c. 1956): 8 episodes/pages, later published as *The Dominator* by Belita–B.N.B. Publishing Company NYC, 1959.

"Twice Subdued," Item #291, a mixed wrestling fantasy (c. 1956): 8 episodes/pages.

*Ultra*, a magazine published by Ultra Sports Co. NYC (1957) which fell between *Exotique* and *Fantasia* (published by Lucian Press), but also focused on "wrestling gals": issues #1 and #2 (signing as "Savage").

*Virgin Co-Ed* by H. Zucca: cover by Bilbrew, illustrations by Stanton (*Ultra* images signing as "Savage"), Paris Press, NYC, 1958.

*The Sex Switch* (Cover plus 24 pages with Steve Ditko): Dunn Publishing Co. NYC, 1958. Connected to Mishkin in 1960 court trial.

*Smooth And Sassy* by Tom Hall (cover with Steve Ditko): No publisher listed, NYC, 1958. Connected to Mishkin in 1960 court trial.

*Her Highness* by Brutus Bloodley (cover with Steve Ditko): states "Privately Printed" on back, NYC, 1958. Connected to Mishkin in 1960 court trial.

*The Violated Wrestler* by Justin Kent (cover): No publisher listed, NYC, 1958. Connected to Mishkin in 1960 court trial.

*Woman Impelled* by Justin Kent (cover): No publisher listed, NYC, 1958. Connected to Mishkin in 1960 court trial.

*Stud Broad* by Justin Kent (cover): No publisher listed, NYC, 1958. Connected to Mishkin in 1960 court trial.

*Touch Me Not* by Justin Kent (cover, front and back): No publisher listed, NYC, 1958. Attributed to Mishkin.

*So Firm and So Fully Packed*, no author listed (cover, front and back): No publisher listed, NYC, 1958. Connected to Mishkin in 1960 court trial.

*Screaming Flesh* by Bob D. Nado (cover): No publisher listed, NYC, 1958. Connected to Mishkin in 1960 court trial.

*Masque* by Justin Kent (cover, interior illustrations): Rainbow Publishing Co., Brooklyn, NY, 1958. Connected to Mishkin in 1960 court trial.

*ToGetHer* by Justin Kent (cover, front and back): Rainbow Publishing, Brooklyn, NY, 1958.

*Impact* by Justin Kent: No publisher listed, NYC, 1958. Attributed to Mishkin.

*Chances Go Round* by Justin Kent (cover and 12 interior illustrations): J K Publishing Company NYC, 1959. Connected to Mishkin in 1960 court trial.

*Bondage Playmates* (10 excellent ink illustrations without text, almost identical in style to *Chances Go Round*): to date discovered unbound.

*Female Sultan* by Stan Reeves (cover and interior illustrations): B.N.B. Publishing Company NYC, 1959. Connected to Mishkin in 1960 court trial.

*Look At Her Motor Turn Over* (cover, interior illustrations): No publisher listed, NYC, 1959. Connected to Mishkin in 1960 court trial.

*Raw Dames* by Justin Kent (cover with Steve Ditko; interior illustrations): No publisher listed, NYC, 1959. Connected to Mishkin in 1960 court trial.

*The Dominator* by Belita (cover and interior illustrations recycled from Gargoyles Sales Co., Item #253, "Boy Meets Girl," a.k.a. "Picnic Pest"): B.N.B. Publishing Company NYC, 1959.

*Gloria* by Marlene D'isty (cover): Ranco Publications NYC, c. 1959.

# Stanley Malkin: Satellite Era Art

(All art produced in 1961/late '62, see chapters twenty-three, twenty-eight)

Mail drop/publishing address for Satellite Publishing Co.: "74 Montgomery Street, Jersey City 2, N.J." (an address also under surveillance by the FBI).

*Bound* #1 ("Stan" cover art shared/co-signed with Eneg): 8 illustrations *Bondage Hotel* Part I (comprising most of the magazine) and 4 pages of *Vixen's Vendetta* cartoon serial.

*Bound* #2 ("Stan" cover art shared/co-signed with Eneg): 6 Nutrix-like illustrations *Bondage Hotel* Part II (comprising most of the magazine), 4 pages of *Vixen's Vendetta* cartoon serial, and 4 pages of samples from Stanton photo sets B-1 to B-16.

*Bound* #3 (cover by Stanton): 6 illustrations *Bondage Hotel* Part III (comprising most of the magazine) and 4 pages of *Vixen's Vendetta* cartoon serial.

*Bound* #4 ("Stan" cover art shared/co-signed with Eneg): 4 pages of *Vixen's Vendetta* cartoon serial.

*Bound*, issues #5 and #6 (cover by Eneg): 4 pages of *Vixen's Vendetta* cartoon serial.

Bound #9 - late 1962 (cover): 6 excellent graphite illustrations by Stanton. No Eneg in this issue.

*Vixen's Vendetta* was completed after the Malkin/Stanton reconciliation and published in digest-sized book form in late 1962 or early 1963. Six installments of the serial appearing in *Bound* were evidently completed in 1961, at the start of the Malkin/Stanton association.

*Correspondence Issue*, no. 1, letters to the publisher (cover): 6 illustrations by Stanton.

"*Bound*" *Correspondence*, no. 2 (cover by Eneg): 3 illustrations by Stanton.

*Vacation at Paradise Lake*, no author listed (cover): 8 illustrations by Stanton.

*How to Tame a Roommate* (cover): 13 illustrations (inked by Steve Ditko).

*Hampered Hercules*, Book 2, no author listed (cover logo and cover): 7 illustrations by Stanton.

*Correspondence Story* No. 1 (an unbound, girl-fighting narrative): 11 illustrations by Stanton (sold separately for $1.00).

*Have Leather Will Fashion*, no author listed (cover): 16 classic illustrations by Stanton.

*Suzanne's Punishment School*, no author listed (cover): 4 graphite illustrations by Stanton.

Satellite fetish photo shoots: "A" and "B" set photos (approximately 300 prints).

*Bound* Series B, volumes 1 and 2: a bound reissue of *Bound to Please*, Item # 245, printed on glossy paper, therefore likely in the late '60s by Pasquale Giordano (a.k.a. Pat Martin/ Martini).

# Leonard Burtman: Full-Sized Magazine Stanton Appearances:

(See chapters twenty-four, twenty-seven, and twenty-nine. Special research credit and thanks goes to Jeffrey A. Kurland)

*Note*: Early magazines without publication dates can be dated by Burtman advertising material.

*Paris-Taboo*, issues #3, #4 (c. 1962): Stanton/Ditko cartoon serial, "Cherie"; issue #4 interior illustrations by Stanton. Selbee Associates, Inc. NYC.

*Diabolique*, issues #1, #2, and #3 (c. 1962): interior illustrations and issue #3 Stanton/Ditko cartoon serial, "Black Widow Sorority." Selbee Associates, Inc. NYC.

*Nocturne*, issues #2, #3 (1962): "E. Stanten" listed as Art Director; interior illustrations and Stanton/Ditko cartoon serial, "Midnight Maiden." Selbee Associates, Inc. NYC.

*Orbit*, issues #2, #3 (1962): "E. Stanton" listed as Art Director; interior illustrations and Stanton/Ditko cartoon serial, "Space Dolls." Selbee Associates, Inc. NYC.

*Pepper*, issues #2, #3, and #4 (c. 1962): interior illustrations (some recycled art) and Stanton/

Ditko cartoon serial, "Miss Patience"; issue #1: Stanton art recycled from *Deborah*. Selbee Associates, Inc. NYC.

*Exotica*, issue #2 (c. 1962): interior illustrations and Stanton/Ditko cartoon serial (2 pages), "The Savage Sisters"; *Exotica* issue #1: "Stan" Stanton art recycled from '50s? Selbee Associates, Inc. NYC.

*High Heels*, vol. 1, issues #1, #2, and #3 (c. 1962): interior illustrations, some recycled; issue #3 Stanton/Ditko cartoon serial, "Spies in Spikes." Selbee Associates, Inc. NYC.

*High Heels*, vol. 2, issues #1 (1962) through #6 (1963): interior illustrations; issues #1 through #4 continuing the Stanton/Ditko cartoon serial, "The Savage Sisters"; issues #4 and #5 with "E. Stanton" listed as Art Director. Selbee Associates, Inc. NYC. Recycled Stanton art appearing thereafter until 1970, in issues #9 through #13 and #15, #16. Consolidated Publishing, Inc. NYC.

*High Heels*, #1, Winter 1970–71, rebooted title (no volume number): interior illustrations, recycled. Eros Publishing Co., Inc. (Eros Goldstripe), Wilmington, DE (Editorial: NYC).

*Leg Show*, issues #1 (1962) through #7 (Spring 1965: the last Stanton contribution): cover logo, interior illustrations; issues #2 through #5, Stanton solo serial, "Case of the Lost Legs." Issue #1: featuring an untitled Stanton/Ditko filler strip involving walking a dog and a "cute meet." Selbee Associates, Inc. NYC.

*Striparama*, vol. 2 (1962) issues #1 through #6 (1963): interior illustrations; issues #1 through #4; Stanton solo serial, "Stormy The Stripper"; issues #2 through #6 listed as Art Director. Interior illustrations and/or marginalia recycled through issues extending past the mid-1960s. Selbee Associates, Inc. NYC.

*Satana*, issues #1 (c. 1962) through #7 (Spring 1965): cover logo, interior illustrations; issues #2 through #5: Stanton solo serial, "Satana." Issue #1: featuring an untitled Stanton/Ditko filler strip featuring a lady at a bar. Selbee Associates, Inc. NYC. Later issues (#10, #12, #13, and #14 published as package deals through Health Knowledge, Inc. NYC) featured rarely seen "Stan" illustrations from the '50s or recycled art.

*Focus On*, issues #1 (1963) through #4 (1964): "E. Stanton" listed as Art Director; 3 different cover logos, interior illustrations, marginalia. Issue #1, *Focus on Bettie Page* (see chapter twenty-seven), features lots of fun Stanton/Ditko Bettie Page line art and the filler strip "Cartoon on Bette Page." Selbee Associates, Inc. NYC.

*Female Mimics* issue #1 (1963): "E. Stanton" listed as Art Director; cover logo, interior illustrations, Stanton/Ditko transvestite line art; a page-by-page panel strip by Stanton/Ditko, and the Stanton/Ditko strip, "The Girls." Selbee Associates, Inc. NYC. Interior illustrations and/or marginalia recycled through issues extending into the 1970

# Burtman Recycled Stanton Art:

*Stocking Parade*, issues #1 through #3 and #5 (July–Aug. 1965 through April–May 1966): interior illustrations; issues #3 and #5 with Stanton cover art. Unique Publications, Ltd. Toronto, Canada (Editorial: NYC).

*III* (Three): issues #1 (Spring 1969), #2 (Winter 1969–70): full page reproductions. Consolidated Publishing, Inc. NYC.

Burtman continued to recycle Stanton art into the '70s and '80s, with his new partner, the now infamous Reuben Sturman. Such magazines, under the "Eros Goldstripe" banner, included the rebooted, now-full-size magazine *Exotique*, plus new titles *Whip 'n Rod* and *Madame Dominque*, and several "bizarre art" tributes (with Gene Bilbrew). Some Burtman-owned, full-color Stanton art also traded hands in California (where Burtman relocated after his time in prison), appearing as Centurian Publishing material issued in the 1980s.

*Bizarre Life*, issues #1 (April–May 1966) through #18 (1972): interior illustrations and/or marginalia; *Sweeter Gwen* serialized in issues #1 through #5; back cover of issue #2 featuring 1962 artwork depicting Meg Miles from Burtman's sexploitation feature film *Satan In High Heels*. (Issue #1, Unique Publications, Ltd. Toronto, Canada; issues #2 through #7, Bilife Publications, Inc. Wilmington, DE; issue #8, Bizcincorp, Inc. Wilmington, DE; issues #9 through #18, Consolidated Publishing, Inc. Wilmington, DE, and NYC (editorial).

*Corporal*, issues #44 (Winter 1968–69) through #54 (1972): minor interior illustrations and the occasional rare Gargoyle Sales Corp.-era art by way of Mishkin (see issues #45 and #47). Issue #44, Bizcincorp, Inc. Wilmington, DE; issues #45 through #54, Consolidated Publishing, Inc. Wilmington, DE, and NYC (editorial).

*Lesbos Review*, issues #2, #3, and #4 (1968): full page/color reproductions. B.B. Sales Company NYC.

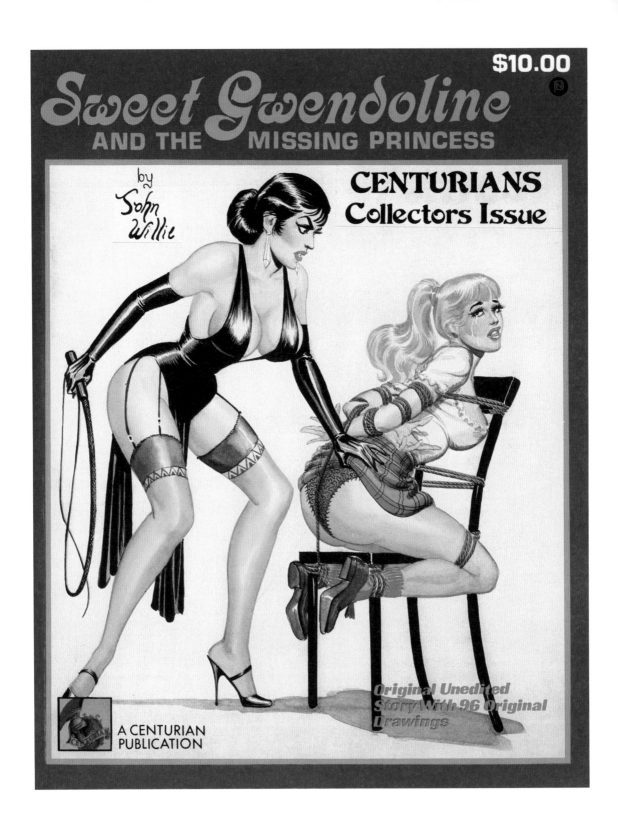

## Leonard Burtman: Digests/Magazines Stanton Appearances:

(See chapters twenty-five, twenty-seven, and twenty-nine)

*Masque*, issues #1 through #4: each featuring 1 "Stan" illustration. With the same interior illustration featured on the back of two issues (#2 and #4). Selbee Associates, Inc. NYC, c. 1960/61.

*Lesbianism* by Edward Podolsky, M.D. and Carlson Wade: interior illustration, recycled Burmel-era art (cover art from *Dominant Desires*). Epic Publishing Co., Inc. NYC, 1961.

*Fantasy in Fashions*, Issue Number One: cover and recycled interior illustrations, two "Stan" illustrations from *Masque*. Back cover Stanton art featuring a masked lady lion tamer. Selbee Associates, Inc. NYC, 1962.

*Exotique* . . . Quarterly, Issue Number One: "Ernest Stanton" listed as Art Director; risqué (i.e., topless) cover logo and cover and interior illustrations, some in a '50s style signed "Stan" plus the first installment of Stanton/Ditko cartoon serial *Sweeter Gwen*. Back cover Stanton art featuring a masked lady lion tamer (as with *Fantasy in Fashions*). Selbee Associates, Inc. NYC, 1962.

*Midnight Nurse*, F-5: Gallery of 13 "Stanten" illustrations from the Burmel period. Selbee Associates, Inc. NYC, c. 1962.

*40+* (Forty-Plus): cover logo/illustration repeated on title page. Selbee Associates, Inc. NYC, 1962.

*Black Stocking . . . Parade*, issues #1 through #3: cover logo and repeated dancing stripper illustration on back cover. Selbee Associates, Inc. NYC, 1963.

*Bombshells of Burlesque*, issues #1 through #3: marginalia plus a repeated dancing stripper illustration on the back cover. Issue #2 Stanton solo serial, "Stormy The Stripper"; Connoisseur Publications, Cleveland, OH, c. 1963.

*Buxom Beauties from . . . France*, v. 1, no. 2: dancing stripper illustration on the back cover. Connoisseur Publications, Cleveland, OH, c. 1963.

*Sweeter Gwen: Captive of Bondage Manor*: cover logo, cover, and complete cartoon serial *Sweeter Gwen* plus the back cover. B.S.F Publishers, Newark, N.J., 1963.

*Bound and Spanked*: cover and interior (graphite) illustrations of fighting gals, with the cover illustration repeated inside and the back cover. B.S.F Publishers, Newark, N.J., 1963.

*Punishment Party*: cover only. Gargoyle Sales Corp. material, including Bettie Page shots (*note*: Bettie Page modeled for Klaw, Burtman, and Gargoyle). B.S.F Publishers, Newark, N.J., 1963.

*Bound to Please*: cover logo, cover, and a (poorly reproduced) reprint of the full Gargoyle Sales Corp. "Stan" serial, *Bound to Please*, Item #245 and back cover. B.S.F Publishers, Newark, N.J., 1963.

*Escape into Bondage*, Book I: cover logo, cover, and interior graphite illustrations, with the cover illustration repeated inside. H-H Associates, 85 West 34th Street, Bayonne, N.J., c. 1963.

*Escape into Bondage*, Book II: cover logo, cover, and interior graphite illustrations, with the cover illustration repeated inside. H-H Associates, 85 West 34th Street, Bayonne, N.J., c. 1963.

*Female by Choice*, No. C-17: cover only. Full serial of *Satan in High Heels*, illustrated by Gene Bilbrew. Selbee Associates, Inc. NYC, 1963.

*Panty Raid*, No. C-18: cover and interior graphite illustrations and back cover. Selbee Associates, Inc. NYC, 1963.

*Deborah*, No. C-19: cover logo, cover, and a reprint of the complete Burmel-era serial plus interior graphite illustrations (in a "Stanton and Bilbrew" portfolio), and back cover. Selbee Associates, Inc. NYC, 1963.

*Forced Femininity*, No. C-20: cover only. Full serial of *Forced Femininity*, illustrated by Gene Bilbrew. Selbee Associates, Inc. NYC, 1963.

*Muscle Man in Silks*, No. C-21: cover logo, cover, and a single interior graphite illustration, repeated on back cover. Selbee Associates, Inc. NYC, 1963.

*Nurse in Rubber*, No. C-22: cover logo, cover, and a single interior graphite illustration, repeated on back cover. Selbee Associates, Inc. NYC, 1963.

*Gambling Vixens*, No. C-23: cover logo, spot illustration, and back cover. Selbee Associates, Inc. NYC, 1964.

*Mistresses of Desire*, No. C-24: cover logo, spot illustration, and the back cover. Selbee Associates, Inc. NYC, 1964.

"AND SHE *STILL* CAN'T FIND A STEADY FELLA!"

*Heat Wave*, No. B-1: cover and interior graphite illustrations, back cover. No publisher listed, Burtman attribution, c. 1963.

*Torrid Zone*, No. B-2: cover and interior graphite illustrations, back cover. No publisher listed, Burtman attribution, c. 1963.

*Bizarre Life*, No. 1: cover and interior illustrations, back cover. Stanton/Ditko cartoon serial, "'Merry MixUp' the Madcap Model," two pages. "S-K Press" listed inside, suggests a fabricated company. Outside: S-K Books. NYC, 1964.

*Bizarre Life*, No. 2: cover and interior illustrations. Stanton/Ditko cartoon serial retitled, "'Merry MixUp' the Model," two pages. "S-K Press" listed inside. Outside: S-K Books. NYC, c. 1964.

*Transvestism Around the World*, No. 1: cover and back cover. "S-K Press" listed inside. Outside: S-K Books. NYC, 1964.

*Guys in Gowns*: famous cover. S-K Books. NYC, 1964.

*Punished in Silk*: cover and assorted recycled illustrations from *Deborah*. S-K Books. NYC, 1964.

*Cherchez La Femme*: cover (color Stan illustration). Selbee Associates, Inc. NYC, 1964.

"I HOPE SHE THROWS THE RIGHT ONE!"

*Devil in Skirts*: interior illustrations and line art. Selbee Associates, Inc. NYC, 1964.

*Discipline Manor*, Books 1 through 6: all feature a famous back cover illustration of a dominatrix, a crop of an image that first appeared in *Focus On*, issue #2 (1963). "S-K Books" listed inside. Outside: Marquis Publishers. NYC, 1966.

*Exotica*, no. 1 through 4 (the third incarnation of the title, this time as a "contact" publication; i.e., personal ads, etc., much like *La Plume* [c. 1963] but with more substance): all feature interior recycled Stanton illustrations and line art, including on the back cover. Most notable for its cover logo of a Stanton dominatrix. Exotique Correspondence Club. NYC, circa 1965.

*The Girl From A.U.N.T.I.E*, Books 1 and 2: repeated cover logo from *Exotica* (above), but used in color for the first time. Epic Publishing Co., Inc., 1967.

*Bizarre Costume Catalog*: recycled (mostly Stan) interior illustrations. Tana & Mara Costumes NYC (later House of Milan, Chicago, IL), c. 1964 (undated, but features "Mod" stylings).

*Bizarre & Unusual Costumes*: "Stan" cover art. A slender continuation of the catalog above. Tana & Mara Costumes. NYC, c. 1964.

# FANTASY
## IN FASHIONS

ISSUE NUMBER ONE

featuring . . .

LIMITED EDITION

FULLY ILLUSTRATED

AN AMAZING CARTOON-STORY OF BONDAGE & PUNISHMENT

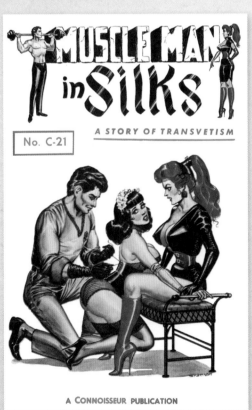

# MUSCLE MAN in SILKS
## A STORY OF TRANSVETISM

No. C-21

A CONNOISSEUR PUBLICATION

# FORCED Femininity

LIMITED EDITION

No. C-20

COMPLETE
CARTOON - STORY
• • •
MAN FORCED INTO
WOMAN

plus:
"BOOTED
BABES"
Photo-Section

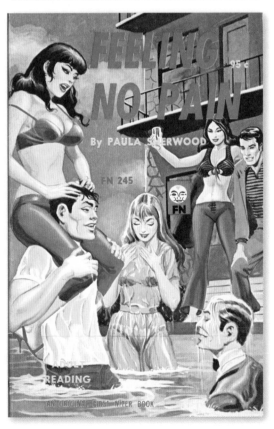

## Stanley Malkin: Published Stanton Sexploitation Paperback Art (1963–1968):

(See chapters twenty-eight and thirty-five; special research credit and thanks goes to Chris Eckhoff.)

**First Niter (forty-six Stanton covers):**

FN101, *Strange Hungers* by Richard Polk, 1963.

FN102, *Running Wild* by Myron Kosloff, 1963.

FN103, *Swapping In Suburbia* by Herb Muller, 1963.

FN104, *Tormented Virgin* by Jon Parker, 1963.

FN106, *Sin Strippers* by Robert Justin, 1964.

FN107, *Camp For Sinners* by Jon Parker 1964. WWNC dist.

FN108, *Lust Ranch* by Myron Kosloff, 1964.

FN109, *Bizarre* by Ivan Tarpoff, 1964.

FN109A, *Passion Doctor* by Grace Gordon, 1964.

FN110, *Dial P For Pleasure* by Myron Kosloff, 1964.

FN110A, *Wicked & Depraved* by Andrew Turner, 1965.

FN111A, *Call Me Later* by Jon Parker, 1964.

FN112, *Sex Takes A Holiday* by Howard Bond, 1964. Connoisseur: Cleveland, OH, address.

FN112A, *Fruit Town* by Monty Farrell, 1965.

FN113, *Twisted* by Richard Allen, 1965.

FN114, *Little Gay Girls* by Bud Conway, 1965.

FN115, *Even Swap* by Pat Conroy, 1965.

FN116, *Sea Madame* by Jon Parker, 1964.

FN217C, *Midnight Peeper* by Richard Allen, 1965.

FN219, *No Man's Land* by Gary Sawyer, 1965.

FN220, *Hole In One* by Peter Willow, 1965.

FN221, *Lesbos Beach* by Monty Farrell, 1965.

FN222, *Intruder* by Anthony Dean, 1965. Cover art with Steve Ditko.

FN223, *Party Swappers* by Bud Conway, 1965.

FN224, *Sex Carnival* by Jon Parker, 1965.

FN225, *Desire & Discipline* by Myron Kosloff, 1965. Cover art with Steve Ditko (Stanton portrait in red).

FN226, *Mask Of Evil* by Charlene White, 1966.

FN227, *Subjected* by Larry Dean, 1966.

FN228, *Hitch Hikers* by Peter Willow, 1966.

FN230, *Ranch Boss* by Bruce Corwin, 1966.

FN231A, *New Bride* by Glenn Allison, 1966.

FN233, *Blueprint For Sin* by Peter Willow, 1966.

FN236, *Free Admission* by Jon Parker, 1966.

FN237, *Over Anxious* by Ellen Dennis, 1966.

FN242, *House Call* by Peter Willow, 1966.

FN243, *Set Up* by Myron Kosloff, 1966.

FN244, *Nature Trail* by Sean Dennis, 1967.

FN245, *Feeling No Pain* by Paula Sherwood, 1967.

FN246, *Money To Burn* by John Carter, 1967.

FN247, *Swamp Spree* by Carol Hylan, 1967.

FN248, *Penthouse Maids* by Paula Preston, 1967.

FN252, *One Too Many* by Jack Fletcher, 1967. Final "Prudential Bldg." address listing.

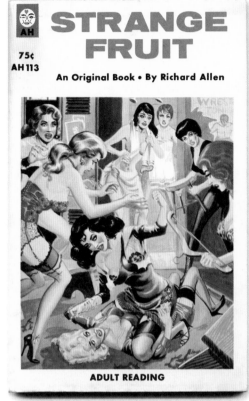

FN253, *The Long Night* by Jon Parker, 1967. "Market Arcade" address.

FN255, *Avalanche Of Lust* by Bob Nelson, 1967.

FN256, *Top And Bottom* by Anthony Dean, 1967.

FN258, *Guest List* by Myron Kosloff, 1967.

### After Hours (forty-three Stanton covers):

AH101, *Twist Me, Kiss Me* by Peter Willow, 1964.

AH102, *Suburban Nymph* by Myron Kosloff, 1964.

AH103, *Peeping John* by Richard Allen, 1964.

AH104, *Hot Lips* by Robert Justin, 1964.

AH105, *Queen Of Evil* by Myron Kosloff, 1964.

AH106, *Rent Party* by Jon Parker, 1964.

AH107, *Sinful Sexpot* by Laurence Foster, 1964.

AH108, *Three's A Crowd* by Bud Conway, 1964.

AH109, *Twice As Gay* by Nan Keene, 1964.

AH110, *Vixens Delight* by Ivan Tarpoff, 1965.

AH111, *Odd Man Out* by Tony Fletcher, 1964.

AH112, *Vice Charmer* by Bud Conway, 1965.

AH113, *Strange Fruit* by Richard Allen, 1965.

AH114, *Prowler* by Barry Grover, 1965.

AH115, *Pleasure Bound* by Ron Horton, 1965.

AH117, *3 Way Split* by Peter Willow, 1965.

AH118, *Miss Behave* by Barry Grover, 1965.

AH119, *Gay Reunion* by Bud Conway, 1965.

AH120, *Talent Scout* by Richard Donalds, 1965.

AH121, *Cycle Sinners* by Bud Conway, 1965.

AH123, *Switch Hitters* by Laurence Fulton, 1965.

AH125, *Ball And Chain* by Bud Conway, 1966.

AH126, *Partner's Choice* by Perry Holloway, 1965.

AH127, *Paradise Isle* by Bud Conway, 1965.

AH128, *Pay The Devil* by Peter Willow, 1966.

AH129, *Joy Ride* by Jon Parker, 1966.

AH130, *Matinee Girls* by Dorian Cole, 1966.

AH131, *Madame Butch* by Edward Marshall, 1966.

AH132, *Private Island* by Dorian Cole, 1966.

AH133, *Down Payment* by Edward Marshall, 1966.

AH134, *Lonely Hearts* by Bud Conway, 1966.

AH135, *S.S. Mardigras* by Yvette Delon, 1966.

AH139, *Mixed Up* by Carol Benning, 1966.

AH141, *Check Room* by Morton Gray, 1966.

AH143, *Bad Girl* by Gerald Werner, 1966.

AH144, *Stand In* by Paul Prentiss, 1966.

AH145, *Not So Funny* by Charlene White, 1966.

AH148, *Quick Change* by Edward Carlisle, 1966.

AH152, *Name Your Pleasure* by Anthony Dean, 1967.

AH155, *Weekend Swappers* by Helon Delon, 1967. Boro Magazine Dist.

AH157, *Lady Boss* by Shawna de Nelle, 1967.

AH162, *Strange Twist* by Jon Parker, 1967.

AH165, *Flashback* by Fred Darwin, 1967.

### Unique Books (twenty Stanton covers thus far recovered):

*Note*: Stanton produced many more cover paintings than appeared in print. Some recovered paintings are even marked on the back for specific titles that may or may not have seen print (e.g., UB166, *Strapped For Time*; UB167, *Discipline Island*). Later UB numbers exist with both Stanton cover art and plain paper covers. Various UB numbers even carried different titles (e.g., UB164: known as *Double Portions* with Stanton art and *Female Avengers* with a plain paper cover). Evidently publishing became chaotic for Malkin, particularly after the Queens warehouse raid (see chapter thirty-five).

UB (unnumbered), *The Gay Rebels*, cover and interior graphite illustrations with Stanton as "C.S.," 1966, digest-sized book.

# HEAT WAVE

FEATURES

No. B-1

THE LUCK OF A SALESMAN

AN ORIGINAL UNIQUE BOOK   **ADULT READING**

# Whippersnapper

By BUD CONWAY    UB 156    95c

## Stantoons Inc.
## (with Stanley Malkin):

(See chapter thirty-one . . .
Stanton/Ditko, 1965–1967)

*Note*: Stantoons Inc. is not to be confused with Stantoons, Stanton's notorious, later published, staple-bound booklets, issued starting in 1982. Stantoons Inc. comics were originally printed unbound on 8.5 × 5.5-in. card stock. Edward Mishkin would later take over Stantoons Inc. distribution in the late 1960s and early 1970s. (Later advertisements for Mishkin's mail order business, Candor Books, also featured "Stantoon Books," staple-bound illustrated narratives listed later in this guide starting with Book "B"–*Legacy Of Pain*.)

1. "My Husband, The Loser"–dominating wife, mixed wrestling: comic.
2. "Dull Day in the Neighborhood"–femme fighting: comic.
3. "My Friend, The Enemy"–femme fighting: comic.
4. "Broken Engagement" part a–femme fighting, female domination: illustrated story.

5. "On A Kinky Hook" Chapter 1–bondage, femme fighting, lesbian: comic.
6. "On A Kinky Hook" Chapter 2–bondage, femme fighting, lesbian: comic.
7. "Correspondence Letter A" (a.k.a. "No Holds Barred"): comic.
8. "Divorce Agreement"–femme fighting: comic.
9. "Kinky Chameleon"–bondage, femme fighting, lesbian: comic.
10. "Broken Engagement" part b–femme fighting, female domination: illustrated story.
11. "Broken Engagement" part c–femme fighting, female domination: illustrated story.
12. "Correspondence Letter B-1"–transvestism: illustrated story/letter.
13. "Correspondence Letter B-2"–transvestism: illustrated story/letter.

*Note*: "Correspondence Letter B-1" and "Correspondence Letter B-2" were later more famously known as *Confidential TV* when it was republished by Eros/Fantagraphics in 1994. "On A Kinky Hook," Chapters 1 and 2, and "Kinky Chameleon" were collected and republished as *The Kinky Hook* by Eros/Fantagraphics in 1991.

## Boone Enterprise
## (with Edward Mishkin):

(See chapter thirty)

The address inside these publications (often rubber stamped) is 220 W. 42nd Street (the address of Kingsley Books, controlled by Mishkin). A second address (often stamped inside of *The Return of Gwendoline*) was Rovin Publications, 5 Quincy Lane, Yonkers, NY. (Mishkin's long term residence was in Yonkers.)

*The Return of Gwendoline*: cover and complete cartoon serial (front cover repeated on back), NYC, c. 1965.
*French Maid*, "The Saga of a Woman Who Was Dominating": cover. NYC, c. 1965.
*Cartoon and Serial Classics*, Book I, II, and III: original color covers (front cover repeated on back) and recycled Peerless Sales material. NYC, c. 1965.
*My Life and Loves* by Frank Harris: original paperback cover (front and back). NYC, c. 1965.

## CARTOON AND SERIAL CLASSICS
### BOOK II

BEATEN AND BOUND · FISTIC FEMMES
WHEN PETTICOATS MEET · DAMES IN A DUEL

# FRENCH MAID

LAVISHLY ILLUSTRATED

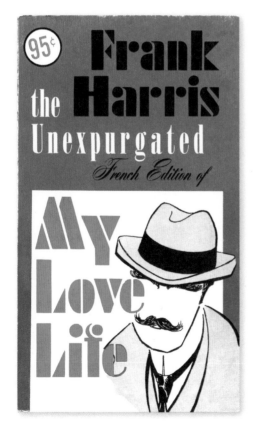

95¢

## Frank Harris
the Unexpurgated
*French Edition of*

My Love Life

### Foreword

At long last I am going back to the old English tradition. I am determined to tell the truth about my pilgrimage through this world, the whole truth and nothing but the truth, about myself and others, and I shall try to be at least as kindly to others as to myself.

**Frank Harris**

## Stantoons Inc. (with Edward Mishkin):

(See chapters thirty-one, thirty-two, and thirty-three)

Listed as they appear in Stantoon Inc. bulletins, which clearly does not reflect actual creation dates (c. 1966–c. 1969). Note that all the books are undated and are published in NYC, initially without a publisher's address (as Mishkin was trying to fly undercover); later they all carried the address of Mishkin's mail order business: Candor Books Inc. Box 822, Madison Square Station, New York, N.Y. 10010. The numbers below continue from earlier Malkin listings (e.g., 11, 12, 13 . . .).

14. "Don't Pick Up Strangers": unbound, illustrated story/letter in the style of Malkin Stantoons, 8 pages.
15. "Submissive Men": 8 loose illustrations on a theme, printed on 6.5 × 4.75 in. card stock.
16. "Submissive Women": 8 loose illustrations on a theme, printed on 6.5 × 4.75 in. card stock.

Below are the illustrated, staple-bound narrative books with Stanton covers:

Book "B"–*Legacy Of Pain*
Book "C"–*Isle of Agony*
Book "D"–*Grip of Fear*
Book "E"–*Hampered By Heather*, with Steve Ditko.
Book "F"–*Suffering Males*
Book "H"–*Pressure Sale* (both parts), with Steve Ditko.
Book "I"–*The Passive Peeper*
Book "J"–*Citadel of Suffering*
Book "K"–*Maid Secured*, with Steve Ditko.
Book "L"–*Horror Pillory*, with Steve Ditko.
Book "N"–*Grotto of the Tortured*.
Book "O"–*Handleman in "V" Pants* [a.k.a. *The Case of the V-pants*], with Steve Ditko
Book "P"–*Mister Sister* by Stanislaus Mell (Bee Dee Publications, 1968).
Book "Q"–*Boy's Boys* by Stanislaus Mell (Bee Dee Publications, 1968).
#1–*Cartoon Classics* (Peerless Sales rehashes: 5.5 × 7 in. booklets).

#2–*Cartoon Classics*

Book "T"–*Don's Degradation* (address of Stantoons Inc. G.P.O. 273, New York, N.Y. 10001).

#3–*Cartoon Classics*

#4–*Cartoon Classics*

#21–*A Man Disciplined* #1: illustrations on a theme, printed on 6.5 × 4.75 in. card stock.

#22–*A Man Disciplined* #2: illustrations on a theme, printed on 6.5 × 4.75 in. card stock.

Book "U"–*Caravan of Cruelty* (address of Stantoons Inc. G.P.O. 273, New York, N.Y. 10001).

Book "V"–*Brutal Sisters Battle* (address of Stantoons Inc. G.P.O. 273, New York, N.Y. 10001).

Book "W"–*Maid Tames Slave* [full title: *Masterful Maid Tames Bondage Slave*] (address of Stantoons Inc. G.P.O. 273, New York, N.Y. 10001).

#24–*Obey or be Bound* (1): a serial, printed on card stock.

#25–*Obey or be Bound* (2): a serial, printed on card stock.

There were a total of six *Cartoon Classics* 5.5 × 7 in. booklets (these recycling Peerless Sales material and including material by other artists Glen and Eneg); the address listed on these was Stantoons Inc. G.P.O. 2573, New York, N.Y. 10001. (PO numbers shared with the later Stantoons address: G.P.O. 273. The "5" would just be whited out in later reprints.)

Stanton's later work for Mishkin emphasized grindhouse style gratuitous violence and psychodrama. Mishkin-commissioned art (listed below) includes the Stanton Archive descriptions:

"Slaveship" Part 1: Fat Fang teaches his girl slaves obedience by rope and whip.

"Slaveship" Part 2: The Sultan buys the best of the lot and whips them into his harem.

"Subjugated Men": Some art poses drawn by Stan and W. Vardon for a sophisticated collector.

"Stella Cravit": Part 1 of the adventures of a female private eye and her girl assistant. Melody gets tied by a brute and his female mistress.

"Stella Cravit" Part 2: Stella fights her way through to save Melody from a fourth degree.

"Obey Or Be Bound" Parts 3, 4: C-28 (order code shared by Mishkin and Stanton Archives), 3.5 by 5 in. color prints. Juvenile thief is caught, beaten, and dominated by a beautiful woman and her cruel daughter.

# DON'S DEGRADATION

## A Tale Of Two Newlyweds

## Oddities for Edward Mishkin:

*Teen age Muscles*, vol. 1, no. 1: gay-themed cover: Steve Ditko as Stanton, NYC 1967.

*Young Muscles*, vol. 1, no. 1: (cover art recycled from interior illustration of Young Danny, 1966), NYC 1967.

*Burlesque Brawl* by B. Fields: cover and interior half-tone illustrations. A girl fighting scenario. No publisher listed. Cover art appears to be from an earlier period, but the interior drawings are c. 1963–65.

## More Stanton Oddities:

*Nightmare In Leather* by Jack Woods (EB-W19), an "Exotik Book" featuring recycled Stanton cover art lifted from *Torrid Zone*, No. B-2, Burtman, c. 1963. This is likely a piracy. (Illustration of the girl in the mirror is by another artist.) Foremost Publishers (the Sturman brothers), Detroit, MI, 1965.

"Kiss of the Unjust!"–a graphite (and ink) filler serial likely produced for Mishkin, judging by its stronger content. The style is consistent with artwork Stanton produced circa 1963–65. Only four pages of this serial have been recovered to date, salvaged in a Leonard Burtman publication, *Whip 'n Rod*, v. 2, n. 2, Winter 1972–73.

*Bellstone Cartoon* #5, "Brawlers"–rare, late '60s girl-on-girl wrestling comic produced for Bellstone/California Supreme, the California-based company that displaced Peerless Sales.

"Leather Lovers," an unpublished pen-and-ink/wash Burtman-era serial filler strip that was likely rejected by Burtman for being too over-the-top. Inking by Steve Ditko. Ten panels recovered to date, c. 1963.

## Final Stanton/Ditko Collaborations (Extending into the 1970s):

Titles include "Beaten by Big Sister," "Beached," "Lez Love Battle," and the X-rated "Savage Wife" (Part 2, pp. 9–16). Stanton pencils also appeared in the Ditko comic narrative, "An Ancient Wrong," *The Many Ghosts of Doctor Graves*, #20, 1970, Charlton. Finally, Ditko inked the cover illustration for the Stanton Archives published anthology

*Pleasure Parade* #1 (1978), in which Ditko even appeared as a comic character (hat, trench coat, and Spider-Man sweater) behind Stanton (p. 263).

"When I met Eric [1968], they were still friends," recalled Britt:

We'd go for dinner or he'd come over to the house for dinner. Around the time I started art school [1972], Steve would come over to teach me how to draw and to draw in perspective. Told me where the horizon is, how to come to one point, how to draw a figure in eight pieces. Y'know, like learning how to draw. He was very interested in having me set it up right, you understand, almost like an architect. So he wanted to teach me. And he seemed all right. But he was a loner, was against everything. He hated religion, marriage, kids, society . . . but he was always like that . . . He would say to Eric and me, when I was pregnant, "How can you bring kids into this horrible world?" After Tommy was born [1974] they would just see less of each other . . .

# Names Used by Stanton

Ernest Stanzoni Jr. (birth name: birth certificate: see chapter one)

Ernest A. Stanzoni (used in high school and the Navy: see chapters one, two)

Ernest Stanton (occasionally used before "Eric" was invented: see chapter four)

Stanton (with Irving Klaw and thereafter: see chapter four)

E. Stanton (with Irving Klaw, Leonard Burtman, and later his own Stanton Archives.)

Ernest Stanten (1951, legal name change: see chapter seven)

Stanten (real name, used during Burmel period with Burtman: see chapter fourteen)

Stan (with Max Stone/Peerless Sales and Mishkin and Malkin/Satellite: see chapters fourteen, eighteen, and twenty-three)

Savage (1957 [with artwork appearing 1957/58], with Mishkin associated publications: see chapter fourteen)

Stranton (Malkin/Satellite Publishing Co., where he also used the name "Stan," likely not to alienate Irving Klaw, see chapter twenty-three)

J. W. Stanton (for *Sweeter Gwen* in tribute to John Willie, 1962: see chapter twenty-five)

C. S. (on several gay-themed Malkin published book interior graphite sketches, c. 1966)

Staton (small Mishkin booklets, Peerless Sales re-prints, and Stantoons Inc. Collectors Cartoon Classics: see chapter thirty-one)

"Eric" Stanton (starting in 1967/68: see chapter thirty-six)

# Notes

*Author's note*: unless otherwise noted, all quotations are from personal interviews conducted between 2011 and 2015.

## INTRODUCTION

10–11. This was the dicey time largely preceding true porn (hardcore or XXX): the tipping point between softcore (or X-rated) material and hardcore (or XXX-rated) material would be *Mona: The Virgin Nymph*, the first commercial XXX content adult film, copyrighted 1970, but which largely played theaters in 1971. For more regarding *Mona: The Virgin Nymph*, see Bill Landis and Michelle Clifford, *Sleazoid Express: A Mind-Twisting Tour Through the Grindhouse Cinema of Times Square* (New York: Fireside, 2002), 42: "Just as the British Invasion finished the Brill Building's reign on the music charts, Ziehm's *Mona* spelled the end of old-style sexploitation." What transpired in adult movies followed in publishing. Printed matter (magazines, books) became graphic/explicit rather than suggestive or "simulated." The classic age of sexploitation ended c. 1971.

11. In this period, operations connected with producing this sort of "smut" were tracked by government agencies; postal inspectors who acted as censors, with strong ties to the local police, even the Catholic church (hugely influential then). Note: I am greatly indebted to Robert V. Bienvenu II for his ground-breaking dissertation, "The Development of Sadomasochism as a Cultural Style in the Twentieth-Century United States" (PhD diss., Indiana University, 1998), henceforth referred to in these notes as simply "Bienvenu." For more on the above, see Bienvenu, 120–142; 162, 163.

11. Leonard Burtman's Manhattan editorial offices: Ibid, 195–201.

## CHAPTER 1

12. Birth certificate of Ernest Stanzoni Jr. and family documents provided by Amber Stanton.

12. Anna's date of birth and the mention of "Nicholas Pelsewski" appeared on her death certificate, dated 25 Nov. 1970. The Social Security Death Index provided additional information about Grandmother Sophie Telesewski; birth: 14 Aug. 1885; died: "Oct 1970."

13. Nikodem Kochengin's first documented appearance, 1926: National Archives and Records Administration (NARA); Washington, DC; Crew Lists of Vessels Arriving at Boston, Massachusetts, 1917–1943; Microfilm Serial: T938; Microfilm Roll: 78. Nikodem's second documented appearance, which includes birth location, port of departure, etc: source Citation: Year: 1927; Microfilm Serial: T715; Microfilm Roll: T715_4129; Line: 2; Page Number: 128.

14. Nephritis and Scarlet Fever, Stanton contracted both: Navy Medical memorandum: 29 July 1944.

14. "I grabbed some comic books": Eric Kroll, *The Art of Eric Stanton: For The Man Who Knows His Place* (Köln: Taschen, 1997), 7.

14. "Let him draw": Ibid.

15. "That's how I kept on drawing": Ibid.

15. "I had control . . . I was king of my world": R. Q. Harmon, "A Conversation with Eric Stanton," *Bondage Life* v. 1 n. 3, August 1978, 24.

15. High school records provided by the Record Office of Franklin K. Lane High; special thanks to Ann Shelley.

15. "an awkward, gawky kid": Stanton, introduction, *Leg Show presents The Fantasy World of Eric Stanton*, 1985, 3.

18. Ernest Stanzoni enlistment information: US Department of Veterans Affairs BIRLS Death File, 1850–2010 [database on-line]. Provo, UT, USA: Ancestry.com Operations, Inc., 2011.

18. Corroborating information provided by Armond Stanzoni phone conversation, 15 April 2012.

## CHAPTER 2

19. "Cheesecake is a good morale factor": Arlene Wolf, "King-Pin of the Pin-ups," the *Daily Mail*, 26 Aug 1943: Hagerstown, Maryland.

20. Ernest Armond Stanzoni: height, weight, and medical details provided courtesy of US Naval documents obtained by the author, dating from 15 Aug. 1944 through 22 June 1946.

20. Twelve cavities filled in a single day: September 25, 1944, with two more fillings on September 28. Surviving US Naval base dental records even feature illustrations.

20. "It was a comic strip about plane recognition": Kroll, *The Art of Eric Stanton*, 7.

20. the ship's surviving "muster roll"—the ship's crew list: 1 Jul 1945, 1 Oct 1945, 1 Jan 1946, 1 Apr 1946, 29 May 1946: Muster Rolls of US Navy Ships, Stations, and Other Naval Activities, 01/01/1939-01/01/1949; A-1 Entry 135, 10230 rolls, ARC 594996. Records of the Bureau of Naval Personnel, Record Group Number 24. National Archives at College Park, College Park, MD.

20. "Immediately following her commissioning": *Dictionary of American Naval Fighting Ships*: online: USS *Turner* (DD-834), currently: http://www.history.navy.mil/research/histories/ship-histories/danfs/t/turner-iii.html

21. "Late in August, the ship returned": Ibid.

21. "A five-inch shell casing": R. Q. Harmon, "A Conversation with Eric Stanton," 57.

22. "I was making a dollar a handkerchief": Ibid., 24.

23. "Who really knows": Ibid., 57.

23. "She operated out of Japanese ports with Task Group 55.4": http://www.history.navy.mil/research/histories/ship-histories/danfs/t/turner-iii.html

## CHAPTER 3

25. Stanton took a stab at applying to college in September 1947: "Adelphi," as noted on his academic school records provided by the Record Office of Franklin K. Lane High.

25. "Women were jumping at me": Kroll, *The Art of Eric Stanton*, 7.

25. Gordon "Boody" Rogers info source: Chance Fiveash, "Boody Rogers: About the Artist," *The Comics Journal* #275, 2006, 128–130.

26. Stanton credit index on Boody Rogers comics: http://www.comics.org/issue/669190/#786610

26. Stanton's year with Boody Rogers: solid evidence of Stanton's hand appeared in *Babe* #3 Oct. 1948 (page 6, bottom left-hand panel—a handbill states: "Vote For Honest Ernest Stanzoni"). The love note to Grace appeared in *Babe, Darling of the Hills* #8, Oct. 1949. Therefore, we know that Stanton worked for Boody Rogers for at least one year, during which time, in 1949, he also contributed to Irving Klaw.

## CHAPTER 4

28. Robert Harrison: Bienvenu, 79–85; also, J. B. Rund, *The Adventures of Sweet Gwendoline* by John Willie (New York: Bélier Press, 1999), 92; see also Dian Hanson, *The History of Men's Magazines*, Vol. 2 (Köln: Taschen, 2004), 43–47.

28. It was likely in spring 1949: before *Cartoon and Pin-Up Parade*, 30th Edition (Nov./Dec. 1949), there were five unnumbered Klaw bulletins. The first of these (c. June 1949) offered four episodes of "Battling Women." Since Stanton's first contribution to Klaw was episode #4 of "Battling Women," we can suggest it was circa April or May 1949, that Stanton first communicated with Klaw.

28. "Whisper or one of those": R. Q. Harmon, "A Conversation with Eric Stanton," 26.

28. "It cost me something like .50 cents a page . . . because I was into fighting girls and the last guy wasn't.": Kroll, *The Art of Eric Stanton*, 7.

28. "What happened was": R. Q. Harmon, "A Conversation with Eric Stanton," 26.

28. "It took me a week": Kroll, *The Art of Eric Stanton*, 7.

28. "I went into bookstores and found some magazines like *Wit*, *It*, *Dash*": Ibid., 7, 8.

29. "Within a month or two, Irving": Ibid., 8.

29. "Pretty soon it didn't take me a week": Ibid., 7.

30. There is evidence to suggest that he toyed with a magician-like variation of "Stanzoni": to amend the early "Stantoni" signatures of several fighting girl episode/pages, Stanton apparently cut the "I" with the tip of a razor, converting it into three stacked dots—a fanciful semi-colon. Future pages, circa 1949/50, were simply signed "Stanton."

30. Who Was Irving Klaw? Plus Irving Klaw Timeline: Bienvenu, 102–119, 143–160. Also contributing J. B. Rund's repeated Klaw introductions appearing in Bélier Press publications: *Bizarre Comix*, *Bizarre Fotos*, *Amateur Bondage*, and *Bizarre Katalogs* (1975–1986).

31. 1910–9 Nov.: Klaw's birth and death dates are inscribed on his tombstone. Irving and his wife, Natalie, are buried in Mount Zion Cemetery, Maspeth (Queens), New York—as confirmed by the author, who paid a personal visit.

31. Born Isadore Klaw (Klau) in Brooklyn: New York State Census, 1915, shows "Isadore Klaw"; however, Irving's son, Arthur, related in a phone interview with publisher J. B. Rund how the family name was originally "Klau." Exactly when the conversion from "Klau" to "Klaw" took place is unknown.

31. Notice of Klaw's marriage license (with mention of Natalie Youdelman): Brooklyn, NY, *Daily Eagle*, 20 May 1938.

31. Irving and Paula had two different mothers, as indicated in the New York State Census, 1915, and United States Federal Census, 1920.

31. 1933–1937: employed as a furrier: Hearings Before The Subcommittee To Investigate Juvenile Delinquency of The Committee On the Judiciary United States Senate, 232.

31. Nutrix Novelty Co. (1935–1936), under the alias, "Irving Leder." The business went by various names: Nutrix Novelty Co., Nutrix Novelty, Nutrix Co. The Klaw alias "Irving Leder" appears in at least three notices in *The Billboard* magazine (7 March, 4 April, 16 May 1936). Magazine ads in 1936 suggest he was, at that point, a wholesaler/pitchman of novelty products looking for jobbers/salesmen. By 1936, mail order products included song books, gag/party tricks, etc. Earlier ads in *Popular Mechanics* (e.g., April 1935, vol. 63, No. 4) focused on magic tricks: "Baffling tricks, easy to perform." "Nutrix Co.," however, was not legally registered as a company until August 25, 1950 (#11946).

31. Enters the fetish art business, Little John: Bienvenu, 105: cites Paula Klaw interview (R. Q. Harmon, "Interview with Paula Klaw,") *The Irving Klaw Years*, 1948–1963, 10, 11, and Karen Essex and James L. Swanson, *Bettie Page: The Life of a Pin-Up Legend* (Santa Monica: General Publishing Group, Inc., 1996) 143, 144. Paula Klaw also elaborated (Gloria Leonard, "Paula Klaw: The First Lady of Bondage," *High Society*, Oct. 1980, 97): "His name was John . . . I'll just leave it at that . . ."

31. "He gave me a bunch of photographs . . . Of course we had John Willie's work to look at and I did": Kroll, *The Art of Eric Stanton*, 8.

31. "The first thing I drew": Ibid. Note: this illustration, labeled #15 of Set #41 (featuring various artists), appeared with the first mention of the name "Stanton" in *Cartoon and Pin-Up Parade* (Nov./Dec. 1949), 27.

32. *The End of Boody Roger*s: Chance Fiveash, "Boody Rogers: About the Artist," *The Comics Journal* #275, 2006, 128–130. Boody Rogers: Social Security Death Index: Born: 8 Sept. 1904, Died: 6 Feb. 1996.

## CHAPTER 5

33. Charles Guyette: Bienvenu, 72–79; see also, *Charles Guyette: Godfather of American Fetish Art* by Richard Pérez Seves ("an illustrated fanzine" with the most complete biographical information on Guyette), available worldwide on Amazon.com.

33. Charles Guyette ad, *London Life*, July 13, 1935 (author's collection).

33. "Offering to supply photographs of boxers": "Held As Exporter of Obscenity," *New York Times*, 20 Aug. 1935. US v. Charles Guyette (Aug. 1935), NARA-NE. Case docket C-97-253: Bienvenu (footnote), 77.

34. To ensure compliance with obscenity standards: Bienvenu, 77.

34. Irving Klaw showed restraint at first: seen in early Klaw ads, but also alluded to by Paula Klaw: R. Q. Harmon, "Interview with Paula Klaw," 11–12. (Q: The pictures . . . did you advertise them as "Bondage Photos?" A: "Damsels in Distress" . . .)

## CHAPTER 6

35. Regarded his high-minded artistic aspirations as a hobby: J. B. Rund, *The Adventures of Sweet Gwendoline* by John Willie (New York: Bélier Press, 1999), vii.

35. Other artists saw Irving Klaw's Hollywood movie stills, pin-ups, and "art studies" as a valuable resource: comic artist Batton Lash e-mail message to author, 1 July 2012: "It was common knowledge among the aspiring comic book people there that cheap movie stills could be bought at Irving Klaw's." Lash would also recall cartoonist great Al Williamson, stating that in the 1950s, he would also visit Irving's in the name of research.

**CHAPTER 7**

37. Stanton's starting/ending attendance dates at C&I, as clearly noted on his VA (Veterans Affairs) forms: 2 April 1951/ 20 May 1953. These exist because the GI Bill paid his tuition.

37. Cartoonists & Illustrators School Timeline: http://www.svaarchives.org/timeline.html.

37. "Stephen John Ditko" is noted on his WW II veteran compensation application. Source: Pennsylvania, Veteran Compensation Application Files, WWII, 1950-1966 [database on-line].

37. While he appears as "Eugene" on the 1930 Federal Census and Social Security Death Index, Bilbrew wrote his name as "Gene Webster Bilbrew" on his World War II Selective Service Registration Card. Source: The National Archives in St. Louis, Missouri; St. Louis, Missouri; Record Group: Records of the Selective Service System, 147; Box: 152.

38. "As a troubleshooting background artist": Jules Feiffer e-mail message to author, 29 July 2012.

38. "Listen, he was a better artist at the time . . . But I think I improved more than he did": R. Q. Harmon, "A Conversation with Eric Stanton," 26.

39. "Fabulous teacher . . . room for improvement": Ibid., 24.

39. "Until I came under the influence of Jerry Robinson": Robert Greene, Steve Ditko Interview, *Rapport* #2, 1966, 12.

39. "You have to learn good planning": R. Q. Harmon, "A Conversation with Eric Stanton," 24.

39. "Yes, Gene was one of the students": 24 Sept. 2012, Steve Ditko hand-written note to the author.

39. "Ogden Whitney": R. Q. Harmon, "A Conversation with Eric Stanton," 24.

39. "Artists which appeared in foreign publications many years ago": Irving Klaw Bulletin #38; *Cartoon and Pin-Up Parade* 30 Edition, Nov./Dec. 1949; *Movie Star News* #29, May/June, 1949.

39. John Coutts's admiration of the fetish artist Carlo is cited in Bienvenu, 76, footnote 47: "heavens what an ingenious bird he is."

40. "Wonder Woman probably had the most satisfying bondage scenes": R. Q. Harmon, "A Conversation with Eric Stanton," 24.

40. Ditko adored Will Eisner's *The Spirit*: Greg Theakston, "The Road to Spider-Man," *The Steve Ditko Reader* V. 1 (New York, Pure Imagination, 2008), unpaginated.

40. Sheena, jungle girl info source: Brent Frankenhoff, *Comics Buyer's Guide Presents: 100 Sexiest Women in Comics*, 41; also see Don Markstein's Toonopedia: http://www.toonopedia.com/sheena.htm

42. Amusingly, while in a cartooning class at C&I: J. B. Rund, *Introduction to Bizarre Comix* v.1 (New York: Bélier Press, 1975), unpaginated. Stanton's widow Britt also personally recounted this story.

42. The chunky wedding album: Rick Vincel shared this album with the author.

42. "Grace Marie Walter of Ozone Park and Ernest Stanten of Cypress Hills are Honeymooning": *The Leader-Observer*, 8 Nov. 1951.

42. Stanton's new Ozone Park address—"116-58 130th Street, South Ozone Park"—appeared on a 1951 tax form. (Stanton's income for 1951 noted as $455.00.) Form provided by Amber.

**CHAPTER 8**

43. "I never was in love with anybody else . . . from a distance.": Kroll, *The Art of Eric Stanton*, 9.

43. "I think I must have placed her too high on a pedestal": R. Q. Harmon, "A Conversation with Eric Stanton," 56.

43. "I just put her in bondage a few times. Only once did I ever do": David Gordon, "The Master's Pieces," *Chic*, Nov. 1997, 42.

43. "Klaw didn't like the artists fraternizing with the other artists": Kroll, *The Art of Eric Stanton*, 9.

43. "Nobody really knew her. Not even Irving . . . You'd sit and talk with her but it was business. All business.": Ibid., 9.

44. "Bettie Mae Page had arrived in New York City for the second time in September 1950": Richard Foster, *The Real Bettie Page* (Secaucus: Birch Lane Press, 1997), 38.

44. "She followed in the path of Cocoa Brown and June King": Ibid., 43.

44. "Harrison's publications, starting in 1951. She eventually made over seventy-five appearances,": Ibid., 52.

44. Camera club photographer that was introduced to Irving Klaw.: Ibid., 55; see also R. Q. Harmon, "Interview with Paula Klaw," 12; see also Paula interview by Gloria Leonard, "Paula Klaw: The First Lady of Bondage," 11.

44. The photo shoots that Eric Stanton recalled generally took place once a month: "Every three

weeks we would pose the models, you know. It was my fun weekend": David Gordon, "The Master's Pieces," 42.

44. "He had two or three different locations": Foster, *The Real Bettie Page*, 58.

44. Irving Klaw, "Charles Guyette was never the photographer: if Klaw was present at all, it was likely to ensure that the material was being produced in compliance with obscenity standards (i.e., no nudity, naughtiness, etc.)." According to Paula Klaw (R. Q. Harmon, "Interview with Paula Klaw," 12.): "Irving was careful to make sure that no pubic hair was showing, that the bra was covering the breasts—no bottomless, no topless. He would always check beforehand to make sure that everything was just right before letting the photographer take the picture . . . He had these standards and they had to be met or no pictures." In this he was simply being practical as a businessman, because if he couldn't re-sell the material, it was worthless to him.

44. The creative end was entrusted to fetish devotees: Bienvenu,106. See also Paula interview by Gloria Leonard, "Paula Klaw: The First Lady of Bondage," 11.

44. "His bondage and fighting girls": R. Q. Harmon, "A Conversation with Eric Stanton," 56.

44. "I did pose a lot of pictures for Irving": Ibid.

44. "Sometimes the models would try and date Stanton": Kroll, *The Art of Eric Stanton*, 9.

44. "I had her make an 8 mm film for me at Irving's": Ibid.

## CHAPTER 9

45. "Klaw asked me to cover . . . Gene didn't like that": Kroll, *The Art of Eric Stanton*, 8, 9; also J. B. Rund, introduction to *Bizarre Comix* v. 1 (New York: Bélier Press, 1975), unpaginated.

45. "I felt miserable": Kroll, *The Art of Eric Stanton*, 10.

48. "He had never once attended the circus": J. B. Rund, introduction to *Bizarre Comix* v. 3 (New York: Bélier Press, 1976), unpaginated.

48. Nutrix Novelty Company, through which he sold magic tricks: *Popular Mechanics* April 1935, vol. 63, No. 4: ad stated "Baffling tricks, easy to perform." *Popular Mechanics* April 1937, vol. 67, No. 4: "12 Amazing card tricks fully explained . . ."

48. Inspired by the 1935 film version: J. B. Rund, introduction to *Bizarre Comix* v. 9 (New York: Bélier Press, 1978), unpaginated.

49. "being the first clear collaboration": I'm using the word "clear" because by my own recent assessment, Ditko (uncredited) may have touched one page of *Duchess of The Bastille*: Episode/page 18.

50. "It was Eric who told me that 'Omar' was Steve Ditko": J. B. Rund, e-mail message to author, 6 Sept. 2012.

50. Al Williamson recalled visiting the shop in those days: comic artist Batton Lash, e-mail message to author, 1 July 2012.

50. "Paper Romance"—appeared in *Gillmor Magazine*'s Daring Love #1: Blake Bell, *Strange and Stranger: The World of Steve Ditko* (Seattle: Fantagraphics, 2008), 20.

50. "We have just re-issued popular artists [*sic*] Stanton's best-selling chapter": *Nutrix Revised Bulletins* #54 and 56, March/April 1962.

## CHAPTER 10

51. Eric was eager to try something new, so he proposed a variation to Klaw: J. B. Rund, "Bondage—The Art of Eric Stanton," *Swank* v. 22, no. 6, 1975, 64.; also J. B. Rund, introduction to *Bizarre Comix* v. 7 (New York: Bélier Press, 1977), unpaginated.

51. Joe Cross, writer on the Buck Rogers radio show: John Dunning, *On the Air: The Encyclopedia of Old-Time Radio* (Oxford: Oxford University Press, 1998), 122; also see https://archive.org/details/BuckRogersInThe25thCentury; also http://www.mwotrc.com/rr2004_04/buckrogers.htm. According to J. B. Rund, who befriended Cross in the early '80s, his "day job" was in advertising.

51. Evidence suggests that in the beginning, B&G made an earnest attempt to illustrate the story himself: At least three versions of *Bound In Leather* exist. One version, which Cross started and Stanton amended; second, the complete Stanton version, showing very little of Cross, published by Bélier Press in 1977, which is the best version; and a third version: a later hybrid (Stanton/Cross) with additional nudity (which Irving Klaw would not permit), published by Taschen in 1997.

51. "I attacked that story": R. Q. Harmon, "A Conversation with Eric Stanton," 26.

54. "You can't wear it on your finger": *Bound In Leather*, 30.

56. "I wasn't really as proud of any of my other work": R. Q. Harmon, "A Conversation with Eric Stanton," 26.

## CHAPTER 11

59. "Love cannot live": Edith Hamilton, *Mythology: Timeless Tales of Gods and Heroes* (New York: Little, Brown & Company, 1942), 129.

59. "Social Register Society": *Bound In Leather*, Book Two, 4.

59. "Subjects and gentlemen": Ibid., 6.

59. "The best of luck, my boy": Ibid., 9.

60. "Little did I realize . . . and you will be given further details": *Pleasure Bound*, Book One, 1.

62. "Dear Joan . . . Your new Mistress, Armande": Ibid., 3.

62. "to the stringent routine": Ibid., 9.

62. "so drastically severe": Ibid., 18.

62. "'gauntlet' of hands and paddles": Ibid., 26.

64. "a magazine devoted to correspondence and articles": Ibid., 1.

64. *Exotica*, v. 1. n. 1: Bienvenu, 176. Two versions of this magazine exist (owned by the author), with one slightly larger, featuring different cover image inserts, unpriced, possibly a piracy. ($5 appears on the original version.)

## CHAPTER 12

65. Evidence to suggest that early on she was sympathetic, encouraging: Rick Vincel shared a photo of his young mother and another woman engaged in girl fighting/wrestling/bondage play, likely posed for Eric's benefit.

66. Klaw was subpoenaed: the Klaw subpoena appeared on page 89 of the printed report: Hearings Before The Subcommittee To Investigate Juvenile Delinquency of The Committee On the Judiciary United States Senate (Printed for the use of the Committee on the Judiciary). The full report is currently available online: https://archive.org/details/juveniledelinque559unit.

66. Estes Kefauver info: http://www.senate.gov/artandhistory/history/common/generic/Featured_Bio_KefauverEstes.htm; http://www.senate.gov/artandhistory/history/common/investigations/Kefauver.htm.
Also: http://bioguide.congress.gov/scripts/biodisplay.pl?index=K000044

66. "I sat with her in Irving's office at the time . . . She was so tearful": Kroll, *The Art of Eric Stanton*, 9.

66. "It was the only time I ever saw Bettie upset": "Bettie Page: The Case of the Vanishing Pinup," *Rolling Stone*, Issue 565: Nov. 16, 1989: archived: http://www.rollingstone.com/culture/features/the-case-of-the-vanishing-pinup-19891116.

66. "I think it is time that this whole sordid business": Hearings Before The Subcommittee To Investigate Juvenile Delinquency of The Committee On the Judiciary United States Senate, 42.

67. "State and Federal income-tax returns": Ibid., 89.

67. "You will remain under continuing subpoena": Ibid., 90.

67. "trussed up in a very unnatural position": Ibid., 224.

67. "Chairman Kefauver: It gives a little example": Ibid., 228, 229.

68. "The photographers have a right": Ibid., 229.

68. "under penalty of contempt of the Senate": Ibid., 229–238

68. "I have a copy of the charges": Ibid., 288.

68. Bandied about as 1.5 million or 1 million annually: the subcommittee hearing quoted 1.5. Ernest A. Miller (who served as special counsel, US Senate Subcommittee to Investigate Juvenile Delinquency) quoted one million in his article, "Exposed! America's Billion Dollar Sex Racket," *Cavalier*, Dec. 1959, 25.

69. Pan American World Airways info: George E. Burns, "The Jet Age Arrives," 2000. Pan American Historical Foundation: http://www.panam.org/. Also see *Aviation News*, Nov., 2011, 50.

## CHAPTER 13

70. "Lovelies, Inc.": (Paula Kramer, Jack Kramer, and Fannie Cronin) #02243; 21 Feb. 1956; Dissolved: 11 May 1959: info J. B. Rund.

70. 16 July 1956: "Dealers Mail Blocked," *New York Times*, 17 July 1956.

70. "Ikay Products, Inc.": (Jack Kramer, Fannie Cronin, and Pauline Kramer) #294:411; 24 Feb. 1956. 799 Bergen Avenue, Room #201, Jersey City 6, New Jersey. (Listed in the Nov. 1956 Edition of the Jersey City Telephone Directory. Not listed in the Nov. 1957 Edition): info J. B. Rund.

70. "Movie Star News, Inc.": (Paula Kramer, Jack Kramer, and Fannie Cronin) #02139; 16 Feb. 1956.

Note: as with Nutrix Co., Klaw tested the name in early 1950s ads.

71. 350 shorts: source, J. B. Rund's repeated Klaw introductions reprinted in Bélier Press publications: *Bizarre Comix, Bizarre Fotos*, et al. (1975–1986); also see Bienvenu, 146, 147. These film shorts, like the photo shoots, were often customer commissions.

71. Mentioned more prominently in the hearing report would be his cheesecake, high heel, lingerie pin-ups, and three burlesque shorts: Bienvenu, 155, 156.

71. "Beautiful Productions, Inc.": (Irving Klaw, Natalie Klaw, and Pauline Kramer) #08702; 31 March 1954. Dissolved: 20 Dec. 1961: info J. B. Rund.

71. Times Square information: Anthony Bianco, *Ghosts of 42nd Street* (New York: William Morrow, 2004), 134–136.

72. "He had a store, actually four different stores": Kroll, *The Art of Eric Stanton*, 10.

72. Mishkin Times Square store info researched/compiled by Jay A. Gertzman and J. B. Rund.

72. Investigated by the IRS (as his lawyer stated) and "all those records" were with them: Hearings Before The Subcommittee To Investigate Juvenile Delinquency of The Committee On the Judiciary United States Senate, 90.

73. "I'd go into all the stores": Kroll, *The Art of Eric Stanton*, 10.

73. Gargoyle Sales Corp., a mail order business in which Mishkin was a partner with Aaron Moses Shapiro, a.k.a. Moe Shapiro, and possibly Leonard Burtman (incorporated 26 Oct. 1954; dissolved 28 June 1957).

73. Starting, by some accounts, as far back as 1953: *Run Girl Run Hard*, published by Mishkin, evidently featured as cover art Eneg's earliest non-Klaw fetish contribution dated 1953.

73. The trade name "The Pin-Up King" owned by Irving Klaw: a notice that appeared inside Irving Klaw monthly bulletins #73–#79, c. 1953.

73. "Ikay Products, Inc." police raid: 31 May 1956, "Dirty—Dirty," *The Journal News*, 31 May 1956. ("The raid on a shop netted the sister of Irving Klaw, alleged kingpin of the lewd picture racket, police reported.")

73. Mail block against "Irving Klaw" remained: Klaw v. Schaffer, Postmaster, New York City. 357 U.S. 346 (1958).

## CHAPTER 14

74. "Savage" appears as Stanton's signature in various issues of the magazine *Ultra*, 1957.

74. According to FBI reports, out of state: e.g., FBI memos dated 14 June 1955, 23 June 1955, and 1 July 1955 obtained through FOIPA (Freedom of Information/Privacy Act).

76. Leonard Burtman timeline: sources include Bienvenu, 167–206; Social Security Death Index; US, Social Security Applications and Claims Index, 1936–2007; two marriage certificates from 1961 and 1964; NYC residency, age nine to nineteen, as noted on 1930 and 1940 US Federal Census; father, Herman, one-time newspaper editor and publisher: the *News-Journal* (Fullerton, Nance County, Nebraska: c. 1912/13–1917), otherwise, his lifelong profession was printing: http://chroniclingamerica.loc.gov/lccn/sn95069058/holdings; father's death: New York, New York, Death Index, also, http://www.jewishgen.org; FBI files obtained under FOIPA.

77. Burtman mail order products: detailed by Bienvenu, 175.

77. Social circle between Burtman and Charles Guyette . . . relationship between Burtman and John Coutts: Bienvenu, 169.

78. Benedict "Ben" Himmel, a former union organizer: Bienvenu, 170, 171.

78. [Himmel] summoned during the Kefauver hearings: 24 May 1955; Hearings Before The Subcommittee To Investigate Juvenile Delinquency of The Committee On the Judiciary United States Senate, 99.

80. Transvestism (one of Leonard's strongest fixations): according to Kim Christy (right hand man/lady and intimate): "He loved the lady boys": http://www.advocate.com/arts-entertainment/photography/2011/02/12/kim-christys-lost-world?page=full.

80. "This is terrible": Kroll, *The Art of Eric Stanton*, 10; Stanton also repeated this story in the foreword for *Brutal Sisters Battle*, v. III (Burbank: Brand × Publishing, 1989), 3.

80. Burtman later got his revenge: e.g., *Burmel Bulletin* #2, items #36–#44, each featuring nine reproductions of Stanton art advertised as "Eneg's exciting and daring drawings." At a later date Burtman also procured the original Stanton artwork of *Sex Switch* from Mishkin.

## CHAPTER 15

81. 22 June 1957: birth dates of sons appear on page two of divorce papers, case no. 103694, Ernest Stanten, Plaintiff vs. Grace M. Stanten, Defendant, filed 3 June 1960, Las Vegas, Nevada.

81. "We met at seaside": Stefano Piselli and Riccardo Morrocchi, *The Art of Eric Stanton: Master of Bizarre* (Firenze: Glittering Images, 1993), 19, 20.

84. "She took the kids, the car": Kroll, *The Art of Eric Stanton*, 9.

## CHAPTER 17

86. "I was a cripple from age 28 to 36": Kroll, *The Art of Eric Stanton*, 9.

86. "From age 28 to 38": Ibid, 12.

## CHAPTER 18

89. Much of what Stanton contributed to Edward Mishkin early on seemed to include fighting and wrestling women: e.g., "Boy Meets Girl" by Stan, Item #253, Gargoyle Sales Corp., Bulletin #9. Fragments of Stanton's ("Stan's") wrestling art would appear in the Burtman-published magazines *Corporal*, #45, #47 (see collector's guide for more details.)

90. "All the pieces I drew for Max Stone": Kroll, *The Art of Eric Stanton*, 11.

90. Both Peerless and Irving sharing advertising space in Harrison's magazines since 1949: e.g., *Wink*, v. 4, n. 4, Jan. 1949.

90. Stone vs. Guyette: Sharing the same business address: 1472 Broadway, room 904, New York: as indicated in a Peerless Sales ad appearing in the magazine *Popular Photography*, Nov. 1946. Guyette used the alias "J. Redwine" primarily to sell fetish footwear, and "Yetta" to sell boxing/wrestling/fencing femme photos. Both J. Redwine and Yetta are featured in advertisements at this address (for J. Redwine: *London Life*, March 25 issue, 1939; for Yetta: *Gay Book* magazine, Dec. 1937).

## CHAPTER 19

93. Kings Tower Building: building since demolished. Studio address appeared on 1962 correspondence between Kinsey Institute director Paul H. Gebhard and Stanton. By 1958, Ditko was already established, churning out volume: 450 pages for Charlton (1957) and "over 430 published pages in 1958": Bell, *Strange and Stranger*, 37, 40.

93. "We had a great working relationship": Greg Theakston, "The Road to Spider-Man," *The Steve Ditko Reader* V. 1, unpaginated.

93. "We just hit it off right away": Ibid.

93. "It was a room about ten feet by twenty": Kroll, *The Art of Eric Stanton*, 10.

94. "Ditko was diagnosed with tuberculosis": Theakston, "The Road to Spider-Man," unpaginated; also see Bell, *Strange and Stranger*, 27.

94. "There were times he would spend twenty hours straight": Kroll, *The Art of Eric Stanton*, 10.

94. "He thought my stuff was funny": Ibid.

94. "Every experience that I had with Steve was terrific": Theakston, "The Road to Spider-Man," unpaginated.

94. Mail block against Klaw ceased in summer 1958: Klaw v. Schaffer, Postmaster, New York City. 357 U.S. 346, 78 S.Ct. 1369, 2 L.Ed.2d 1368 (1958). Decided June 23, 1958.

94. Jani Sales Co. #38727; 1 April 1957; Discontinued 5 Feb. 1959: info J. B. Rund.

94. "Nutrix Co.," established in New York City and used briefly to sell mail order novelties: "Nutrix Co." and "Nutrix Novelty Company" advertised tricks/party novelties in the early '40s; "Nutrix Co.," officially registered as a company on 25 Aug., 1950 (#11946). Consummate mail order marketer, Klaw also "tested" the name "Nutrix Co." in early '50s ads (along with "Movie Star News") using his 212 East 14th St. address. One Nutrix bulletin—bulletin #9, featuring mostly cheesecake material—was issued from the 212 NYC address prior to establishing his New Jersey operation.

95. Bettie Page, December 1957: Bettie Page wrote in a 1992 letter: "I quit modeling in December 1957 when I left New York for good. I was tired of my life as it was and wanted to try something else . . .": Foster, *The Real Bettie Page*, 89; also see: Karen Essex and James L. Swanson, *Bettie Page: The Life of a Pin-Up Legend*, 223.

95. "We have employed a new artist named Jon Bee": *Nutrix Co. Bulletin*, unnumbered but stating "Latest Bulletin 1958."

95. J. Kodti/Kotdi (e.g., "J. Kodti": *Black Fury* #18, April 1959; "Kotdi:" cover, *Mysteries Of*

*Unexplored Worlds* #11, Jan. 1959) and "Space Mann:" (e.g., *Space Adventures*, Feb. 1959).

## CHAPTER 20

97. Mishkin seemed to have no critical standards whatsoever: Kroll, *The Art of Eric Stanton*, 11; also this is plainly visible to the average collector in virtually everything Stanton contributed to Mishkin.

98. "I think I always wanted to be a calendar artist . . . I really wasn't into comic books": Theakston, "The Road to Spider-Man," unpaginated.

99. Sometimes split jobs 50/50 with his studio mate: Kroll, *The Art of Eric Stanton*, 10.

99. "He introduced me to the work of bondage artist Eric Stanton": http://strangenessofbrendanmccarthy.blogspot.com/2008_03_01_archive.html.

100. "Wash is achieved with various degrees": Bell, *Strange and Stranger*, 103.

100. The use of wash appeared in Charlton's *Mad Monsters* #1, 1961: Ibid.

100. "How he developed his expertise in such short order at Warren": Ibid.

## CHAPTER 21

103. The raid, which occurred on the cusp of the new decade 1959/'60 between December 29, 1959 (the police raid on Mishkin's store headquarters, Publisher's Outlet), and March 10, 1960 (Mishkin's widely publicized arrest). Likely it was January 1960.

103. "Yes, I remember some of the police raid": Steve Ditko letter to the author, 18 May 2013.

103. "Everything that belonged to me": Kroll, *The Art of Eric Stanton*, 10.

103. "Yonkers Man Called 'Largest' Smut Dealer" (Headline) and text: "A man described": *The Herald Statesman*, 10 March 1960.

103. "Hogan said that immunity might be granted": "Smut King Suspect Trapped in DA's Sweep Held in 25Gs," *Long Island Star-Journal*, 10 March 1960.

103. "Mishkin's arrest developed from a joint investigation": "'Kingpin' of Smut Seized by Hogan," the *New York Times*, 10 March 1960.

104. For more on the earliest known Tijuana bible arrests (in Terre Haute, 1926): Tom Roznowski, *An American Hometown: Terre Haute, Indiana, 1927* (Indiana: Indiana Univ. Press, 2009). For more on stag films featuring XXX content see Al Di Lauro and Gerald Rabkin, *Dirty Movies: An Illustrated History of The Stag Film, 1915–1970* (New York, Chelsea House).

104. The "prurient" interest of a select few, or, as ultimately determined: Mishkin v. New York, 383 U.S. 502: "Where the material is designed for and primarily disseminated to a clearly defined deviant sexual group, rather than the public at large, the prurient-appeal requirement of the Roth test is satisfied if the dominant theme of the material taken as a whole appeals to the prurient interest in sex of the members of that group."

104. "Sexually morbid, grossly perverse": Ibid., Footnote 4.

105. Ernest Stanton [sic], having been called as a witness: Note: the name "Stanten" appears erroneously as "Stanton" in the printed transcript of the court case, People v. Mishkin, 26 Misc.2d 152 (1960), 477–490.

105. "What I said instead helped the defense . . . they told me everything was burned": Kroll, *The Art of Eric Stanton*, 10.

105. "When Ernie came back from the police station": Steve Ditko letter to the author, 18 May 2013.

106. 5 ft. 3 in. Eddie Mishkin (a.k.a. Ed Lantz): FBI memo (obtained through FOIPA), 17 Aug. 1961, 3.

106. Mishkin Rap Sheet (1936–1959): "alleged to have accepted bets on horses": "3 Found Guilty in Bookmaking," *Long Island Daily Press*, 21 Nov. 1936.

106. "Mishkin had been accused by Detective Louise Nebb": "Mishkin Discharged In Obscene Art Case," the *Herald Statesman*, 7 Jan. 1953. The author could find no hard evidence of a 1952 conviction later alluded to in the media, nor does it appear on the FBI Mishkin rap sheet dated 17 July 1961, 4. However, an article from *The Herald Statesman*, 15 Dec. 1960, states: "Mishkin was convicted only once before. That was in 1952 when he was fined $1,600 and received four suspended jail sentences."

106. "Mishkin has been able to operate with impunity": FBI memo (obtained through FOIPA), 8 June 1955, 2.

106. "When he walked into a bookstore": "Mishkin Freed In New York Vagrancy Case," the *Herald Statesman*, 8 Jan. 1960.

106. "Fifty books are involved in this case. They portray sexuality in many guises": Mishkin v. New York, 383 U.S. 502.

107. "'Kingpin' of Smut Gets Stiff Term" (Headline) . . . (text) Edward Mishkin, a man described": "'Kingpin' of Smut Gets Stiff Term" the *New York Times*, 15 Dec. 1960.

107. On 172 criminal counts. Sixty of those counts related to Stanton: listed in Mishkin v. New York, 383 U.S. 502.

107. "Assistant District Attorney Melvin Stein, who prosecuted the case, called Mishkin": "'Kingpin' of Smut Gets Stiff Term," the *New York Times*, 15 Dec. 1960.

## CHAPTER 22

108. "Cross Examination by Mr. Kern": printed transcript of the court case People v. Mishkin, 26 Misc.2d 152 (1960), 489.

110. "The word 'Amazon' became a key": Stefano Piselli & Riccardo Morrocchi, *The Second Book of Stanton* (Firenze: Glittering Images, 1997), 8.

111. "Inhabited only by Amazon type girls": *Tame-Azons Subdue and Subjugate Man*, v. 1, (New York: Nutrix, 1960), 18.

111. "Roughly throwing her captive man to the floor": italicized text represents an abridged version of the original text of *Tame-Azons Subdue and Subjugate Man*, 28–62.

112. "Swear allegiance to her cause": Ibid., 38.

114. "Subdue and vanquish": *Men Tamed to Submission by Tame-Azons*, (New York: Nutrix, 1960), 4.

115. "This time Potentia was determined to break down Dan's will": Ibid., 24.

115. "The tedious bent-over position": Ibid.

115. "Part of the deal was that the mysterious employer of the Tame-Azons": Ibid, 6.

115. "Sadomasochism, a way people can forget themselves . . . Masochism is a set of techniques for helping people temporarily lose their normal identity": Marianne Apostolides, "The Pleasure of Pain," *Psychology Today*, 1 Sept. 1999; archived online: https://www.psychologytoday.com/articles/199909/the-pleasure-pain.

115. "Gender performativity": a term attributed to gender theorist Judith Butler.

115. "His one-time air of braggadocio": *Men Tamed to Submission by Tame-Azons*, 58.

116. "You know, this whole area of fantasy in our field is considered": R. Q. Harmon, "A Conversation with Eric Stanton," 25.

116. "Going to nightclubs and drinking most of the night": *Bondage Artist Dominated By Tame-Azon*, (New York: Nutrix, 1961), 4.

118. "Crestfallen and embarrassed": Ibid., 58.

## CHAPTER 23

119. "I met Stanley through Mishkin": Kroll, *The Art of Eric Stanton*, 12.

119. Stanley Malkin, in 1957, is listed as a principal partner for The Little Book Exchange, 228 W. 42nd Street: an address also associated with Mishkin: 1957-B, Stanley Malkin & Frank Adler, #08727. Among Malkin's other businesses, according to Malkin's daughter, Jane Konigsberg (as per 19 March 2015 phone conversation), a restaurant, The Spindletop, and a topless bar that Times Square historian Jay Gertzman also alludes to: "Softcore Publishing: The East Coast Scene," *Sin-A-Rama*, 23.

119. Satellite Publishing Co., entity ID #7923023500, Incorporation date: 24 Jan. 1961, New Jersey: courtesy of https://www.njportal.com/DOR/BusinessNameSearch/Search/EntityId.

119. "We printed some things. I did some good work for them": Kroll, *The Art of Eric Stanton*, 11, 12.

120. First appearance of the word "dominatrix" in a fetish context: page 50. (Oxford English Dictionary wrongly states the first appearance of "dominatrix" was in 1967: http://www.oed.com/view/Entry/56699.)

120. Stanton would also direct Satellite's first fetish photo sessions: sets marked "A" and "B."

121. FBI memo dated 15 Dec. 1961: the subject of FBI memo (obtained through FOIPA) was "Stanley Malkin."

121. FBI investigation (8 May 1961): subject of FBI memo (obtained through FOIPA): "Ed Mishkin."

121. "It appears that the magazine is designed to appeal to a perverted female mind," noted one FBI agent: the memo (3 July 1961, pg. 2) further states: "it may be that the newsstands involved would sell copies more readily to a woman. It is, therefore, suggested that this matter be discussed with cooperative local police in an effort to have a policewoman of proper appearance attempt to purchase the magazine at suspected newsstands . . ."

The memo further urges (on pg. 3) that Satellite Publishing Co. be further investigated through "obtaining telephone toll calls, a mail cover, reliable informants, spot check surveillances, and interviews of express agencies."

## CHAPTER 24

124. In 1962, Eric Stanton's productivity for Irving Klaw: Stanton's final contribution to Klaw appeared in spring 1962: *Tales of Female Domination Over Man*, Vol. 5.

124. The Trials of Leonard Burtman: Bienvenu, 120–142, 194–201.

124. Kaysey Sales imprint: would fold, but "Kaysey Sales Co., Inc." continued as a mail order business into the 1960s.

124. Divorce from Tana Louise: Divorce Certificate Number 8223. Florida Department of Health. Florida Divorce Index, 1927–2001. Jacksonville, FL, USA.

125. Selbee Associates & Masque: Bienvenu, 176.

125. The new sexploitation era (*Playboy*, *Modern Man*, "heel & hose" magazines, etc.): Dian Hanson, *The History of Men's Magazines*, v. 2, 205–239; 295–298; also see *The History of Men's Magazines*, v. 4 (Köln: Taschen, 2005), 89, 90; 153–160.

126. Steve Ditko's heavy reliance on pen and ink over pencil: Bell, *Strange and Stranger*, 50.

## CHAPTER 25

137. "Bizarre" social circles (like those connecting Coutts to the likes of Charles Guyette): Bienvenu, 168,169.

137. As it turned out, Burtman got it half right: J. B. Rund, introduction to *Sweeter Gwen & The Return of Gwendoline* (New York: Bélier Press, 1976), unpaginated.

137. "I roughed out 30 pages . . . He loved it and that was it": Kroll, *The Art of Eric Stanton*, 10.

137. The full narrative would appear for sale in a Burtman catalog that summer: "As to the Original edition of the Serial, I have a clipping from a flyer (from Kaysey Sales Company, Aug. 1962) which offers it in '3 Chapters' for '$5.00 per chapter / $12.00 complete.' "(Each chapter contains 8 drawings.) / (3 chapters are available.)": J. B. Rund, e-mail message to author, 8 July 2012.

138. "I am now completing the GREATEST THING": 1962 letter from Stanton to the Kinsey Institute, courtesy of J. B. Rund.

138. Willie had some difficulty with pacing narratives and in correspondence expressed his dissatisfaction: J. B. Rund, *The Adventures of Sweet Gwendoline* by John Willie (New York: Bélier Press, 1999), 134.

139. "Sir d'Arcy d'Arcy," the bungling, dastardly villain Willie based on himself, was renamed "Sir Dystic d'Arcy" in the 1958 reworked version of the *Sweet Gwendoline* comic.

139. "Stanton" was none other than Steve Ditko: "The 'rumor' was printed in *Les Filles de Papier* by Jacques Sadoul (Paris: *Editions Elvifrance*, 1971). I think that was the original source, which after appearing there, just spread.": J. B. Rund, e-mail message to the author, 26 Nov. 2013. The rumor was repeated in *Le Supersexy Del Fumetto* (Bologna: EP EdiPeriodici / Elvipress, 1971) by the same author, according to Hans Siden, *Sadomasochism in Comics* (San Diego: Greenleaf Classics, Inc., 1972), 188. Also Stanton in a 1988 interview with Theakston: "Somebody else said, 'There is no Eric Stanton. His name is Steve Ditko'": Theakston, "The Road to Spider-Man," unpaginated.

## CHAPTER 26

143. "For me, the Spider-Man saga began": *Steve Ditko, A Mini-History*: 13. "Speculation," The Comics v 14 #8, Aug. 2003, 1.

143. "Kirby had penciled five pages": Steve Ditko, "An Insider's Part of Comics History: Jack Kirby's Spider-Man," *Avenging World* (Bellington: Robin Snyder and Steve Ditko, 2002), 57, 58.

143. The character evidently resembled Captain America: Ditko illustrations (with a side-by-side comparison: Captain America vs. Kirby's Spider-Man) accompany the article above: Ibid.

144. "Stan never told me who came up with the idea": Ditko, "Speculation," 1.

144. "Almost all the bits of this 'creation'": Ditko, "An Insider's Part of Comics History: Jack Kirby's Spider-Man," 58.

144. Assumed that Stan Lee alone was the creator as he had the "idea": Ditko, "Speculation," 2.

144. "I created the character": Jack Kirby, Gary Groth, "Jack Kirby Interview," the *Comics Journal* #134, Feb. 1990, 82.

144. "Spider-Man" was not designed at Marvel Comics: the offices of Marvel were located at 625 Madison Avenue.

144. "The first thing Ditko did was to redesign the costume": Theakston, "The Road to Spider-Man," unpaginated.

144. "I did it because it hid an obviously boyish face": Ditko, "An Insider's Part of Comics History: Jack Kirby's Spider-Man," 57.

144. "It is interesting that Spider-Man": Amber Stanton, "A Tangled Web," *The Creativity of Ditko* (San Diego: IDW Publishing, 2012), 89.

144. "The idea of the web shooting out": Ibid., 87.

146. *Exotique Quarterly* #1 was advertised in the mail order Kaysey Sales, Co. catalog #62–4, April 1962, which coincided with the creation of the first eleven pages of Spider-Man. We can assume that Stanton also had early access to copies of *Exotique Quarterly*.

146. "A 1 or 2 page synopsis": Steve Ditko, "Tsk! Tsk!" *Avenging World*, (Bellington: Robin Snyder and Steve Ditko, 2002), 68.

146. "Draw me a Spider-man!": Theakston, "The Road to Spider-Man," unpaginated. (Author's correction of Theakston's misspelling "Spiderman" in caps.)

146. *Exotique* #6, featuring the Bilbrew spider webbing idea, circa 1956.

146. "There have been earlier uses of the spider 'idea'": Ditko, "An Insider's Part of Comics History: Jack Kirby's Spider-Man," 59.

146. "Black Widow Sorority," published in 1962: *Diabolique* #3: though undated, the issue shares identical back-magazine Burtman publication advertising appearing in *Orbit* #3, dated 1962, *Exotique Quarterly* #1 (1962) among the items advertised.

146. From "back-up features" fantasy artist to "lead story" front man: "The back-up features (five-pagers) were drawn by me": Ditko, "An Insider's Part of Comics History: Jack Kirby's Spider-Man," 57.

146. The choices were made by the colorist at Marvel (Stan Goldberg), who chose cherry red and dark cobalt: Sean Howe, *Marvel Comics: The Untold Story* (New York: Harper, 2012), 42.

146. "My original color combination was a warm red orange on the webbing section and a cool blue on the body parts": Steve Ditko, "A Mini-History #3: The Amazing Spider-Man #1" *The Comics!*, Vol. 12, No. 11, Nov. 2001, 1.

148. "The use of the spider theme": Ditko, "An Insider's Part of Comics History: Jack Kirby's Spider-Man," 58.

150. "By suggesting the Spider-signal": Theakston, "The Road to Spider-Man," unpaginated.

150. "Together he and Ditko would have 'skull sessions'": Ibid.

150. "Many of the issues suggest Stanton's hand in the mix": Ibid.

150. "My dad explained that he wanted to protect the family by keeping a low profile": Amber Stanton, e-mail message to author, 12 Jan. 2012; variation later used in *The Creativity of Ditko*, Amber Stanton essay, "A Tangled Web," 88.

**CHAPTER 27**

152. "Real Smoky Mountain Tennessee": R. Q. Harmon, "Interview with Paula Klaw," 14.

152. Satellite publication *Bound and Transformed* (an undated magazine) was among the items confiscated in a December 5, 1962, police raid on the Malkin-related Main Street Book Shop, Inc., at 626 Main Street in the city of Buffalo, NY. [Stengel v. Smith: 37 Misc.2d 947 (1963)]. First appearance of the Spider-Man half-face was in 1963: *The Amazing Spider-Man* #1, March. *Adonis in High Heels*, a 1959 Burtman publication, also featured a Bilbrew variation of Klaw's *Femme Mimics* idea. We should not forget that Ditko also knew Bilbrew and might have followed his art.

155. "The first time somebody approached me to do a homosexual story": *Brutal Sisters Battle*, v. II, Stanton interview excerpt: "Delving Below The Surface," (Burbank: Brand X Publishing, 1989), 3.

158. Adding to his deep bitterness regarding Burtman: J. B. Rund, introduction to *Sweeter Gwen & The Return of Gwendoline* (New York: Bélier Press, 1976), vii.

**CHAPTER 28**

165. Bound had proven a disappointment: evidence of poor sales appears in an FBI memo (obtained through FOIPA) involving informants dated 7 July 1961: Cover Page "C": "PCI stated that this book is not presently being sold by the Primrose Book Store, 130 West 42nd Street, NYC. He said the reason this book is not on the shelves of this bookstore is not because of its obscenity, but because it is not a good seller."

165. "He was the best I ever worked for": Kroll, *The Art of Eric Stanton*, 12.

167. "Carlson Wade" = Burtman: Bienvenu, 171.

167. Attracting potential distribution: in the beginning, Malkin erratically went through various distributors, including the Sturman brothers, based in Cleveland, Ohio. FN104, *Tormented Virgin* (1963) shows a mysterious stamped west coast address: 6006 Coolidge Ave., Culver City, CA— evidently the first distributor.

167. "Notorious for ignoring the rules": Chris Eckhoff, "After Hours Books," *Paperback Parade* #20, April 1996, 25.

167. Malkin was legally liable: "Nitey Nite Books Inc . 20,000 shares. Incorporators are Loretta and Stanley Malkin, 204 Court, Rochester; William J. Smith, 525 Delaware Ave." listed under "Incorporations:" *Buffalo Courier-Express*, 20 July 1963.

167. The Sturman brothers, based in Cleveland: Joe Sturman and Rueben "Ruby" Sturman, the latter who became the greatest "kingpin" of them all. For a first-hand account of the Sturman brothers, see Mike Resnick, "Me and the Kingpin," author's blog, February 2007: http://novelspot.net/node/1519

167. "After Hours": "Incorporation, Aug. 12: After Hours Books Inc., 200 shares. Incorporator is William J. Smith, 525 Delaware Ave.": *Buffalo Courier-Express*, 13 Aug. 1964.

## CHAPTER 29

177. Suggested even the most modest raise: "an increase in the per-page payment, from $35.00 to $40.00—a raise of $5.00": J. B. Rund, introduction to *Sweeter Gwen & The Return of Gwendoline* (New York: Bélier Press, 1976), unpaginated.

177. Non-payment from a secondary distributor, Chicago-based All-States News Co.: Bienvenu, 191, 192. (Note: evidence suggests 1964, rather than "circa 1965," as stated by Burtman attorney Monte-Levy.)

177. City-wide anti-smut campaign kicked into high gear by Catholic priest and moral entrepreneur Father Morton A. Hill: Bienvenu, 141, 142; 201–206.

177. On 28 Jan. 1964, a 66 count indictment: Bienvenu, 204.

177. In 1964, only three full-sized Selbee magazines would be published, as opposed to seventeen from the previous year: 1963–*Striparama* #3, #4, #5, #6; *Satana* #5, #6; *Leg Show* #4, #5, #6; *High Heels* #3, #4 ,#5, #6; *Focus On* #1, #2; and *Female*

*Mimics* #2, #3. 1964: *Striparama* (zero); *Satana* (zero); *Leg Show* (zero); *High Heels* (zero); *Focus On* #3, #4; and *Female Mimics* #4 (Fall).

177. Stanton's name as art director was listed inside two of them: *Focus On* #3, #4.

177. S-K Books, evidently fabricated "S-K Press" appears printed inside, suggesting this was a sham (or unregistered) publishing imprint.

178. During this period (1964/65) that Stanton provided his final 1960s artwork: two "new" Stanton illustrations appear in 1965 Burtman magazines (one inside *Leg Show* #7, one inside *Satana* #7), however, it is unknown when these were actually created by the artist. Possibly 1964? Other Stanton art inside these issues was recycled material.

178. Rely on "package deals" offered by secondary distributors to produce his magazines: e.g., a subsidiary company of secondary distributor Acme News Company was Health Knowledge Inc.—set up to partner/produce/print magazines for publishers like Burtman. See: Earl Kemp (Editor), Luis Ortiz (Editor), *Cult Magazines: A to Z: A Compendium of Culturally Obsessive & Curiously Expressive Publications* (New York: NonStop Press, 2009), 7, 8.

## CHAPTER 30

180. "Klaw was in an office there at a desk": United States v. Klaw 227 F. Supp. 12 (1964) United States of America, v. Irving Klaw and Jack Kramer, Defendants. 63 Cr. 580.

180. "Having knowingly used the mails to distribute": 350 F.2d 155 United States of America, Appellee, v. Irving Klaw and Jack Kramer, Defendants-Appellants, No. 70, Docket 28887.

180. Part of a Nutrix anthology in June 1962: *Tales of Female Domination Over Man*, Vol. 5.

181. "Striking simultaneously at various locations": "13 Stores Raided For Pornography," the *New York Times*, 19 Jan. 1961.

181. "Conspiring to import from England pornographic books and pictures": "Smut Charge Is Denied By Mishkin," *The Herald Statesman*, 9 Sept. 1962.

181. "A present from the boys in England": United States v. Edward Mishkin, 317 F.2d 634 (2d Cir. 1963).

181. "Mishkin tried to set up a smuggling operation": "Smut Dealer Gets Federal Prison Term," the *Herald Statesman*, 23 Nov. 1962.

181. Upheld his first case—his 1960 conviction—on all but thirty-two counts: those relating to the general business law: "Anonymous Books Upheld By Court," the *New York Times*, 4 Dec. 1962.

184. *My Life and Loves* (actually a copyright-free reprint of the original one-volume 1931 edition): this same text, same title, as it was in the public domain, was also published by Greenleaf: *My Love Life* by Frank Harris (San Diego: Greenleaf Classics, 1966), #GC 208.

184. Payment, this time, would be modestly improved at $100 cash: J. B. Rund, introduction to *Sweeter Gwen & The Return of Gwendoline*, unpaginated.

## CHAPTER 31

185. Incorporated in September 1965: "Stantoons Inc., 200 shares. William Smith, 525 Delaware Ave."; listed under "Incorporations:" *Buffalo Courier-Express*, 25 Sept. 1965.

185. At odds with Marvel publisher Martin Goodman over royalties and his recent work on Spider-Man, and no longer on speaking terms with Stan Lee: Howe, *Marvel Comics: The Untold Story*, 53–56, 62, 63, 66; Greg Theakston, "The Road to Spider-Man," unpaginated; Bell, *Strange and Stranger*, 89–97.

185. Edward D. Wood Jr. under the pen name "Charlene White": http://rmc.library.cornell.edu/EAD/htmldocs/RMM07779.html.

187. "On A Kinky Hook" was the original title. It was advertised as *Stantoons* #5 "On a Kinky Hook" Chapter (1), #6 "On a Kinky Hook" Chapter (2), #9 "Kinky Chameleon," later collected into a single comic magazine, *The Kinky Hook*, published by Eros Comix/Fantagraphics, 1991.

187. Which would eventually vie for popularity with *Sweeter Gwen*: as a bound comic magazine published in the 1990s, *The Kinky Hook* would go through various printings (first printing on glossy paper and the rest on standard, porous comic stock). Eros Comix/Fantagraphics would also reprint *Sweeter Gwen* and other Stantoons Inc. Stanton/Ditko comics.

187. As long as Malkin's First Niter and After Hours books kept the Prudential Bldg., Buffalo address: Malkin's "mail drop" Buffalo New York address would change from "1009 Prudential Bldg." to "Market Arcade 617 Main St." with the paperback *The Long Night*, FN253, 1967. So 1967 would mark the end before Mishkin picked up Stantoons, Inc. with installment #14.

187. Stantoons Inc. *Collectors Cartoon Classics*: would feature the name "Staton" and advertise Stanton/Ditko Stantoons as well as Mishkin commissioned material, indicating a change of the guard. *Stantoons* #14, "Don't Pick Up Strangers!" would bear a New York City address: G.P.O. Box 2573, an address associated with Mishkin. Mishkin later absorbed Stantoons Inc. material, half of which he commissioned, into his 1970s mail order business Candor Books Inc. (for more see collector's guide).

## CHAPTER 32

194. A progressive interplay between the area's aberrant film culture and the bookshops: "The adult bookstores led the way toward 42nd Street's X-rated future, with the movie theaters following cautiously a few steps behind": Bianco, *Ghosts of 42nd Street*, 137; as a side note regarding bookstore concentration in Times Square, according to Bianco, 169: "the number of adult bookstores more than doubled to sixty-eight in 1970, from about thirty in 1967."

194. "A new symbol of victory for democracy": Anonymous, *The Case of The V-Pants*, 35.

196. "Like a baby, What gives": Anonymous, *Grip of Fear*, 3.

197. "Bell-like, girlish": Ibid., 21.

197. "Come on over, Audrey, dear": Ibid., 23.

197. "Now, Paula, I want you to take": Ibid., 29.

197. "Of being puny, a sissy, a push-over": Ibid., 27.

198. "Exhausted, emotionally shattered": Ibid., 31.

198. "She was dressed again, freshly made-up": Ibid., 34.

199. "Don't look now, June": Anonymous, *The Passive Peeper*, 1.

199. "Apparently he's going to keep": Ibid.

199. "Suppose we could lure him": Ibid., 2.

199. "Let's see how much fight you have": Ibid., 10.

199. "Since he likes my panties so much": Ibid.

199. "She hitched up her skirt": Ibid.

201. "C'mon to bed with me": Ibid., 18.

201. "I'll do anything, but let's keep this": Ibid., 31.

201. "A sore-muscled, pained, and rueful man": Ibid., 28.

201. "A flag of victory to the girls": Ibid., 32.

## CHAPTER 33

203. His "smuggling" conviction of 1962 would be affirmed in '63: United States v. Mishkin No. 337, Docket 27900. 317 F.2d 634 (1963).

203. In 1964, while conducting appeals, he would be arrested again: mention of another arrest: 2 Dec. 1964: "Pornography Case Dropped," the *Herald Statesman*, 17 Feb. 1965.

203. The highly publicized decision would be upheld, six to three: "Pornography Verdict Jails Dealer Here," the *Herald Statesman*, 22 March 1966. Also see: "Supreme Court Actions," the *New York Times*, 22 March 1966.

203. The history of Miskin's major obscenity case (1960–1966) was summarized in Mishkin v. New York, No. 49., 383 U.S. 502 (1966): "This case, like Ginzburg v. United States, ante, p. 463, also decided today, involves convictions under a criminal obscenity statute. A panel of three judges of the Court of Special Sessions of the City of New York found appellant guilty of violating § 1141 of the New York Penal Law by hiring others to prepare obscene books, publishing obscene books, and possessing obscene books with intent to sell them. 26 Misc.2d 152, 207 N.Y.S.2d 390 (1960). He was sentenced to prison terms aggregating three years and ordered to pay $12,000 in fines for these crimes. The Appellate Division, First Department, affirmed those convictions. 17 App. Div. 2d 243, 234 N.Y.S.2d 342 (1962). The Court of Appeals affirmed without opinion. 15 N.Y.2d 671, 204 N.E.2d 209 (1964), remittitur amended, 15 N.Y.2d 724, 205 N.E.2d 201 (1965). We noted probable jurisdiction. 380 U.S. 960. We affirm."

203. Bookstore arrest in April: 5 April 1966: "Smut Case Figure is Arrested Again," the *New York Times*, 6 April 1966.

203. In 1967, Mishkin hired a new legal team: People v. Mishkin 20 N.Y.2d 716 (1967).

203. "Late in 1959 and early in 1960, New York City police conducted": United States v. Thomas 68 Civ. 464. 282 F. Supp., 729 (1968), United States ex rel. Edward Mishkin, Petitioner, v. James A. Thomas, Warden of the City Penitentiary of the City of New York, Respondent.

203. April 1968, Mishkin was released: "The court orders today the termination of petitioner's confinement": Ibid., according to footnote 12.

"Petitioner was freed on bail by order of this court on March 25, 1968."

204. An aborted attempt at another trilogy, *Grotto of The Tortured* concludes with the note: "For the further adventures of personalities first encountered in this work, look for its sequel: *Mount Mansquirm*."

## CHAPTER 34

207. Irving Klaw won on appeal, July 1965: 350 F.2d 155, United States of America, Appellee, v. Irving Klaw and Jack Kramer, Defendants-Appellants. No. 70. Docket 28887.

207. "Irving's attorney thought it might make a good impression": R. Q. Harmon, "Interview with Paula Klaw," 56.

207. Natalie would die of a sudden heart attack; Irving Klaw, peritonitis: *The Irving Klaw Years, 1948–1963*, 1976, 7.

207. His most fragile son, Jeffrey, this according to Arthur Klaw, his brother.

207. Natalie Klaw's death date is inscribed as 28 Oct. 1965 on her tombstone. Irving Klaw's death is listed as 8 Sept. 1966, as verified by the author in a personal visit to their graves in Maspeth, Queens.

207. "His whole life was in his business": Paula interview by Gloria Leonard, "Paula Klaw: The First Lady of Bondage," 95.

207. Her own nephew, Jeffrey Klaw, would sue her: Klaw v. Kramer, 56 Misc.2d 173 (1968), Jeffrey H. Klaw, Plaintiff, v. Pauline K. Kramer, as Executrix of Irving Klaw, Deceased, Defendant.

207. "His wife was a little jealous of me": Paula interview by Gloria Leonard, "Paula Klaw: The First Lady of Bondage," 95.

207. "I think whatever Klaw hadn't sold": R. Q. Harmon, "A Conversation with Eric Stanton," 56.

## CHAPTER 35

208. "He had observed a quantity of partially burned photographic film . . . .": People v. Bosco, Misc.2d 1080 (1968).

208. "Armed with this second warrant": Ibid.

209. Jay Gertzman, Liberty Bookshop: "Softcore Publishing: The East Coast Scene," *Sin-A-Rama* (Los Angeles: Feral House, 2005), 23.

209. "He owned a bookstore on Times Square. It was Mafia connected": Lynn Monroe online interview with Gil Fox: http://www.lynn-munroe-books.com/list55/midwood.htm.

209. William Smith, police raid in Buffalo: "the manager and operator": Stengel v. Smith, 37 Misc.2d 947 (1963).

209. "626 Main Street" would also appear under the heading "After Hours Books, Inc."—rubber stamped inside select Malkin paperbacks: one such example owned by the author: *Vixens Delight*, AH110, 1965.

210. "We are sure that Stanley Malkin individually": Articolor Graphic Co., Ltd., Appellant, v. After Hours Books, Inc., et al., Defendants, and Stanley Malkin, respondent, 13 (of court transcript).

210. "At his direction, the bills would be made out": Ibid., 15, 16.

210. "The initials on the billing indicates": Ibid., 16.

210. "The statement of Jan. 10, 1967": Ibid.; Note: "First Nite Books, Inc." is not a typo, as this appears to be the legal name of the imprint (not "First Niter Books, Inc." as appears printed in the books).

210. "Stanley Malkin made all the payments": Ibid., 17, 18.

210. "The fact is that the Defendant, Stanley Malkin": Ibid., 33.

210. "Albert Bosco was never considered": Ibid., 33.

210. "He indicated that all of these corporations": Ibid., 34.

210. "Stanley Malkin is not now": Ibid., 24.

210. "Stanley Malkin states": Ibid., 30.

210. "There is no writing sufficient to indicate": Ibid., 42.

210. "I am not and never have been an officer, director or shareholder": Ibid., 8.

211. "Massachusetts vs. *Memoirs of a Woman of Pleasure*": (a.k.a. "the U.S. Supreme Court's Fanny Hill decision"), Bienvenu, 205; also, Stephen J. Gertz, "West Coast Blue," Sin-a-rama (Los Angeles: Feral House, 2005), 27.

211. "Involving as it did a massive seizure of constitutionally protected matter": People v. Bosco, 56 Misc.2d 1080 (1968)

## CHAPTER 36

213. "It was 7:30 in the morning": Kroll, *The Art of Eric Stanton*, 13.

213. "Yoga. Thank God for yoga": R. Q. Harmon, "A Conversation with Eric Stanton," 57.

213. Eric may have paraphrased Hittleman: "'Self' is another word for 'God,'" Richard Hittleman, *Yoga for Health* (New York: Ballantine Books, 1983), 185. (This concept of self was alluded to in many of Hittleman's books, but also his *Yoga For Health* TV program, which first aired in New York in 1966: Robert Love, "Fear Of Yoga," *Columbia Journalism Review*, Nov. 2006.)

213. 1968, "Eric" would also stop sharing studio space with Steve Ditko: Greg Theakston, "The Road to Spider-Man," *The Steve Ditko Reader* v. 1, unpaginated; Britt also corroborated, stating that when they had met Eric had just gone "solo," using his small bedroom as his working studio. But the split was not because of Britt.

215. "High lieutenant of the Genovese Mafia family": "Mafia Figure Indicted on Charge of Bribery in Pornography Case," the *New York Times*, 22 May 1969. Note: the incident occurred on 29 April 1968. Court case: 428 F.2d 86, United States of America, Appellee, v. Charles Tourine et ano., Defendants, and Leonard Burtman and Benedict Himmel, Defendants-Appellants.

# Index